METAMORPHOSIS IN MODERN GERMAN LITERATURE
TRANSFORMING BODIES, IDENTITIES AND AFFECTS

LEGENDA

LEGENDA is the Modern Humanities Research Association's book imprint for new research in the Humanities. Founded in 1995 by Malcolm Bowie and others within the University of Oxford, Legenda has always been a collaborative publishing enterprise, directly governed by scholars. The Modern Humanities Research Association (MHRA) joined this collaboration in 1998, became half-owner in 2004, in partnership with Maney Publishing and then Routledge, and has since 2016 been sole owner. Titles range from medieval texts to contemporary cinema and form a widely comparative view of the modern humanities, including works on Arabic, Catalan, English, French, German, Greek, Italian, Portuguese, Russian, Spanish, and Yiddish literature. Editorial boards and committees of more than 60 leading academic specialists work in collaboration with bodies such as the Society for French Studies, the British Comparative Literature Association and the Association of Hispanists of Great Britain & Ireland.

The MHRA encourages and promotes advanced study and research in the field of the modern humanities, especially modern European languages and literature, including English, and also cinema. It aims to break down the barriers between scholars working in different disciplines and to maintain the unity of humanistic scholarship. The Association fulfils this purpose through the publication of journals, bibliographies, monographs, critical editions, and the MHRA Style Guide, and by making grants in support of research. Membership is open to all who work in the Humanities, whether independent or in a University post, and the participation of younger colleagues entering the field is especially welcomed.

ALSO PUBLISHED BY THE ASSOCIATION

Critical Texts
Tudor and Stuart Translations • *New Translations* • *European Translations*
MHRA Library of Medieval Welsh Literature

MHRA Bibliographies
Publications of the Modern Humanities Research Association

The Annual Bibliography of English Language & Literature
Austrian Studies
Modern Language Review
Portuguese Studies
The Slavonic and East European Review
Working Papers in the Humanities
The Yearbook of English Studies

www.mhra.org.uk
www.legendabooks.com

GERMANIC LITERATURES

Editorial Committee
Convenor: Professor Ritchie Robertson (University of Oxford)
Dr Barbara Burns (Glasgow University)
Professor Jane Fenoulhet (University College London)
Professor Anne Fuchs (University of Warwick)
Dr Jakob Stougaard-Nielsen (University College London)
Professor Annette Volfing (University of Oxford)
Professor Susanne Kord (University College London)
Professor John Zilcosky (University of Toronto)

Germanic Literatures includes monographs and essay collections on literature originally written not only in German, but also in Dutch and the Scandinavian languages. Within the German-speaking area, it seeks also to publish studies of other national literatures such as those of Austria and Switzerland. The chronological scope of the series extends from the early Middle Ages down to the present day.

APPEARING IN THIS SERIES

1. *Yvan Goll: The Thwarted Pursuit of the Whole*, by Robert Vilain
2. *Sebald's Bachelors: Queer Resistance and the Unconforming Life*, by Helen Finch
3. *Goethe's Visual World*, by Pamela Currie
4. *German Narratives of Belonging: Writing Generation and Place in the Twenty-First Century*, by Linda Shortt
5. *The Very Late Goethe: Self-Consciousness and the Art of Ageing*, by Charlotte Lee
6. *Women, Emancipation and the German Novel 1871-1910: Protest Fiction in its Cultural Context*, by Charlotte Woodford
7. *Goethe's Poetry and the Philosophy of Nature: Gott und Welt 1798–1827*, by Regina Sachers
8. *Fontane and Cultural Mediation: Translation and Reception in Nineteenth-Century German Literature*, edited by Ritchie Robertson and Michael White
9. *Metamorphosis in Modern German Literature: Transforming Bodies, Identities and Affects*, by Tara Beaney
10. *Comedy and Trauma in Germany and Austria after 1945: The Inner Side of Mourning*, by Stephanie Bird
11. *E.T.A. Hoffmann's Orient: Romantic Aesthetics and the German Imagination*, by Joanna Neilly
12. *Structures of Subjugation in Dutch Literature*, by Judit Gera

Managing Editor
Dr Graham Nelson, 41 Wellington Square, Oxford OX1 2JF, UK
www.legendabooks.com

Metamorphosis in Modern German Literature

Transforming Bodies, Identities and Affects

Tara Beaney

LEGENDA

Germanic Literatures 9
Modern Humanities Research Association
2016

*Published by Legenda
an imprint of the Modern Humanities Research Association
Salisbury House, Station Road, Cambridge* CB1 2LA

ISBN 978-1-909662-84-1 (HB)
ISBN 978-1-781883-24-2 (PB)

First published 2016

All rights reserved. No part of this publication may be reproduced or disseminated or transmitted in any form or by any means, electronic, mechanical, photocopying, recording or otherwise, or stored in any retrieval system, or otherwise used in any manner whatsoever without written permission of the copyright owner, except in accordance with the provisions of the Copyright, Designs and Patents Act 1988, or under the terms of a licence permitting restricted copying issued in the UK by the Copyright Licensing Agency Ltd, Saffron House, 6–10 Kirby Street, London EC1N 8TS, *England, or in the USA by the Copyright Clearance Center, 222 Rosewood Drive, Danvers MA 01923. Application for the written permission of the copyright owner to reproduce any part of this publication must be made by email to legenda@mhra.org.uk.*

Disclaimer: Statements of fact and opinion contained in this book are those of the author and not of the editors or the Modern Humanities Research Association. The publisher makes no representation, express or implied, in respect of the accuracy of the material in this book and cannot accept any legal responsibility or liability for any errors or omissions that may be made.

Trademark notice: Product or corporate names may be trademarks or registered trademarks, and are used only for identification and explanation without intent to infringe.

© *Modern Humanities Research Association 2016*

The chapter images are from Maria Sibylla Merian, Swamp Immortelle with Giant Silk Moth, *watercolour and bodycolour on vellum, 35.9 × 28.5cm, 1701–03; Royal Collection Trust/*© *Her Majesty Queen Elizabeth II 2015.*

Copy-Editor: Nigel Hope

CONTENTS

	Acknowledgements	ix
	Introduction	1
	Central Questions	2
	Approaching Metamorphosis	11
1	Inner Realms: The Painful Pleasure of Metamorphosis in E.T.A. Hoffmann	19
	Metamorphosis and the Romantic Individual	19
	Animato: Metamorphic Fantasies in 'Der goldne Topf'	22
	Miserere: Distortions of the Night in 'Der Sandmann'	33
	Scherzo: Metamorphosis as Social Satire	40
	Conclusion	50
2	Being Animal: Kafka and the Wordless World	54
	Metamorphosis and Modernism	54
	Extraordinary Change	56
	Animal Existence	65
	Languages of Affect	74
	Conclusion	82
3	Cocooned from the Past: Temporal Subversion in Marie Luise Kaschnitz and Jenny Erpenbeck	87
	Metamorphosis and Socio-Political Change	87
	Marie Luise Kaschnitz, 'Das dicke Kind'	88
	Jenny Erpenbeck, *Geschichte vom alten Kind*	98
	Comparative Analysis	110
	Conclusion	116
4	Metamorphoses under the Influence: Transformation Politics, Poetics, and Affects in Yoko Tawada	120
	Movement and Metamorphosis	120
	Transformation Politics	122
	Transformation Poetics	131
	The Affects of Transformation	141
	Conclusion	153
	Endings and Beginnings: Towards a Conclusion	159
	Bibliography	171
	Index	182

For my parents

ACKNOWLEDGEMENTS

This book began as a doctoral dissertation carried out at the graduate school of the Cluster of Excellence 'Languages of Emotion' at the Free University of Berlin from 2009 to 2013. The doctoral scholarship provided was essential to making this book possible, as was the inspiration and guidance received from countless people throughout its development. I would like to thank, in particular, my primary supervisor, Stefan Keppler-Tasaki, for his generous engagement with my work, and my second supervisor Jutta Müller-Tamm for her insightful comments. I would also like to thank the rest of my dissertation committee for their feedback: Irene Albers, Anne Fleig, and Tim Lörke.

Some of my work in progress was presented at conferences (at the University of Michigan, Edinburgh University, Cornell University and the University of Giessen) and in colloquia (including the 'Languages of Emotion' and Friedrich Schlegel graduate schools of the Free University of Berlin), and I would like to thank the organizers, those with whom I discussed ideas, and those who provided funding for me to attend ('Languages of Emotion', the Dahlem Research School and the DAAD). I would especially like to thank my colleagues at the 'Languages of Emotion' graduate school for their supportive and critical engagement with my work throughout the doctoral process.

Work on this book was also carried out at Cornell University during the academic year 2011–12, where I held a visiting research scholarship. I am grateful to Cornell University, the Berlin Consortium for German Studies, and the exchange programme at the Free University of Berlin for providing this opportunity. I would also like to thank all of those at Cornell whose discussions helped shape my thinking, in particular Leslie Adelson for her detailed comments on my early written work for chapters 3 and 4, and Brett de Bary, for discussing with me an early version of chapter 4.

The process of transforming the dissertation into a book was carried out at Aberdeen University between 2014 and 2015, during which time I received helpful advice from several colleagues, including Julia Biggane and Edward Welch. Aberdeen University also assisted with publication costs. At Legenda, Graham Nelson was an excellent editor, and series editor Ritchie Robertson's attention to detail was exceptional. I would also like to thank Jim Hardy at the Royal Entomological Society for information on the cover image, used also for the chapter images. Translations in the text are my own, unless otherwise indicated.

I have been particularly lucky to have had an additional *Doktormutter* and *Doktorvater* in my parents, Sharon Macdonald and Mike Beaney, whose comments and advice were extremely valuable. My husband Erdem Osman has been supportive throughout, and has made possible the most miraculous of transformations to have occurred since completing the dissertation: the new existence of our daughter Iris.

T.B., Aberdeen, November 2016

INTRODUCTION

❖

The idea of transforming into a radically different body may seem strange and unlikely. Yet the strange and unlikely has been a source for some of the most affectively and intellectually powerful works of literature. A fascination with animal existence, and even with humans crossing over into animal form, can be traced back to the earliest known works of human art. Painted over 30,000 years ago in the Chauvet caves, we find the image of a woman's legs merging with the torso of a bison.[1] Whether this is a hybrid figure, or a depiction of metamorphosis, a process of moving from one form to another, is unclear. Yet in early mythology, both hybrid and metamorphic figures suggest a world in which the boundaries between humans and others are constantly being challenged. As in Ovid's *Metamorphoses* (AD 8), stories of transformation between humans, animals, plants, and inanimate matter sit naturally alongside creation myths, expressing a world that is constantly subject to change. While Ovid's epic poem is often regarded as a major influence on later tales of metamorphosis across Europe and the West, the origins of metamorphosis stories are diverse. In the Arabian Nights, with its roots in ancient and medieval Middle Eastern and South Asian folklore, metamorphosis is often brought about through sorcery or disguise. In many folktales, metamorphosis provides the anagnorisis, or key moment of recognition, that helps to generate narrative satisfaction.

Many of the myths, folktales, and fairy tales involving metamorphosis served as inspiration for Romantic writers as they engaged with the individual predicament of being caught between different modes of existence. If we understand modern literature as placing emphasis on the individual as an autonomous agent, then Romantic tales, with their exploration of inner thoughts and feelings, offer a decidedly modern outlook. Even as literature moves away from the myths and folktales in which metamorphosis is a casual occurrence, there is still a place for metamorphosis. In the fantastic literature of the past two centuries, metamorphosis has surprised, provoked, and challenged. Though tales of metamorphosis have originated in diverse places, this book focuses on German literature from the Romantic period to the present, a period starting during the upheavals of the Napoleonic wars and progressing through two world wars, through the division and reunification of the country. With its changing borders, Germany provides particularly fertile ground for tales of changing bodies and identities. An experience of displacement through political and social upheaval or through moving geographically and culturally is something shared by all the writers explored in this book, and it is these experiences that inform their writing of metamorphosis.

Literature is rich in tales of metamorphosis. But what it is about metamorphosis that excites the imagination? Perhaps it is that metamorphosis engages with what it is to change, thereby challenging the identity of a person, or because it throws into relief our assumptions about the distinction between humans and other animals. It also forces attention onto bodies and affects, and in narrating bodily transformation, a parallel with literary transformation and creation frequently arises. All of these issues are addressed in this book. Metamorphosis is explored in diverse forms, but what all the literary texts have in common is the depiction of an extreme and rapid change of form. The terms 'transformation' (from the Latin) and 'metamorphosis' (from the Greek) are often used interchangeably to mean 'change of form', but I make a distinction in using 'metamorphosis' for extreme change that goes beyond ordinary processes of growth and maturation, or is far more rapid than evolution, and that therefore lies outside the bounds of ordinary experience.

A comparison with the use of 'metamorphosis' as a biological term is illuminating: 'complete metamorphosis' describes the radical bodily change of many insects, marine creatures, and amphibians, which also adopt a different diet and habitat in their nymph and adult forms. The metamorphosis of such creatures is alluded to in some of the texts I examine. In these texts, the most common term for radical change is 'Verwandlung' [often translated as 'transformation']. 'Metamorphose', meanwhile, is confined mainly to scientific use, as well as being the familiar translation for the title of Ovid's epic poem. 'Verwandlung' means a movement from one state to another (a 'Wandlung') that is in some sense more extreme: the prefix 'ver-' can have an intensifying effect (as in 'verlieben' [to fall in love] versus 'lieben' [to love] or 'versprechen' [to promise] versus 'sprechen' [to speak]), but it can also modify the verbal stem to produce a more negative action (as in 'verachten' [to disdain] or 'verdrehen' [to distort]). The idea of 'Verwandlung' can thus have a negative connotation of something gone awry. Certainly in some of the texts I examine, metamorphosis is a horrific experience, but it can also be a positive one. As I will argue, the last two centuries of German literature have seen some very different understandings of what it is to change one's body and identity, and some fascinating ways of writing metamorphosis.

Central Questions

Metamorphosis invites questions about the status of the individual, the human, and the body, as well as about literature and affect. While these questions are pertinent to all of the texts I explore, each of the chapters deals centrally with one of these issues: models of self and individuality in chapter 1; what it is to be human or animal in chapter 2; chapter 3 deals with bodies undergoing temporal change; and chapter 4 examines the connection between metamorphosis and the production of literature. All of the chapters consider metamorphosis as an affective process. In introducing the central questions below I also provide an overview of the chapters.

Identity and the Boundaries of the Self

One of the most longstanding questions in Western philosophy is the question of identity: how can something change form, and yet maintain its identity? Particular problems arise in the case of personal identity: how can a person maintain their identity through temporal or physical change? If we can talk of a person staying the same despite radical changes, then what is it that remains the same, and at what point is one no longer the same person?

Literary texts may use metamorphosis to support the view of personal identity being maintained despite radical corporeal change, or conversely, metamorphosis may raise doubts about the possibility of personal identity. The former view is articulated in Ovid's epic poem, the *Metamorphoses* (AD 8), when the philosopher Pythagoras claims that although everything is constantly changing, and physical forms are moulded and remoulded like wax, the spirit or soul persists intact throughout:

> omnia mutantur, nihil interit. errat et illinc
> huc uenit, hinc illuc, et quoslibet occupat artus
> spiritus eque feris humana in corpora transit
> inque feras noster, nec tempore deperit ullo.
> utque nouis facilis signatur cera figuris,
> nec manet ut fuerat nec formas seruant easdem,
> sed tamen ipsa eadem est, animam sic semper eandem
> esse sed in uarias doceo migrare figuras.[2]
>
> [Everything changes; nothing dies; the soul
> Roams to and fro, now here, now there, and takes
> What frame it will, passing from beast to man,
> As yielding wax is stamped with new designs
> And changes shape and seems not still the same,
> Yet is indeed the same, even so our souls
> Are still the same for ever, but adopt
> In their migrations ever-varying forms.][3]

The idea that the soul persists while the body changes is exemplified in the many metamorphoses of Ovid's characters: Narcissus becomes the flower that seems to gaze downwards, talkative Echo is punished by being turning into an echo, beautiful Io can only reveal the crime against her through the doleful eyes of a heifer. Each transformation encapsulates the character's spirit in some way.

However, metamorphosis can also be used to explore anxieties over the idea of personal identity. The idea of the persisting spirit as criterion for personal identity came under particular pressure during the Enlightenment, with new attempts to account for personal identity without assuming an immortal soul. Empiricist John Locke, for example, defined personal identity as consisting in the continuity of consciousness.[4] That is, you are the same person now as you were before if you can trace a continuity of consciousness between now and then. However, consciousness is far more fragile a notion than that of the soul, since it can be broken by numerous sleeping, drunken, irrational, or dream states. Such states raise the possibility of losing one's personal identity, of transforming into someone else. It is no surprise that following the Enlightenment, and, in particular, from the Romantic period onwards, tales of metamorphosis explore the possibility of personal identity being ruptured during states of loosened consciousness.

This book begins with Romantic literature, which might be seen as standing at the beginning of a modern approach to metamorphosis in the emphasis on the individual experience of unstable identities. If Charles Taylor, in *Sources of the Self: The Making of Modern Identity* (1989),[5] is right in identifying a distinct form of 'modern identity', then the anxieties, hopes, and instabilities within modern identity might well be explored through tales of metamorphosis. It may not be possible to identify a clear beginning of modern literature and modern identity, but certainly by the European Enlightenment, with the development of scientific methods, the challenge to established doctrines, and the emphasis on the individual as a rational, autonomous agent, a modern outlook is apparent. Yet as the secure autonomy and identity of the individual are put under pressure, literature turns again towards metamorphosis and the new movement of Romanticism delights in uncovering alternatives to mundane, everyday reality.

This book begins with late Romantic writer E. T. A. Hoffmann, focusing on two of Hoffmann's best-known tales ('Der goldne Topf' [The Golden Pot], 1815, and 'Der Sandmann' [The Sandman], 1816), as well some tales of human–animal metamorphosis from his *Fantasiestücke in Callots Manier* [Fantasy pieces in the style of Callot] (1814–15).[6] Through an analysis of these texts in chapter 1, I examine key uses of metamorphosis in Hoffmann's work: as part of a Romantic longing for a 'higher self', as an articulation of the threat of unstable identity, and as part of a satire on those who lack the individuality, inner life and feeling characteristic of the Romantic artist. In these texts, emotions intimate access to a 'higher' or 'deeper' self, but are also configured as potentially uncontrollable external forces threatening the self. I argue that this influential model of emotion emerges alongside a configuration of 'modern identity' as unstable and open to metamorphosis.

As well as raising the philosophical problem of personal identity, metamorphosis also challenges social concepts of identity. Social identity, meaning the way in which people position themselves within a social group, may include categories such race, class, nationality, and sexuality. All of these can be understood as historically changing, but also as distinctly modern concepts, emerging only during the Enlightenment.[7] Such forms of social identity tend to take place only when constructed against a newly realized 'other', against alternative social practices or bodily qualities, against different people, groups or modes of being.[8] In this sense, literary depictions of metamorphosis, with their engagement with alternative forms of bodily existence, bring identities into question, either to reinforce or to undermine certain forms of social identity.

Uncertain positioning within social groups can also be a result of social or geographical transition. Since metamorphosis involves a transition between bodies and identities, it has been related to experiences of geographical boundary crossing and movement between different social or cultural environments. In her book *Fantastic Metamorphoses, Other Worlds*, Marina Warner suggests that tales of metamorphosis may arise in particular at 'crossroads, cross-cultural zones, points of interchange on the intricate connective tissue of communications between cultures'.[9] I examine Warner's link between metamorphosis and the crossing of geographical, social, and cultural spaces by considering the concerns articulated in the modern German texts that I discuss and the experiences that their authors draw upon.

Humanity and Language

Metamorphosis not only raises questions about what it is to be a person, but about what it is to be a human rather than another animal. Transformation into an animal can mean losing characteristics considered uniquely human, but can also mean gaining new, animal attributes. Stories of metamorphosis can therefore provide insight into how understandings of what it is to be human have changed historically. As critical theorists Theodor Adorno and Max Horkheimer put it: 'die Idee der Menschen in der europäischen Geschichte drückt sich in Unterscheidung von Tier aus' [the idea of the human in European history is expressed in the way in which he is distinguished from the animal].[10]

Stories of metamorphosis may undermine human–animal distinctions, though they may also reinforce them. Some studies of metamorphosis focus exclusively on the former, seeing metamorphosis crucially as a challenge to human–animal difference.[11] However, metamorphosis can also reinforce human–animal difference by positioning animals as fundamentally different or 'other'. The idea of animals as non-rational and humans as rational can be traced back as far as Plato and Aristotle, though the concept of humans as *essentially* rational beings has roots in early Enlightenment thought. Descartes, for example, describes himself as fundamentally a being that thinks ('cogito ergo sum'). For Descartes, animals do not share the capacity for rational thought, and are little more than machines. When rationality is valued, and animals are devalued, as has been common in modern Western thought, then the idea of transforming into an animal is likely to be a horrific and degrading prospect, as Hegel claims, citing examples of metamorphosis from Augustine and Dante.[12]

However, becoming animal is not degrading if we get rid of the assumption of human hierarchy over animals. Instead, becoming *human* can be a degrading prospect, as some tales of ape–human metamorphosis make clear. Franz Kafka's 'Bericht für eine Akademie' (1917) [A Report to an Academy] reveals the influence of evolutionary theory, but counters his contemporaries' outrage over the idea that humans evolved from ape-like ancestors with a sceptical exploration of what it means to be human. For Kafka, writing from the perspective of alternative, animal existences is central to his work as a whole. Metamorphosis is not only subject matter but belongs to his literary practice of closely entering alternative perspectives.

The second chapter thus turns to Kafka as one of the best-known writers of metamorphosis in modern German literature. Focal scholarly concerns are situated within a wider investigation of the use of metamorphosis in literature, with a view to gaining a better understanding of identity, humanity, corporeality, and affect in

Kafka's work. As well as 'Ein Bericht für eine Akademie' (1917), *Die Verwandlung* (1912) [Metamorphosis] is examined in depth, alongside consideration of some of Kafka's other animal stories.[13]

One of the major aspects of becoming animal is the loss of verbal language. Language has not only been regarded as a uniquely human attribute, but has been seen as a key marker of what it is to be human. In many accounts of human origin, the acquisition of language marks the transition from animal to human.[14] Through examining Kafka's 'Die Verwandlung' in chapter 2 I consider what it means to lose language: whether it poses a degrading prospect, or the way forward to alternative, non-linguistic modes of existence.

Bodily and Temporal Change

Many studies of metamorphosis address only human–animal transformations, but transformations into another human form, perhaps of a different sex or age, are also important forms of metamorphosis. Rather than engaging with what it means to be human rather than animal, these metamorphoses help to understand how specific bodily forms shape identities, and help to examine the behavioural characteristics that are culturally associated with particular physical forms.

Studies of metamorphosis often subordinate issues of bodily difference and corporeal change to those of personal identity and psychological continuity. However, without recourse to the body, and to the bodily and affective nature of the change, the psychological effects of the metamorphosis cannot be fully understood. Unlike tales of metempsychosis, which emphasise continuity of the spirit, metamorphosis continually refers to the body as a central locus of affective engagement, and as fundamentally connected to the psyche.[15]

Metamorphosis forces attention onto the body, an aspect of existence that has long been neglected in Western philosophical thought, in which the body has traditionally been regarded as a hindrance to thinking.[16] With feminist thinkers calling for greater attention to women's bodies and experiences, more awareness has arisen about the effects that a person's body has on the way in which they are treated, and the identity they are ascribed in society. As part of negotiating a new place for women in society, literary writers were called upon to affirm women's experience in all its physicality, or to 'write their bodies', as Hélène Cixous put it. Cixous's call was taken up with works such as Verena Stefan's bestselling feminist novel *Häutungen* (1970). The metaphor of sloughing off old skin ('Häutungen') suggests a process of metamorphosis in which the negative associations ascribed to female bodies are left behind, and a positive, new existence is embraced.

My third and fourth chapters turn to tales of female metamorphoses in which the bodily experience of girls and women is firmly in the foreground. Chapter 3 is based on a comparative reading of Marie Luise Kaschnitz's short story 'Das dicke Kind' (1951) [The fat child][17] and Jenny Erpenbeck's novella *Geschichte vom alten Kind* (1999) [Story of the old child].[18] Both stories revolve around the metamorphosis of a fat girl, which reveals a different identity than supposed. A major focus of my analysis is on the girls' positioning as abject figures, which I relate both to cultural inscriptions of fatness and to the repression of the past.

In both cases, metamorphosis is not only a corporeal change, positioned around the affectively saturated transition from girl to woman, but a radical temporal rupture. Metamorphosis often acts as temporal reversal or regression to a past state, or alternatively as rapid acceleration into an older body. Unlike the gradual progress and evolution characteristic of a Bildungsroman, stories of metamorphosis deal with moments of personal crisis. Mikhail Bakhtin, writing about Apuleius' *The Golden Ass*, claims:

> Metamorphosis serves as the basis for a method of portraying the whole of an individual's life in its more important moments of *crisis*: for showing *how an individual becomes other that what he was*. We are offered various sharply differing images of one and the same individual, images that are united in him at various epochs and stages in the course of a life.[19]

Rather than depicting a gradual progression towards a final state, metamorphosis emphasizes the sharp contrasts within an individual's life, and depicts change as one of destruction and renewal. In the non-linear narratives examined in chapter 3, the girls' abrupt transformations can be read as a radical break from the past, or as a forcible reminder of an unwanted past.

As well as dealing with metamorphosis as corporeal experience, chapter 3 also examines the relationship between personal, individual change, and larger-scale political and social change. The comparison between a post-war and a post-reunification text allows for an exploration of changing attitudes towards difficult pasts and the integration, or non-integration, of past and present identities. Metamorphosis stories have been observed to emerge particularly during periods of political and social instability, in which individual identities become subject to breakdown, while in periods of political stability where there is slow change, and perhaps horror of change, metamorphosis goes underground.[20] Such a claim suggests that nineteenth- to twenty-first-century German literature may provide a particularly fertile source of metamorphosis stories, given the radical social and political changes experienced by German-language writers.

Literary Practices

Metamorphosis means confronting alternative existences, a process akin to literary production itself. To write, authors must transform themselves imaginatively and affectively into their characters. According to writer Elias Canetti, literary authors should act as 'Hüter der Verwandlung' [guardians of transformation], both in the sense that they look after and pass on metamorphosis stories, and in the sense that they have the ability to become any being.[21] Affective identification is central to literary production, and metamorphosis stories are prime examples of literature's capacity to engage with other existences. The bodily transformations within literary texts might be thus seen as experiments in the empathic or mimetic process that is at the origin of the literary imagination. For many writers, metamorphosis is a way of engaging with the process of writing literature itself.

The connection between metamorphosis and literary creation as imaginative transformation has a long tradition in German literature. An early example can be found in an episode reworked from Hans Sachs in Grimmelshausen's *Simplicissimus* (1668), in which the narrator encounters the strange metamorphic creature Baldanders. Baldanders is at first is a stone statue, but later becomes an array of different things (he is 'bald anders' [soon another]). Not only is Baldanders a metamorphic figure, but he also promises to illuminate the art of literary production, which means conversing with all things and creating linguistic puzzles. To this end he writes in the narrator's book: 'Ich bin der Anfang und das Ende und gelte an allen Orten' [I am the beginning and the end and apply to all places], before uttering a series of cryptic words and then transforming in rapid and bewildering succession.[22] Baldanders' words suggest the limitlessness of change, and open up the possibility of transformation as an allegory for writing. Later literary works have drawn upon this episode, for example in W. G. Sebald's *Die Ringe des Saturn* [The Rings of Saturn], in which metamorphosis is also used as an allegory for writing.[23]

The fact that Baldanders continually makes reference to Hans Sachs' tale about the same figure suggests another key feature of many metamorphosis texts: their reflection upon the process of rewriting and transforming existing texts as another form of metamorphosis. To understand the literary process as a form of metamorphosis means rejecting the idea of literature as creation *ex nihilo*, and instead paying attention to processes of refashioning existing material. Indeed, tales of metamorphosis are often richly intertextual, thereby making reference to the fact that the text itself is a form of transformation. Considering the text as a transformation of previous texts raises questions of relationship: is the text to be understood as reproducing material from an original, as replacing it, engaging with it, answering it or continuing it? Such questions have been explored extensively in translation studies, and the discussion of textual transformation in chapter 4 is informed by debates within translation studies.

Chapter 4 addresses the relationship between bodily and textual transformation in the work of contemporary author Yoko Tawada, with focus on *Opium für Ovid: Ein Kopfkissenbuch von 22 Frauen* (2000) [Opium for Ovid: a pillow book of 22 women].[24] Since Tawada engages with stories of metamorphosis by authors such as Ovid, Hoffmann, and Kafka, this chapter revisits the older models of metamorphosis discussed in chapters 1 and 2, and considers Tawada's reconfiguration of metamorphosis. In particular, the chapter relates Tawada's use of metamorphosis to changing models of literature, identity, subjectivity, and affect.

Not only are many metamorphosis texts about literature as a transformative activity, but the stories are also often created through linguistic transformation. The possibility of metamorphosis, imagined in literary texts as a real experience, often arises from language play. For example, a tale of metamorphosis from human to pig, as in Marie Darrieussecq's *Truismes* [Pig Tales], might draw on metaphorical expressions comparing humans to pigs, or a transformation from ape to human might draw on the expression 'to ape' ('nachäffen'), as is the case in Hoffmann's tale of the ape Milo, examined in chapter 1. In chapter 2 I examine the claim that Kafka's metamorphosis in *Die Verwandlung* is a literalization of the insult 'Ungeziefer' [vermin]. The physical metamorphoses in the tales often have a basis in the creative possibilities that language opens up through metaphor, metonymy, or linguistic ambiguity. Such language-play works best when it surprises through the use of unexpected connections, which is also what metamorphosis texts do when they take affectively laden language, such as insults or jokes, and turn them into radical corporeal experience.

Affect

Changing bodies means learning to inhabit a new identity, dealing with the loss and gain of defining physical characteristics, and often confronting existential questions about who we are. The horror, anxiety, desire, or confusion that metamorphosis evokes is fundamental to the experience of bodily transformation, and to its literary representation.

However, literary studies have traditionally tended to neglect affect. Doubts about the aesthetic value of affect can be traced back to long-standing philosophical debates. For Plato, it is affect that makes the poetic arts so dangerous, since these appeal to the lowest part of the soul and obscure knowledge based on reason. However, Aristotle's work opens up an alternative view of affect, with pity and fear being vital to our identification with the characters, and thereby contributing to a greater understanding of human nature. The problem of whether the affects articulated within and created through the poetic arts detract from our understanding of the work, or are essential to it, has been ongoing ever since.

Modern literary criticism and theory has its roots in an anti-affective tradition, however, based on the inheritance of structuralist approaches. Structuralists place emphasis on the language and structure of literary texts, but disregard anything that may carry the threat of subjectivism, such as the affects articulated within and through the language of the texts. As literary theory became an established academic field, from around the 1950s onwards, affect continued to be regarded as unimportant to the study of literature, a by-product rather than as essential to what literature is and does.[25]

However, with the affective turn of the mid-1990s literary studies increasingly started attending to affect. Examining the affects within literary texts became a way of understanding the ways in which affects shape identities and inter-personal relationships and affect social dynamics. Understood as important socio-cultural phenomena that are implicated in the politics of social life, affects could be investigated in multiple ways. Cultural theorists Lila Abu-Lughod and Catherine Lutz claim that a particularly fruitful line of investigation for those who are interested in emotions as socio-cultural phenomena is to historicize them. One might thereby trace the genealogy of emotion in order to understand 'how emotions came to be constituted in their current form, as physiological forces, located within individuals, that bolster our sense of uniqueness and are taken to provide access to some kind of inner truth about the self'.[26] This study is not a genealogy of emotion as such, but I do examine different understandings of affect within the literary texts. In doing so, I am able to trace some changes in affective style and in understandings of affect across the texts, and relate such changes to changing understandings of personal identity and subjectivity. In metamorphosis texts, the affects involved in changing identity provide insight into what it means to lose or gain identity, and into understandings of the self and the nature of change. Considering the underlying model of affect — for example, as external, threatening forces, or as rational responses — also provides insight into the model of the self within these texts.

At this point, it is necessary to clarify my use of the term 'affect', since the terms 'affect' and 'emotion' have been used in diverging ways in contemporary scholarship, and have also had different meanings or connotations in different historical periods.[27] I use 'affect' as an umbrella term to cover the whole range of affective phenomena running from feelings and moods to passions and emotions. Similar terminology is used in Charles Altieri's *The Particulars of Rapture: An Aesthetics of the Affects*.[28] Within the broad category of affect, it is possible to draw further distinctions. Emotions can be distinguished from feelings in that emotions are intentional, that is, they have a direct object or are *about* something, and therefore involve the construction of attitudes. Moods are more diffuse modes of feeling, where feeling merges into something closer to atmosphere. The term 'passion' in its contemporary sense, might be described as a type of emotion 'within which we project significant stakes for the identities they make possible'.[29] As well as using affect in a broad sense, the term can also be useful when talking about affective phenomena that do not clearly fit into established categories or that are not clearly marked as distinct, nameable emotions or feelings, as used, for example by Anna Parkinson, in discussing a text by Anne Duden that evokes 'a diffuse affective charge that lacks a socially identifiable form'.[30]

By using the terms 'affect' and 'emotion' as outlined above, I diverge from alternative contemporary usage. For example, Jonathan Flatley distinguishes between emotions as personal, and affects as interpersonal: 'Where emotion suggests something that happens inside and tends towards outward expression, affect indicates something relational and transformative. One *has* emotions; one is affected *by* people or things.'[31] However, although affect carries the connotation of affecting and being affected, and emotion carries the connotation of moving outwards (from the Latin 'emovere', meaning to move out, remove, or agitate), Flatley's internal versus relational distinction is not upheld in ordinary usage. We may speak of *having* emotions (as in 'having a fear of heights') but we also speak of emotions as *having us* (as in 'being possessed by fear'). Emotions are not consistently regarded as things that one *has* and then expresses, but may also be seen as part of a dialogue with the world.

However, considering different understandings of emotion and affect is important within this study. Emotions have been understood historically both as objects that one has, and as lenses through which one perceives the world, or even as forms of judgement or appraisal, as recent theorists have argued.[32] Tracing the etymology and changing historical usage of affect terms such as 'emotion' or 'passion' can be one way of providing insight into different conceptualizations of affect.[33] For example, affect has been regarded both as something that one suffers passively (as the word 'passion' suggests, and as a violent, active force that move out of us — as in 'emotion').[34] In this study, I examine different understandings of affect in literary texts ranging over a broad historical period, and specifically consider the relationship between changing understandings of affect and changing models of identity and subjectivity.

As well as identifying the types of affect and affective styles of the literary texts, I also argue that affect is particularly important in understanding metamorphosis. Since affect, like metamorphosis, transforms bodies, narratives of bodily transformation are often at the same time narratives of affective transformation. Not only is bodily change often a highly emotional process, but it may also involve profound affective change, and indeed, metamorphosis may serve as a representation of our capacity to be changed affectively. While I examine the importance of affect in metamorphosis texts, concepts of transformation or movement between bodies have been used in cultural theory to characterize affect. For example, in the introduction to *The Affect Theory Reader* Melissa Gregg and Gregory J. Seigworth claim:

> Affect arises in the midst of in-between-ness: in the capacities to act and be acted upon [. . .] That is, affect is found in those intensities that pass body to body (human, nonhuman, part-body and otherwise) in those resonances that circulate about, between, and sometimes stick to bodies and worlds, *and in the very passages or variations between these intensities and resonances themselves.*[35]

If affect arises between bodies, as highlighted here, then the process of transforming from one body to another opens up particular potential for affect. In describing affect in terms of passages between bodies, metamorphosis can even be used as a conceptual tool for understanding the dynamism of affective practices, a dynamism that Patricia Clough identified as the most provocative and enduring contribution of the affective turn.[36]

Cultural studies of affect tend to emphasize the ways in which affects arise and are transformed in the passages between bodies. Following such an approach, this study attends to the types of affect that arise during metamorphosis, the characters' changing affective state, the positioning of and reflection upon affect within the text, and the affective style of the narrative. The diverse forms of affect that emerge reflect the different prospects posed by metamorphosis, which can be degrading or elevating, a threat to established order or an opportunity for change.

Approaching Metamorphosis

Amongst the dozen or so English and German language books dealing with metamorphosis, the topics of identity, human–animal difference, language, temporality, and allusions to literary practice come to the fore. None, however, foreground the affective nature of the corporeal change, which I claim is vital to understanding the significance of metamorphosis.

Though I offer a unique approach, I also examine the central questions identified above, which have been addressed in various ways in studies of metamorphosis. For example, questions of personal identity are central in Harold Skulsky's *Metamorphosis: The Mind in Exile* (1981),[37] written in the wake of renewed philosophical interest in the nature of personhood, and influenced in particular by Thomas Nagel's 1974 essay 'What is it like to be a bat?',[38] which considers whether we can understand the subjective experience of beings with very different bodies. Skulsky asks whether personhood is to be identified with body, mind, or behaviour,[39] a question that he approaches through a discussion of around ten well-known European metamorphosis texts from Ovid's *Metamorphoses* to Virginia Woolf's *Orlando*.

Irving Massey adopts a similarly broad diachronic approach to the study of metamorphosis in his *The Gaping Pig: Literature and Metamorphosis* (1976),[40] also discussing a dozen or so European texts. Massey's central claim is the idea that metamorphosis involves a 'critique of language' that occurs after being transformed into an animal and losing language.[41] Later studies have also foregrounded language and language-play in tales of metamorphosis. In her *Poetiken der Verwandlung* (2008) [Poetics of Transformation],[42] Monika Schmitz-Emans links metamorphosis to the problem of unrepresentability in the modern period. She draws on a wide range of mainly European works, some pre-twentieth century, but mostly twentieth century.

Questions of human–animal difference are particularly prominent in studies dealing specifically with human–animal transformations. These often relate metamorphosis to theories of evolution, and claim that both metamorphosis and evolution destabilize the boundary between humans and other animals. For example, in *Aspects of Metamorphosis: Fictional Representations of the Becoming Human* (2001), D. B. D. Asker argues that stories written before Darwin anticipate evolution in that they depict the possibility of transgressing the human–animal boundary, and claims that later understandings of the human–animal distinction have been hugely influenced by evolutionary theory.[43] Asker's book ranges over European and non-European texts, categorized in terms of the animals involved: wolves, monkeys, dogs and horses, ending with a discussion of animal rights.

A similarly taxonomic approach is also adopted by David Gallagher in his *Metamorphosis: Transformations of the Body and the Influence of Ovid's Metamorphoses on Germanic Literature of the Nineteenth and Twentieth Centuries* (2009), currently the only study in English of metamorphosis in German-language texts. Gallagher groups texts on 'ascending evolutionary scale', starting with 'Arachnids, Invertebrates and Lepidoptera' (ranging from Gotthelf's *Die schwarze Spinne* [The Black Spider] and Kafka's *Die Verwandlung*, to butterflies in works by Thomas Mann, Hermann Hesse, and Nelly Sachs). He progresses as far as 'Melusinas, Nymphs, Water Spirits and Undinas' before a final chapter on Christoph Ransmayr's *Die letzte Welt* [The Last World].

Asker's and Gallagher's taxonomic approach may have the potential to offer insight into the significance of particular animals in metamorphosis texts, but it provides less scope for understanding writers' engagement with the problems of being human that arise under particular socio-cultural conditions. My approach is instead to discuss texts chronologically with attention to the ways in which understandings of identity and change, human–animal difference, corporeality, and the role of literature and emotional expression have changed historically. One insightful study of historically changing attitudes towards personal identity is medievalist Caroline Walker Bynum's *Metamorphosis and Identity* (2001).[44] Bynum discusses metamorphosis in medieval literary and factual texts, revealing changing views about the nature of personal identity and change in medieval culture. For example, she identifies the replacement of a model of temporal change as evolution or development in the late twelfth century with a new notion of radical change, bringing with it a proliferation of metamorphosis tales.[45]

Another monograph dealing with changing concepts of change is Pascal Nicklas's extensive *Die Beständigkeit des Wandels: Metamorphosen in Literatur und Wissenschaft* (2002) [The Permanence of Change: Metamorphosis in Literature and Science].[46] Nicklas's book links literary metamorphosis texts to understandings of transformation in the history of science, first in relation to Ovid, then in texts by H. G. Wells, Joseph Conrad, and Kafka, which he examines in connection with Goethe's and Darwin's departure from creation models, before finally exploring metamorphoses of the psyche in Joyce and Broch alongside Freud's *Die Traumdeutung* [The Interpretation of Dreams]. Friedmann Harzer's *Erzählte Verwandlung: Eine Poetik epischer Metamorphosen (Ovid, Kafka, Ransmayr)* (2000) [Narrated Transformation: a poetics of epic metamorphoses],[47] also addresses temporality in metamorphosis texts, though with the aim of theoretically classifying types of temporality in metamorphosis texts, for example as discontinuous, involving abrupt breaks, or as continuous.

As well as relating metamorphosis to historically changing understandings of identity and change, humanity and corporeality, I also address the relationship between metamorphosis and geographical movement, a link that is central in Marina Warner's *Fantastic Metamorphoses, Other Worlds* (2002). Warner's suggestion that tales of metamorphosis often arise in spaces of cross-cultural transfer prefaces a discussion of a wide range of literary texts, myth, painting, and natural history with particular focus on the encounter with the Americas as fertile ground for tales of metamorphosis.

In identifying ways in which metamorphosis alludes to literary processes of transformation, I am able to draw upon existing studies of the relationship between metamorphosis and literature. In particular, Bruce Clarke's *Allegories of Writing: The Subject of Metamorphosis* (1995) reads the metamorphic bodily changes within texts as allegories of the metamorphic changes of texts that happen in the process of writing.[48] Clarke makes a case for this claim by examining texts ranging from Homer, Plato, Apuleius, and Shakespeare to Keats, Kafka, and Calvino. Clarke's second book on metamorphosis, *Posthuman Metamorphosis: Narrative and Systems* (2008), takes a different approach by using posthumanism, narratology, and second-order systems theory to read metamorphosis in modern and postmodern science fiction, particularly that which involves cybernetic or human–machine metamorphosis.[49]

Other studies of the relationship between metamorphosis and writing include Ursula Reber's *Formenverschleifung: Zu einer Theorie der Metamorphose* (2009) [Form Blurring: Towards a Theory of Metamorphosis], which provides four major case studies, on Ovid, Clemens Brentano, Richard Beer-Hofmann, and Alban Nikolai Herbst. In doing so, Reber attempts to identify a type of metamorphic writing that spans across a broad historical period. Reber focuses on intertextuality, but also draws on visual theory in her consideration of conceptual questions about identity, alterity, individuality, dividuality, and t(r)opology.

The variety of approaches to metamorphosis detailed above has informed both the content and approach of this study. My focus, however, is a select corpus of texts written over the last two turbulent centuries of German history. In examining these texts chronologically, my aim is not to provide a canon of metamorphosis texts, or indeed to lay out a distinct literary tradition, but to shed light on why writers turn to metamorphosis and how they envision the central concepts of identity, change or humanity, as well as demonstrate particular relationships towards corporeality and affect.

In focusing on German-language texts I provide scope for attending to the intertextual dialogue between texts, while also tracing the shifting conditions within which German-language literature has been produced. All of the writers I explore have lived, at least for some time, outside the area that now constitutes Germany. So while I will not be referring to German literature in the sense of a national tradition, I will be exploring the changing social conditions and experience of radical political change that are so pertinent to writers of German language literature as they write from both inside and outside the shifting borders of Germany.

The book begins in the modern period with Romantic texts. Although many diachronic studies of metamorphosis start with classical literature, particularly with Ovid's *Metamorphoses*, this book focuses on texts in which metamorphosis is bound up with doubts and anxieties about the nature and integrity of the self, which might be seen as problems concerning 'modern identity' in Charles Taylor's sense. In particular, I explore the affective conflicts of the individual facing the prospect of changing bodies and identities. By focusing on a small corpus of texts, I am able to examine in detail the significance of metamorphosis within an author's work. In the first chapter, on E. T. A. Hoffmann, I argue that metamorphosis is used in a variety of ways, involving different affects: the longing for a higher existence, the horror over the breakdown of the self, and the comedy that is needed to reconcile ourselves with the gap between the ideal and reality. The second chapter, on Franz Kafka, examines another canonical author of texts involving metamorphosis, with the aim of identifying core debates surrounding Kafka's use of metamorphosis, whilst situating Kafka's use of metamorphosis in a wider context of metamorphosis writing, and also providing new insight into metamorphosis and affect in Kafka's work.

The third and fourth chapters turn to texts by women writers which also deal with the metamorphoses of female protagonists. Texts involving female metamorphosis, or indeed written by women, tend to play a very minor role, or none at all, in studies of metamorphosis. Yet an account of the role of metamorphosis in literature is lacking without the perspective of women, particularly women writing after the advent of feminism, with its emphasis on women's identities and bodily experience. The few studies that do include analysis of texts by and about women tend also to subordinate the writers' specific engagement with female bodily transformation to the studies' central concerns with issues such as personal identity, language, geographical movement, or intertextuality. This book, however, engages with the corporeal and affective nature of specifically female metamorphosis. At the same time, chapter 3 also addresses the relationship between metamorphosis and social and political change, while chapter 4 deals with the connection between metamorphosis and the process of writing literary texts. The final chapter also revists Hoffmann and Kafka as intertexts in Tawada's writing of metamorphosis. The conclusion returns again to the central questions identified in this introduction as well as highlighting some major confluences and shifts in the use of metamorphosis and in understandings of identity and its affects.

The cover image for this book, that of the life-cycle of a silk-worm, was drawn by Maria Sibylla Merian (1647–1717), a German-born naturalist and scientific illustrator, known in particular for her major work *Metamorphosis Insectorum Surinamensium* [The Metamorphosis of the Insects of Suriname] (1705). As a leading entomologist of her time, Merian contributed significantly to understanding the process of metamorphosis. The illustrations that accompany the chapters can be considered a reminder of the process of metamorphosis as it continually reappears from one life-cycle to the next. The illustrations also serve as a reflection on the structural progression of the book: in the first chapter, the shuffling off of an old caterpillar skin works as metaphor for a new concept of inner identity hidden beneath; in chapter 2 the experience of being a voracious, abject animal is central; in chapter 3, the silkworm becomes a motionless pupa, which in the case of this species would normally remain buried beneath the earth until the adult form suddenly emerges; in chapter 4, the vibrant process of metamorphosis is central, though here the illustration shows not the process, but the plant that nourishes the metamorphic creature; and finally, in the conclusion, a moth emerges again, though while a male moth is depicted in the introduction, after having progressed from male to female metamorphosis it is only appropriate to conclude with the larger female moth and with her potential to generate further life and further metamorphosis.

Notes to the Introduction

1. Jean Clottes, *Chauvet Cave: The Art of Earliest Times*, trans. by Paul G. Bahn (Salt Lake City: University of Utah Press, 2003); Werner Herzog, dir., *Cave of Forgotten Dreams* (IFC Films/ Sundance Selects, 2010).
2. Ovid, *Metamorphoses*, Oxford Classical Texts (Oxford: Oxford University Press, 2004), book XV, lines 165–72, p. 452.
3. Ovid, *Metamorphoses*, trans. by A. D. Melville (Oxford: Oxford University Press, 1987) p. 357.
4. John Locke, *An Essay Concerning Human Understanding* [1690], (Penguin: London, 1997), Book II, Chapter XXVII, pp. 296–313.
5. Charles Taylor, *Sources of the Self: The Making of Modern Identity* (Cambridge, MA: Harvard University Press, 1989).
6. All references to Hoffmann's work are taken from E. T. A. Hoffmann, *Sämtliche Werke*, 6 vols, ed. by Wulf Segebrecht and others (Frankfurt a.M.: Deutscher Klassiker, 1985–2004).
7. Linda Martín Alcoff, 'Introduction: Identities: Modern and Postmodern', in *Identities: Race, Class, Gender and Nationality*, ed. by Linda Martín Alcoff and Eduardo Mendieta (Malden, MA: Blackwell, 2003), pp. 1–8 (p. 5–6).
8. Edward Said in his book *Orientalism* (1978) claims that collective identities involve 'the construction of opposites and "others" whose actuality is always subject to the continuous interpretation and re-interpretation of their difference from us' (New York: Vintage, 1994), p. 332.
9. Marina Warner, *Fantastic Metamorphoses, Other Worlds: Ways of Telling the Self* (Oxford and New York: Oxford University Press, 2002), p. 17.
10. Theodor Adorno and Max Horkheimer, *Dialektik der Aufklärung* (Frankfurt a.M.: Fischer, 1986), p. 262.

11. E.g. D. B. D. Asker, *Aspects of Metamorphosis: Fictional Representations of the Becoming Human* (Amsterdam: Rodopi, 2001).
12. Georg Wilhelm Friedrich Hegel, *Vorlesungen über die Ästhetik II*, in *Werke*, XIV, ed. by Eva Moldenhauer and Karl Markus Michel (Frankfurt a.M.: Suhrkamp, 1999), p. 36.
13. All references to Kafka's literary work are taken from Franz Kafka, *Gesammelte Werke*, Kritische Ausgabe, 12 vols, ed. by Hans-Gerd Koch (Frankfurt a.M: Fischer, 1994).
14. Giorgio Agamben, *The Open: Man and Animal* (Stanford: Stanford University Press, 2004), p. 35.
15. Ursula Reber, *Formenverschleifung: Zu einer Theorie der Metamorphose* (Paderborn: Fink, 2009), pp. 54–55.
16. Plato claimed that: 'if we are ever going to know anything purely, we must be rid of [the body] and must view the objects themselves with the soul as itself' (*Phaedo*, trans. by David Gallop (Oxford: Oxford University Press, 2009), 11.65c–67d, p. 12).
17. Marie Luise Kaschnitz, *Das dicke Kind und andere Erzählungen*, Text und Commentar, ed. by Asta-Maria Bachmann and Uwe Schweikert (Frankfurt a.M: Suhrkamp BasisBibliothek, 2002).
18. Jenny Erpenbeck, *Geschichte vom alten Kind*, Text und Commentar, Buchners Schulbibliothek der Moderne (Bamberg: Buchners, 2008).
19. M. M. Bakhtin, 'Forms of Time and of the Chronotope in the Novel: Notes towards a Historical Poetics', in *The Dialogic Imagination: Four Essays*, trans. by Caryl Emerson and Michael Holquist (Austin: University of Texas Press, 2004), pp. 84–258 (p. 115).
20. Carla Dente and others, *Proteus: The Language of Metamorphosis* (Aldershot: Ashgate, 2005), p. 18.
21. Elias Canetti, *Das Gewissen der Worte: Essays* (Munich: Hanser, 1983), p. 253.
22. Hans Jakob Christoffel von Grimmelshausen, *Der abenteuerliche Simplicissimus Teutsch* (Stuttgart: Reclam, 1986), p. 619 ('Continuatio', ch. 9).
23. W. G. Sebald, *Die Ringe des Saturn: eine englische Wallfahrt* (Frankfurt a.M.: Eichborn, 2001), p. 32.
24. Yoko Tawada, *Opium für Ovid: Ein Kopfkissenbuch von 22 Frauen* (Tübingen: Konkursbuchverlag, 2000).
25. On the rejection of affect within literary studies: Ildiko Csengei, *Sympathy, Sensibility and the Literature of Feeling in the Eighteenth Century* (Basingstoke: Palgrave Macmillan, 2012), esp. p. 15; Burkhard Meyer-Sickendiek, *Affektpoetik: Eine Kulturgeschichte literarischer Emotionen* (Würzburg: Könighausen und Neumann, 2005), esp. p. 10.
26. Lila Abu-Lughod and Catherine Lutz, eds, *Language and the Politics of Emotion* (Cambridge: Cambridge University Press), 1990), p. 103.
27. For an account of historical changes in German emotion terms see Ute Frevert and others, *Gefühlswissen: Eine lexikalische Spurensuche in der Moderne* (Frankfurt a.M.: Campus, 2011).
28. Charles Altieri, *The Particulars of Rapture: An Aesthetics of the Affects* (Ithaca: Cornell University Press, 2003).
29. Ibid., p. 2.
30. Anna Parkinson, 'Aptitudes of Feeling: Ekphrasis as Prosthetic Witnessing in Anne Duden's *Judas Sheep*', *New German Critique*, 112 38 (2011), 39–63 (p. 45).
31. Jonathan Flatley, *Affective Mapping: Melancholia and the Politics of Modernism* (Cambridge, MA: Harvard University Press, 2008), p. 12.
32. Philosopher Robert Solomon has claimed that emotions are judgements (e.g. in his book *The Passions: Emotions and the Meaning of Life* (Indianapolis: Hackett, 1976), p. 125); psychologist Klaus Scherer has developed an appraisal theory of emotion (e.g. in his article 'Appraisal Theories', in *Handbook of Cognition and Emotion*, ed. by Tim Dalgleish and Mick Power (Chichester: Wiley, 1999), pp. 637–63.
33. E.g. Frevert, *Gefühlswissen*.
34. Susan James, *Passion and Action: The Emotions in Seventeenth-Century Philosophy* (Oxford: Oxford University Press, 1997).
35. Melissa Gregg and Gregory J. Seigworth, 'Introduction', in *Affect Theory Reader*, ed. by Melissa Gregg, Gregory J. Seigworth, and Sara Ahmed (Durham, NC: Duke University Press, 2010), pp. 1–28 (p. 1).
36. Patricia T. Clough, 'The Affective Turn: Political Economy, Biomedia and Bodies', *Theory,*

Culture and Society, 25.1 (2008), 1–22 (p. 1).
37. Harold Skulsky, *Metamorphosis: The Mind in Exile* (Cambridge, MA and London: Harvard University Press, 1981).
38. Thomas Nagel, 'What is it like to be a bat?', *The Philosophical Review*, 84.4 (1974), 435–50.
39. Skulsky, p. 2.
40. Irving Massey, *The Gaping Pig: Literature and Metamorphosis* (Berkeley, Los Angeles, and London: University of California Press, 1976).
41. Ibid., p. 1.
42. Monika Schmitz-Emans, *Poetiken der Verwandlung* (Innsbruck: Studienverlag, 2008).
43. D. B. D. Asker, *Aspects of Metamorphosis: Fictional Representations of the Becoming Human* (Amsterdam: Rodopi, 2001), p. 5.
44. Caroline Walker Bynum, *Metamorphosis and Identity* (New York and Cambridge, MA: Zone/MIT Press, 2001).
45. Ibid., pp. 23–25.
46. Pascal Nicklas, *Die Beständigkeit des Wandels: Metamorphosen in Literatur und Wissenschaft* (Hildesheim: Olms, 2002).
47. Friedmann Harzer, *Erzählte Verwandlung: Eine Poetik epischer Metamorphosen (Ovid, Kafka, Ransmayr)* (Tübingen: Niemeyer, 2000).
48. Bruce Clarke, *Allegories of Writing: The Subject of Metamorphosis* (Albany: State University of New York Press, 1995), p. 2.
49. Bruce Clarke, *Posthuman Metamorphosis: Narrative and Systems* (New York: Fordham, 2008).

CHAPTER 1

Inner Realms: The Painful Pleasure of Metamorphosis in E.T.A. Hoffmann

Metamorphosis and the Romantic Individual

One might suppose that tales of strange, irrational metamorphoses would go into decline in the modern period, at least, certainly after the Enlightenment with its emphasis on rational thinking and faith in human progress. Other literary forms such as the eighteenth-century *Bildungsroman*, which charts the development of an individual, might seem more appropriate to an age based on human advancement. In contrast, tales of metamorphosis, with their depiction of sudden, radical change, undermine individual autonomy and progress. Yet tales of metamorphosis flourished, particularly in German Romantic literature of the period around 1800.

To understand the appeal of metamorphosis during the Romantic period, some aspects of the social landscape might be considered. First, the political fragmentation of the German lands led to an attempt to establish a sense of cultural unity, for example, through promoting tales that were perceived to belong to a German folk tradition. The *Kinder- und Hausmärchen* [*Fairy Tales*] of the brothers Grimm, first published in 1812 and in five further revisions until 1858, can be seen as part of the attempt to establish a German cultural heritage. Such *Märchen* tend to be set in a magical, fictionalized past in which metamorphoses are commonplace. In the *Kinder- und Hausmärchen*, metamorphoses may be caused by magic, or through appearances having been deceptive, or they may be based on animism.[1] They may also be embedded within a moral framework, for example, when they are enacted as punishment or when they reveal animals to have been human, and therefore demanding of certain behavioural expectations.[2]

Secondly, metamorphosis may serve an articulation of individual instability, which can be related to Enlightenment concerns with autonomy, rationality, and personal identity. By raising the need for new philosophical and scientific understandings of what it is to be a person, uncertainties about the integrity of the individual are also opened up. Romantic literature explores such uncertainties through unstable and metamorphic figures. As well as human–animal transformations, literature of this period presents diverse ways in which individuals may be subject to radical physical or psychological change. Popular Romantic figures such as Doppelgänger (one person split in two), vampires (in-between living and dead), mermaids (lacking a human soul), and puppets (lifelike but soulless) all contest the boundaries of the individual, and can be seen as part of negotiating a new understanding of the modern individual.

The use of metamorphosis to articulate individual instability and inner conflicts is particularly apparent in the work of late Romantic E. T. A. Hoffmann (1776–1822). Hoffmann's own frequent geographical displacement, financial insecurity, and radical changes of circumstance both through personal troubles and through socio-political upheaval, attest to a particularly unsettled life. Hoffmann's literary work is only part of his creative output: he aspired primarily to a career as musician and composer, but was also a talented caricaturist and illustrator, occupations which he often pursued alongside his work in the legal profession. At the age of twenty, Hoffmann was sent from his home town of Königsberg to Glogau, in the Prussian provinces, following a scandal caused by a love affair. After a move to Płock in New East Prussia, following another scandal caused by his caricatures of military officers, Hoffmann obtained a job in Warsaw in 1804, which he lost when Napoleon captured Warsaw in 1806. After a move to occupied Berlin, and then to Bamberg to work as stagehand, decorator and playwright at the Bamberg theatre, Hoffmann began to write as a music critic. His innovative musical reviews and stories about music led to further literary pieces. His first collection of stories, the *Fantasiestücke in Callots Manier*, was published in 1814, the same year as his opera *Undine* was performed to great acclaim. By this time, Hoffmann had also worked as musical director of an opera company in Dresden, and witnessed the horrors of the battle of Dresden in 1813. Over the following decade, until his death at the age of forty-six, Hoffmann became a prolific writer of tales. His work often draws on fantasy genres such as *Märchen*, but blends *Märchen* characteristics with satirical portrayals of contemporary society. As such, Hoffmann's tales are sometimes considered to be situated on the cusp between Romanticism and later Realism, with its psychological narratives.[3]

While Hoffmann has been considered a key author of Romantic tales of metamorphosis,[4] the kinds of metamorphosis found in his work often differ from those of myth and more straightforward *Märchen* in that their reality may be subject to doubt. It is not always clear whether the metamorphoses have really taken place, or are only imagined. Yet the ambiguity surrounding metamorphosis does not mean that Hoffmann's texts should be discounted from a study of metamorphosis. On the contrary, uncertainly over reality is a central feature of modern metamorphosis texts, which often belong to the genre of fantastic literature. Hoffmann's work also exhibits a great variety of metamorphoses, and characters who undergo numerous metamorphoses. Some scholars have distinguished between literature that involves such a protean capacity for metamorphosis and that which places emphasis on single, specific metamorphoses.[5] In Hoffmann's work the dualistic transition from one state or bodily form to another might be seen as part of a wider picture of constant tensions, dualities, and metamorphoses.

When metamorphosis explores the tensions inherent in modern identity, then it is an affective process, articulating both anxieties and desires over becoming other. The association between Romantic writing and a particularly intense form of affectivity has become commonplace. Indeed, the term 'romantic', referring to the affective style, has etymological roots in the highly affective forms of prose narrative from which the novel ('Roman') stems. Although affect is crucial to understanding Romantic literature, critical studies prior to the past couple of decades have tended to disregard affect, as discussed in the introduction. Highly affective literary work such as Hoffmann's has often been considered disreputable, even within Hoffmann's own time. Goethe, for example, regarded Hoffmann's work as mentally deranged,[6] while Heinrich Heine, writing in 1830 as German Romanticism was drawing to a close, cited Hoffmann's intensely affective style as a reason for his fall from fashion. Heine claimed that Hoffmann used to be much read, but only by those whose nerves were too strong or too weak to be affected by gentle chords.[7] The more recent reappraisal of Hoffmann, as more than just an author of 'Unterhaltungsliteratur' [light fiction], has tended to come from areas such as narratology,[8] rather than from a reappraisal of affect itself.

The Romantic emphasis on feeling is not straightforwardly a reaction against the excessive rationality of the Enlightenment, but rather stems in part from Enlightenment thinkers' attempt to understand human nature in its affective as well as rational capacity.[9] The emancipation of the individual from religious precepts and social bonds also means a turn towards the inner self and its feelings. Indeed, feelings become markers of subjectivity, and grounds for realizing one's individuality: for example, Herder writes in 1769 'Ich fühle mich! Ich bin!' [I feel! I am!].[10] Yet if feelings are markers of the self, we might ask: what happens to feelings when the self is called into question, as in tales of metamorphosis? We might expect to find both positive affects, when metamorphosis is a way of realizing the self, and negative affects when metamorphosis poses a threat to the self. By investigating the varied affects involved in metamorphosis, this chapter aims to gain insight into configurations of self and affect during the late Romantic period, as well as to examine the role of metamorphosis in the work of one major writer of this period.

The division of the chapter into three parts reflects the different forms of metamorphosis in Hoffmann's work, and the different affective states with which they are associated. I structure the chapter as musical movements to reflect Hoffmann's understanding of literature as part of a broader and integrated system of art. The first part explores the metamorphoses of 'Der goldne Topf' [The Golden Pot], which are situated within a wonderful utopian fantasy. At the opposite end of the spectrum are metamorphoses that belong to darker, dystopian fantasies, which I explore through 'Der Sandmann' [The Sandman] in the second part. Besides these opposing forms of metamorphosis, as wonderful possibility or as horrific breakdown, Hoffmann's work contains a third type of metamorphosis, as a humorous and satirical process, which I explore in particular through the tales of Milo and Berganza in the *Fantasiestücke in Callots Manier* [Fantasy Pieces in the Style of Callot]. If, as scholars claim, Hoffmann's dualities find their resolution through humour, as a way of accepting the conflicts and tensions of the individual, then the third part of the chapter examines this resolution.[11]

Animato: Metamorphic *Fantasies* in 'Der goldne Topf'

'Der goldne Topf' (1815, revised 1819) was published in Hoffmann's first collection of tales entitled *Fantasiestücke in Callots Manier*. The title of the collection alludes to popular baroque illustrator Jacques Callot (1592–1635). The preface to the collection contains a discussion of particular features of Callot's visual art that might be compared to Hoffmann's literary work. For example, the narrator admires Callot's ability to fill a small space with an abundance of objects and figures without allowing the gaze to become lost or confused.[12] Such multiplicity also characterizes Hoffmann's approach to metamorphosis, which is never of a single character, but which happens to a varied assortment of figures and objects. Hoffmann also identifies a quality in Callot's figures that he calls 'etwas fremdartig bekanntes' (II, 17) [something strangely familiar]. This almost paradoxical combination of the familiar and the strange forms an underlying dialectic in Hoffmann's work as well. 'Der goldne Topf' provides a particularly clear example. The story, which Hoffmann subtitles as a 'Märchen aus der neuen Zeit' [A Modern Fairy-Tale], begins in the familiar, contemporary reality of Dresden on ascension day at three o'clock in the afternoon, but moves rapidly into a strange 'Märchen-like' world in which figures are not what they first seem. Many of the figures encountered by the hero Anselmus turn out to have alternative forms, and the capacity to transform into animals and things. In exploring the role of metamorphosis in this tale, I situate the metamorphoses within Hoffmann's wider artistic project, while particularly considering the importance of affective expression.

Animistic Metamorphoses: The Transformative Power of Feeling

Scholars have frequently discussed the interplay of the ordinary and the wonderful in 'Der goldne Topf', but what implications does this have for the representation of metamorphosis? Most importantly, it means that, in contrast to myth and traditional 'Märchen', magical transformations are not simply taken for granted. Rather, the central protagonist, Anselmus, has to be initiated into the wonderful realm and to become convinced that he is not suffering from a delusion before he can accept the metamorphoses as real.

The process of initiation into the wonderful, metamorphic realm is not simply a matter of encountering this other realm, but requires affective transformation. The initiation process begins early in the tale, when Anselmus knocks into an old woman, who spills her basket of apples and cries 'Ins Kristall bald dein Fall' (II, 229) [into glass you'll soon pass (p. 1)]. Though encountered within the everyday reality of Dresden, the old woman turns out to be a metamorphic figure, an evil adversary who takes forms such as a door-knocker, a witch, a nurse-maid, and a mangel-wurzel, and her cry prefigures a magical episode later in the tale. However, Anselmus only starts to become aware of the magical realm to which this figure belongs when he sits down to bemoan his fate under an elder-tree. In a famous passage that marks Anselmus's initiation into the wonderful realm, Anselmus begins to hear soft whispering sounds that seem like words:

> Zwischen durch — zwischen ein — zwischen Zweigen, zwischen schwellenden Blüten, schwingen, schlängeln, schlingen wir uns — Schwesterlein — Schwesterlein, schwinge dich im Schimmer — schnell, schnell herauf — herab — Abendsonne schießt Strahlen, zischelt der Abendwind — raschelt der Tau — Blüten singen — rühren wie Zünglein, singen wir mit Blüten und Zweigen — Sterne bald glänzen — müssen herab — zwischen durch, zwischen ein schlängeln, schlingen, schwingen wir uns Schwesterlein. —
> So ging es fort in Sinne-verwirrender Rede. (II, 233–34)
>
> [Through the trees, through the leaves, through the swelling blossoms, we slip and slide and slither — sisters, little sisters, slither through the shimmering sunshine — up and down — the evening sun shoots its beams, the evening breeze breathes and stirs the leaves — the dew descends — the blossoms are singing — let's raise our voices, and sing with the blossoms and the breeze — soon stars will be shining — we must descend — through the leaves, slip and slither, little sisters.
> And so it went on, bewilderingly.][13]

The sibilance in this lyrical passage conveys the sense of leaves rustling, thereby blending the auditory impression of wind in the tree with intelligible words, and making Anselmus and the reader uncertain as to whether he is hearing words or the sound of the wind. The disconnected phrases make use of repetition, giving a sense of movement, and suggest images of nature and make reference to sisters ('Schwesterlein'), even while no speaker is apparent.

It is in this state of uncertainty and heightened sensorial awareness of nature that Anselmus encounters the metamorphic figure of Serpentina. Their encounter is preceded by a sound like a trio of crystal bells and the sight of three snakes gleaming in gold and green. Although Anselmus is inclined to distrust his senses (he explains the snakes away as the evening sun playing in the tree), the sight of Serpentina produces a profoundly affective shock:

> Da fuhr es ihm durch alle Glieder wie ein elektrischer Schlag, er erbebte im Innersten — er starrte hinauf und ein Paar herrliche dunkelblaue Augen blickten ihn mit unaussprechlicher Sehnsucht an, so daß ein nie gekanntes Gefühl der höchsten Seligkeit und des tiefsten Schmerzes seine Brust zersprengen wollte. (II, 234)
>
> [An electric shock seemed to penetrate his entire body, he trembled inwardly; he stared upwards, and saw a pair of magnificent dark-blue eyes looking at him with inexpressible yearning, so that a mixture of happiness and intense pain, which he had never felt before, made his heart almost burst. (p. 5)]

In Hoffmann's day, electricity was considered to be a kind of life-force, or as Maria Tatar claims, 'a magical power that promised to renew health by renewing the harmony between man and nature'.[14] In the passage above, the sensation of the electric shock is a way of suggesting a powerful, life-giving, affective force. The inner shock that Anselmus feels is an experience of profound affective transformation. It transforms Anselmus's state from one of mundane despondency and disbelief, to one of intense affective conflict, a mixture of pleasure and pain that threatens to split his breast. Thus, the initiation into the wonderful realm not only involves an affective transformation, but the new affective state threatens the loss of bodily integrity.

The new feeling of intense, co-existing pleasure and pain is characteristically Romantic. According to G. H. Schubert, whom Maria Tatar describes as 'one of Hoffmann's mentors in psychological matters' the distinct combination of bliss and pain surfaces when the cerebral nerves, which serve as the seat of consciousness, yield control to the ganglionic nerves, governing unconscious behaviour. That is, semi-conscious states of mesmerism, intoxication and madness are also states in which bliss and pain are intensified.[15] Under the elder tree, smoking a pipe and lost in thought, Anselmus succumbs to his unconscious, and discovers a Romantic sensation of love, akin to an experience of the sublime. The popular Romantic concept of the sublime can be both an aesthetic quality of nature and an affective state of an individual.

Kant's account of the sublime in 1790 was more sophisticated than that of Edmund Burke in 1757, since rather than seeing the sublime simply as a mixture of pleasure and pain, Kant sees the two as intimately interconnected. When experiencing the sublime in nature, for example in viewing immense heights, Kant claims that the fear we experience also affords a kind of pleasure because we are able to recognize ourselves as being outside of nature, and are thereby able to transcend our fear. In other words, while we feel ourselves to be threatened, we also gain an accentuated sense of that self that is threatened.[16]

Anselmus's encounter with wonderful figures brings him into a sublime state of painful bliss or blissful pain, which also heightens his sense of self. Thinking upon his recent acquaintance with Archivist Lindhorst, he also experiences such a state: 'Er fühlte, wie ein unbekanntes Etwas in seinem Innersten sich regte und ihm jenen wonnevollen Schmerz verursachte, der eben die Sehnsucht ist, welche dem Menschen ein anderes, höheres Sein verheißt' (II, 252) [He felt some unknown force stirring within him and causing that blissful pain, that yearning, which assures humanity of another and higher existence (p. 21)]. Through his encounters with the wonderful, metamorphic figures of Serpentina and Lindhorst, Anselmus is transformed affectively, and initiated into a new state of being.

For Hoffmann the sublime is found not only in nature but in art, particularly music. The sound of bells preceding Anselmus's first encounter with Serpentina is an example of music providing initiation into a higher state of being. Hoffmann's early tales, focusing mainly on musical experiences, deal centrally with the sublime experience elicited by music. In 'Don Juan', which is both an innovative opera review and a fantastic tale, the narrator is overwhelmed by hearing the voice of Donna Anna, and feels an 'unaussprechlicher, himmlischer Schmerz wie die unsäglichste Freude der entzückten Seele' (II, 96) [unspeakable, heavenly pain like the most inexpressible pleasure of the enraptured soul]. The adjectives 'unaussprechlich' and 'himmlisch' point towards an inexpressible, higher realm. However, Donna Anna's extreme affective state also leads to her death after the performance. With its conflicting affects, sublime artistic sensibility threatens to destroy the body. Thus, in Hoffmann's 'Rat Krespel' (1819), Antonie's sublime voice is said to be the result of an organic flaw in her breast, which will also lead to her early death. While sublime affects heighten the self, they also lead to bodily destruction.

Anselmus's encounter with Serpentina is experienced not only as an affective transformation, but as a transformation of nature. The tree seems to come alive and speak to him, saying: 'Du lagst in meinem Schatten, mein Duft umfloß Dich, aber Du verstandest mich nicht. Der Duft ist meine Sprache, wenn ihn die Liebe entzündet' (II, 234) [You lay in my shade, surrounded by my fragrance, but you did not understand me. The fragrance is my language, when it is kindled by love (p. 5)]. Through love, the language of the natural world — the scent of the elder-tree, the breeze of the evening wind, the glow of the sun's rays — becomes perceptible. The enlivening of nature culminates in Anselmus staring longingly into the snake's blue eyes: 'Da regte und bewegte sich alles, wie zum frohen Leben erwacht' (II, 235) [Then everything around him began to stir, as though waking into joyous life (p. 6)]. The process of 'ins Leben treten' [coming to life], as Hoffmann calls it in a letter to his publisher in 1813, might be described as a form of animistic metamorphosis, and is something that is central to Hoffmann's wider poetics of transformation as a way of access to another, higher, form of existence.[17]

The idea of nature becoming animate is a common Romantic trope, which Eichendorff's short poem 'Wünschelrüte' [Divining Rod] (1835) encapsulates particularly succinctly:

> Schläft ein Lied in allen Dingen,
> Die da träumen fort und fort
> Und die Welt hebt an zu singen,
> Triffst du nur das Zauberwort.[18]

[A song is sleeping in all things, | That are dreaming on and on, | The world is lifted into song, | if only you find the magic word.]

In Eichendorff's poem, things become animate through the magical properties of language. The poem might be read as an account of the poetic capacity for bringing things to life. For the musician, artist, and writer Hoffmann, it is not only language that brings things to life but the intense affective state that is at the basis of all Romantic art. Sublime romantic love transforms nature and brings things to life. In this way, Anselmus's affective transformation is integral to his ability to become aware of the wonderful possibilities of another, higher realm.

Perceptual Metamorphoses: Affective Spaces

Intense affect not only provides the impetus for the animistic metamorphosis in 'Der goldne Topf', but also underlies the processes of perceptual metamorphosis in this tale. The idea of perceptual metamorphosis, in which transformations are not situated clearly within reality, but are connected to the protagonist's state of mind, is key to understanding Hoffmann's poetics. Perceptual metamorphosis is at work when Anselmus first goes to Archivist Lindhorst's house and attempts to knock on the door. Upon doing so, the face on the bronze door-knocker grins at him and Anselmus recognizes the woman whose apples he had knocked over ('da verzog sich das metallene Gesicht im ekelhaften Spiel blauglühender Lichtblicke zum grinsenden Lächeln. Ach! Es war ja das Apfelweib vom schwarzen Tor', II, 243–44) [its metal features were hideously obscured by fiery blue rays and contorted into a grin. Alas! It was the apple-woman from the Black Gate! (p. 14)]. Anselmus experiences the animistic metamorphosis of the door-knocker as real, and ends up running away. However, the next time he goes to Lindhorst's house, he wonders whether the previous transformation was merely an effect of the strong liqueur he had drunk. The reality of the metamorphosis thus becomes subject to doubt.

Another example of Anselmus calling his perception into question is when he watches Lindhorst walk away into the dusk and then sees a white-grey kite in the air. He realizes that the flutter of white that he had assumed was Lindhorst's cloak must have been that of the kite, although he cannot understand where Lindhorst can suddenly have gone. Anselmus's confusion leads him to consider the possibility of metamorphosis:

> 'Er kann aber auch selbst in Person davongeflogen sein, der Herr Archivarius Lindhorst,' sprach der Student Anselmus zu sich selbst; 'denn ich sehe und fühle nun wohl, daß alle die fremden Gestalten aus einer fernen wundervollen Welt, die ich sonst nur in ganz besondern merkwürdigen Träumen schaute, jetzt in mein waches reges Leben geschritten sind und ihr Spiel mit mir treiben.' (II, 258)

> ['But he may have flown away in his own person, Archivist Lindhorst,' said Anselmus to himself, 'for I can see and feel that all the strange figures from a distant world of wonders, which before I saw only in rare and remarkable dreams, have now entered my waking life and are making me their plaything.' (p. 25)]

Anselmus's uncertain reasoning process is captured in the long, conjoined phrases of this passage. Gabriela Brunner-Ungricht highlights this passage as a classic example of Hoffmann's narrative technique, which shifts from the everyday to the wonderful through making use of a gaze that may be the product of unclear, subjective perception.[19] Yet what has not been adequately stressed in scholarship addressing the subjective nature of Hoffmann's metamorphoses is the way in which perception is modulated affectively. Anselmus's interpretation of the apparent metamorphoses fluctuates between disbelief and belief according to his affective state. To explain this in more detail, I take as an example Anselmus's changing experience of Lindhorst's house.

Every time Anselmus visits Lindhorst's rooms they appear different, sometimes wonderful, metamorphic, and animistic, and sometimes ordinary. The first time Anselmus enters Lindhorst's house he has remained sober and is inclined to disbelieve the transformation of the door-knocker on the previous occasion. On the other hand, he is hopeful of meeting the wonderful figure Serpentina. When Anselmus enters Lindhorst's garden in this state of mingled doubt and hope, he sees wonderful flowers bathed in a magical light, hears strange sounds and notices glorious scents. He also starts to hear voices mocking him and ridiculing his appearance (II, 269–70). His experience of the room correlates with the way in which, at this stage of the tale, Anselmus has become aware of a wonderful realm, but feels awkward and uncertain and in a state of conflict over whether he believes in wonderful occurrences such as metamorphosis. After he has been mocked, Anselmus sees the fire-lily bush move towards him and transform into Lindhorst: 'er sah, daß es der

Archivarius Lindhorst war, dessen blumigter in gelb und rot glänzender Schlafrock ihn nur getäuscht hatte' (II, 270) [At that moment the orange lily walked towards him, and he saw that it was Archivarius Lindhorst, and that the brilliant red and yellow flowers on the Archivist's dressing-gown had deceived his sight (p. 38)]. This time, the narrative, which is focalized through Anselmus's perspective, rules out an actual metamorphosis. Instead, Lindhorst's transformation is positioned as only an apparent metamorphosis. The dismissal of potential wonder continues when Anselmus is taken to Lindhorst's writing room, where Anselmus seems to see Serpentina reflected in a bronze statue. However, Lindhorst tells Anselmus that Serpentina is elsewhere taking her piano lesson. In this way, Anselmus's previous experience of Serpentina as a golden snake is undermined by her inclusion within the ordinary bourgeois world. The reality of wonder and metamorphosis is thus called into doubt.

Anselmus's subsequent visits to Lindhorst's house help to confirm a correlation between the appearance of the rooms and Anselmus's state of mind. The second time Anselmus enters the garden room, after having worked for Lindhorst for several days, Anselmus is again able to grasp 'alle Wunder einer höheren Welt' (II, 284) [all the wonders of a higher world (p. 50)]. This time he is not only amazed by the wonder of the garden, but also sees things he had not previously noticed:

> er sah nun deutlich, daß manche seltsame Blüten, die an den dunklen Büschen hingen, eigentlich in glänzenden Farben prunkende Insekten waren [. . .] Dagegen waren wieder die rosenfarbenen und himmelblauen Vögel duftende Blumen, und der Geruch, den sie verbreiteten, stieg aus ihren Kelchen empor in leisen lieblichen Tönen die sich mit dem Geplätscher der fernen Brunnen, mit dem Säuseln der hohen Stauden und Bäume zu geheimnisvollen Akkorden einer tiefklagenden Sehnsucht vermischten. (II, 285)

> [he could now perceive that many of the strange flowers hanging on the dark bushes were in fact little insects resplendent in gleaming colours [. . .] As for the rose-pink and sky-blue birds, they had turned into fragrant flowers, and the scent they emitted rose from their cupped petals in soft, lovely tones, which mingled with the whisper of distant fountains and the murmuring of the lofty trees and shrubs to form mysterious chords that uttered a deep, sorrowful yearning. (p. 51)]

The metamorphic qualities of the plants and animals are central to the wonder of the garden. This time Anselmus is able to see that some of the strange petals are insects and that the birds are flowers. These objects undergo a perceptual transformation that is made possible by Anselmus's renewed receptivity to alternative possibilities opened up by wonder. Like Anselmus's multi-sensorial experience under the elder-tree, in this passage, Anselmus's experience of things having wonderful, alternative forms is mediated through a particular affective mood evoked through multiple senses. The Romantic longing ('Sehnsucht') described in this passage intimates secret depths (the longing is 'geheimnisvoll' and 'tiefklagend'), pointing towards the affectively charged promise of alternative existence.

This impression of the garden contrasts markedly with its appearance on the day after Anselmus has drunk punch at Konrektor Paulmann's house. On this occasion, Anselmus is feeling grateful towards Veronika for having dispelled his foolishness ('albernen Grillen'), and has resolved to become a privy councillor and to marry Veronika. Now the garden appears ordinary, and even unpleasant:

> Als er nun mittags durch den Garten des Archivarius Lindhorst ging, konnte er sich nicht genug wundern, wie ihm das Alles sonst so seltsam und wundervoll habe vorkommen können. Er sah nichts als gewöhnliche Scherbenpflanzen, allerlei Geranien, Myrtenstöcke und dergleichen. Statt der glänzenden bunten Vögel, die ihn sonst geneckt, flatterten nur einige Sperlinge hin und her, die ein unverständliches unangenehmes Geschrei erhoben, als sie den Anselmus gewahr wurden. (II, 300)
>
> [At noon, walking through the Archivist's conservatory, he was astonished that the objects there should ever have seemed to him so strange and wondrous. He could see nothing but ordinary potted plants, various kinds of geraniums, myrtle-bushes, and so forth. Instead of the brilliantly coloured birds that had teased him in the past, there were only a few sparrows fluttering to and fro, which made an unintelligible and unpleasant noise on catching sight of Anselmus. (p. 65)]

Once Anselmus starts to entertain the bourgeois ideals of social status and married life, he is no longer open for the experience of Romantic love and the awareness of a higher world. The garden then loses all sense of wonder. Anselmus can no longer understand the birds, and when he attempts to copy the manuscripts for Lindhorst he finds his task impossible. Whereas he previously found himself able to not only copy, but even to understand the strange characters, he now becomes completely confused and ends up blotting the original (II, 301).

Anselmus's affectively changing perception makes the things in Lindhorst's house appear different every time, not simply in their degree of pleasantness, but in terms of their actual form. As readers, we do not know whether Lindhorst's garden is full of magical flowers and talking birds, whose language Anselmus occasionally fails to comprehend, or whether the birds' talking is only in Anselmus's mind. Since the narrative is focalized through Anselmus's perspective, the reader has no access to an objective reality, and it is therefore impossible to distinguish between what the garden is really like, and how it appears to Anselmus.

By foreclosing the possibility of an objective reality, the text can be seen as reflecting contemporary philosophical debates about the nature of the external world. Though Hoffmann does not deeply engage with philosophy or literary theory like many other Romantic writers, he did attend some of Kant's lectures while growing up in Königsberg, and he read with considerable interest some of Schelling's works. Both of these philosophers addressed the issue that Hoffmann problematizes through his narrative technique, namely the problem of whether we can know an objective reality, independent of a subject's perception. Kant attempted to deal with this problem by identifying in detail the ways in which the external world is accessible through our conceptual structures. However, the problem for idealists such as Schelling was that Kant appeared to give no account of how a subject that has these conceptual structures can exist as a free subject within a determinate nature. For idealists, Kant's account appeared to create a duality between subject and nature, which they hoped to resolve. To do so, one possibility is to reject the idea of objectively existing nature, or alternatively to consider nature as in some sense subjective.[20] Schelling adopted the latter position in the late 1790s through his important contribution to the idealist movement of *Naturphilosophie*, which had become popular in Romantic circles by the 1800s. Schelling famously argued for the unity of nature and mind: 'Die Natur soll die sichtbare Geist, der Geist die unsichtbare Natur sein. Hier also, in der absoluten Identität des Geistes in uns und der Natur außer uns, muß das Problem, wie eine Natur außer uns möglich sey, auflösen' [Nature must be the visible mind, mind the invisible nature. Here, therefore, in the absolute identity of the mind within us and the nature outside of us, the problem of how it is possible for nature to exist without us must disappear].[21]

Hoffmann studied Schelling's *Von der Weltseele* [On the World Soul] in 1813, shortly after completing the *Fantasiestücke*,[22] but the idea of a correspondence between nature and mind can already be seen in 'Der goldne Topf'. Anselmus's affectively changing perspective filters the reader's impression of the garden in such a way that the garden cannot be grasped as an objectively existing entity. The metamorphic changes of the natural environment parallel the affective changes of Anselmus's subjectivity. In a state of love, longing, or the sublime, states that for Romantics heighten subjectivity, nature appears to come alive, while unfeeling bourgeois pragmatism reduces awareness of nature. If nature is identical with mind, as proponents of *Naturphilosophie* claim, then nature must be subject to the same kind of metamorphic changes as our minds are through the operation of the affects.

The new understanding of the external world, which underlies Hoffmann's text, leads to a fundamentally different form of metamorphosis than those of myth or *Märchen*, whose reality tends not to be called into question. In Hoffmann's work, metamorphosis does not simply take place within an independent external reality, but rather, it happens through perception, and, as I have claimed, through the affective modulation of perception.

Utopian Metamorphoses: Escapism or Allegory?

'Der goldne Topf' marks a new, modern way of narrating metamorphosis in the sense that the metamorphosis is not situated in a wonderful realm in which such events are commonplace. Rather, the fact that Anselmus is unsure whether Lindhorst or the door-knocker have really transformed marks the text as belonging to the genre of the fantastic. According to structuralist critic Tzvetan Todorov, fantastic literature characteristically involves hesitation over whether to interpret events as real or supernatural.[23] In 'Der goldne Topf' Anselmus's hesitation finds a form of resolution through his own feeling. It is his strength of feeling that convinces him that his wonderful encounters are real. For example, reflecting upon the snake in the elder tree Anselmus claims:

> 'Das alles,' schloß der Student Anselmus, 'habe ich wirklich gesehen und tief in der Brust ertönen noch im hellen Nachklange die lieblichen Stimmen, die zu mir sprachen; es war keineswegs ein Traum und soll ich nicht vor Liebe und Sehnsucht sterben, so muß ich an die goldgrünen Schlangen glauben' (II, 254–55).

> ['I saw all this,' concluded Anselmus, 'with my own eyes, and deep in my heart I can still hear the echo of the delightful voices that spoke to me; it was certainly not a dream, and if I am not to die of love and yearning, I have no choice but to believe in the green and gold snakes (p. 23)]

Anselmus's assertion that the experience was not a dream is based on the strong longing aroused in him that seems to intimate access to a deeper existence ('tief in der Brust'). Having experienced this, Anselmus expresses a need for these feelings to have a basis in reality. We might read this as an assertion of the emotional need for wonder.

The need for wonder renders the text susceptible to a charge that is often posed against fantasy or fantastic literature: that it is escapist, a flight from the everyday world rather than an engagement with it.[24] Since 'Der goldne Topf' ends with Anselmus going to live in the blissful realm of Atlantis with Serpentina, it might seem that the trajectory of this tale is an escapist one, and the metamorphoses are also escapist processes, enacting a transition into a wonderful fantasy realm. However, the tale is not escapist in the sense of avoidance of reality, since Anselmus's gradual awareness of and metamorphic immersion into this wonderful realm is positioned as part of what it is to have a poetic imagination. This becomes clear when we consider the ending, which is not simply an account of Anselmus's departure for Atlantis, but an account by a first-person narrator, an impoverished writer, of the difficulty of describing Anselmus's blissful new life. In the writer's midst of despair, Lindhorst intervenes by inviting him to finish the tale in his blue writing room. After the narrator has succeeded in expressing the wonders of Atlantis, and is again reminded of his own meagre life, Lindhorst again provides support by encouraging him to find satisfaction in the poetic vision afforded to him. The tale ends with Lindhorst's question: 'Ist denn überhaupt des Anselmus Seligkeit etwas anderes als das Leben in der Poesie, der sich der heilige Einklang aller Wesen als tiefstes Geheimnis der Natur offenbaret?' (II, 321) [Indeed, is Anselmus's happiness anything other than the life in poetry, where the holy harmony of all things is revealed as the deepest secret of nature? (p. 83)]. Through this question, Lindhorst positions Atlantis not as unattainable utopian fantasy, but as poetic construction (as 'das Leben in der Poesie'). By reflecting upon Anselmus's newfound bliss as an attainment of poetic insight, the text articulates Romantic irony, a practice of making apparent the constructedness of literary texts. Romantic irony results from the condition of the Romantic writer, who is caught in the dialectic between the everyday world and a longing for a higher realm of existence. To avoid being made miserable by the unattainablity of this other realm, in which deeper awareness becomes possible, the writer has to be able to see the higher realm as attainable through the imagination. In this way, the transformations of mundane everyday reality into wonderful bliss are not simply escapist, but are a way of articulating the value of poetic imagination.

Thus, the trajectory of the tale can be seen not as escapist but as a learning process. It is significant that Anselmus is constantly referred to as a student, despite never being shown to be engaged in university study. What Anselmus is learning is to transform himself into the 'Leben in der Poesie', to become aware of the wonderful realm. He does this by copying manuscripts for Lindhorst. In his *Romantische Metamorphosen*, Detlef Kremer argues that the process of copying is integral to cabbalistic or alchemical metamorphoses, to which the text alludes.[25] Both cabbala and alchemy involve repeating ritualistic words and following a master, in this case Lindhorst. By having Anselmus study under the guidance of such a figure, it becomes clear that Anselmus is being instructed in the art of metamorphosis. As Andrew Webber points out, many of Hoffmann's heroes are poets, artists, or musicians, and their quest involves seeing the way to a truer sense of life through its aesthetic simulation.[26]

In learning the art of metamorphosis, Anselmus also needs to learn to adopt the right kind of affective state. When Anselmus is filled with love for Serpentina he finds the task of copying easy, but after resolving to become a privy councillor he struggles. In order to be able to read and reproduce the written characters Anselmus needs to adopt a poetic sensibility made possible through his longing for Serpentina. The importance of this affective state as a way of accessing the wonderful realm is also reflected in the overall trajectory of the tale, which is not only a narrative of learning poetic awareness but a narrative of affective transformation. The tale starts with Anselmus in a despondent state of self-pity after losing his money, but ends with his having achieved a wonderful life of bliss. The many forms of metamorphosis in this tale, from the bodily transformations to Anselmus's affective transformation, are all ways of expressing the poetic capacity for imaginative transformation.

A number of scholars have highlighted the connections between metamorphosis and poetic imagination or writing. For example, Bruce Clarke reads metamorphosis as an allegory of writing.[27] Although Clarke does not discuss Hoffmann, his idea is applicable to 'Der goldne Topf', with its parallel between copying manuscripts and physical and affective metamorphosis. However, the idea of metamorphosis as an *allegory* of writing might be called into question. 'Der goldne Topf' itself invites debate on how to interpret metamorphosis and other wonderful occurrences by having the characters themselves contest the issue. In particular, the text raises three possible ways of interpreting wonderful occurrences: as madness, as allegory, or as real.

The more prosaic characters, firmly situated in the bourgeois world, tend to dismiss tales such as Lindhorst's account of Atlantis as mad. This is the view held by Sub-Rector Paulmann ('orientalischer Schwulst, werter Hr. Archivarius', II, 246; 'ich will indessen glauben, daß es die Liebe ist, die Euch in dem Gehirn spukt, das gibt sich aber bald in der Ehe, sonst wäre mir bange, daß auch Sie in einigen Wahnsinn verfallen, verehrenswürdiger Herr Hofrat', II, 315). Counsellor Heerbrand is similarly inclined, but when Veronika starts talking about the victory of the salamander he is unwilling to dismiss her as mad and instead opts for the claim that her story is 'wohl nur eine poetische Allegorie — gleichsam ein Gedicht, worin sie den gänzlichen Abschied von dem Studenten besungen' (II, 314) [no more than a poetic allegory — a metrical work, so to speak, telling of her final and entire parting from the student (p. 77)]. The particle 'nur' [only] suggests that by interpreting Veronika's narrative as a poetic allegory, it loses importance and affective power. Heerbrand thus avoids charging Veronika with madness. Veronika supports Heerbrand's view, claiming that he is welcome to consider it as 'einen recht albernen Traum' (II, 314) [a silly dream]. While Heerbrand does not want to dismiss the truth of the tale completely, it is soon forgotten, and they get engaged before the soup has had time to get cold.

While one extreme is to interpret the tales as madness, a milder course is that of poetic allegory, and at the other extreme is the claim that such narratives are true. Lindhorst holds the latter view, claiming that his account of the creation of Atlantis is the 'Wahrhaftigste, was ich Euch auftischen kann' (II, 247) [the truest story I can regale you with (p. 17), and that 'Euch mag wohl das, was ich freilich nur in ganz dürftigen Zügen erzählt habe, unsinnig und toll vorkommen, aber es ist dessen unerachtet nichts weniger als ungereimt oder auch nur allegorisch gemeint, sondern buchstäblich wahr' (II, 247) [you may well think it mere crazy nonsense; nevertheless, it is very far from absurd or even allegorical, but literally true (p. 17)]. Lindhorst explicitly denies that the story is an allegory, but claims it as true to the letter. By drawing attention to the written word ('buchstäblich') Lindhorst raises the issue of the tale's textual dimension. Yet the truth, Lindhorst suggests, is to be sought within the text, rather than outside it, as it would be to claim the text as an allegory of something else.

The debate over how to read fantastic texts, which Hoffmann instigates within his work, is also one with which Hoffmann's critics engage. Detlef Kremer argues that Hoffmann may claim to be communicating meaning through allegory, but this is deceptive. Rather, Hoffmann's fondness for multi-stranded narrative perspectives signifies a lack of closure and makes multiple, indeterminate readings inevitable.[28] Hilda Brown responds to Kremer's deconstructionist reading by providing an alternative. She begins from the assumption that 'a 'polyphonic' perspectivism does not itself spell *dis*harmony'.[29] Brown argues that Hoffmann's 'polyphonic' or multi-stranded narratives, as well as his use of irony, do not stem from despair about meaning. Rather, they suggest an 'awareness and acceptance of the contradictions with which human beings (and especially authors) are confronted, and a recognition that there are nonetheless meaningful patterns to be discerned'.[30] Brown's idea is supported by the desire for unity expressed in many of Hoffmann's texts, such as in last line of 'Der goldne Topf'.

The distrust of allegory, a form that had become disreputable by the end of the eighteenth century, also reflects a concern that allegorical interpretations reduce the story to mere riddles to be solved.[31] Heerbrand's view of Veronika's story as 'only' a poetic allegory resonates with the poetics professor's claim in 'Der Sandmann'. The professor attempts to dispel the unease over discovering that Olimpia was an automaton by saying: 'Hochzuverehrende Herren und Damen! Merken Sie denn nicht, wo der Hase im Pfeffer liegt? Das Ganze ist eine Allegorie — eine fortgeführte Metapher!' (III, 46) [My most esteemed ladies and gentlemen! Don't you see what lies behind all this? The entire matter is an allegory — an extended metaphor (p. 115)]. In both cases, the idea of allegory is used to neutralize the affective content of the story, and to dismiss its importance. Hoffmann's texts satirize this dismissive approach, since it means an inability to engage with the tale affectively and thereby to discover the wonder accessible through aesthetic experience. The notion of allegory that Hoffmann satirizes is that of allegory as extended metaphor (following Quintilian). Reading a tale as extended metaphor is to read a particular point of comparison sustained throughout the tale, which is not how Hoffmann's tales function. Detlef Kremer claims that neither 'Der Sandmann' nor the other Hoffmann tales he discusses can be categorized as allegories in this sense. However, Kremer calls for a different definition of allegory, based not on metaphor but on metonymy.[32] This would mean that no one-to-one correspondence is assumed, but rather a loose correspondence based on association. For Irving Massey, it is a metonymic process that is at work in tales of metamorphosis, not that of metaphor (p. 218). Similarly, Rosemary Jackson claims that the fantastic is not metaphorical.[33] In Hoffmann's texts, wonderful processes such as metamorphosis are not metaphors, standing for a determinate meaning, but forms of affective engagement.

Miserere: Distortions of the Night in 'Der Sandmann'

While the metamorphoses of the *Fantasiestücke* collection allow access to the wonders of a higher realm, in Hoffmann's next collection, the *Nachtstücke* (1816–17) [Nocturnes], metamorphoses expose the demonic side of human nature. Attention to both is essential to understanding Hoffmann's work.

Like the *Fantasiestücke in Callots Manier*, the title of the *Nachtstücke* references painting. 'Nachtstücke' are paintings of night-time scenes, with very little light or with artificial light from one direction, such that colours and forms appear altered from their day-time appearance. The distortion of vision plays an important role in the *Nachtstücke*, particularly in 'Der Sandmann', the first and most famous in the collection. If, in 'Der goldne Topf' metamorphosis is the result of successful poetic perception, in 'Der Sandmann' identities become problematized (doubled, split, subject to uncertainty) through distorted perception. In this respect, metamorphosis is similarly enacted, but as though transposed into a more ominous, minor key.

'Der Sandmann' revolves around a confusion of identities in the mind of the main protagonist Nathanael, who feels that the barometer-seller Coppola is his father's acquaintance Coppelius, whom Nathanael associated with the horrific figure of the Sandman. Nathanael's confused perception becomes apparent after he falls in love with the automaton Olympia, and is led gradually into madness.

Animistic Metamorphoses: Misaligned Passions

Like 'Der goldne Topf', 'Der Sandmann' centres upon a young man who undergoes a profound affective transformation after being confronted with the possibility of alternative identities and things not being what they seem. However, whereas Anselmus's sudden awareness of these other possibilities comes during a sublime experience under the elder-tree where he confronts the beautiful Serpentina, Nathanael's revelation comes as a horrific shock after encountering Coppola, whom Nathanael is convinced is Coppelius, a horrific figure from his past. This horrific encounter is introduced in the letter with which the story begins, in which Nathanael speaks of being 'in der zerrissenen Stimmung des Geistes, die mir bisher alle Gedanken verstörte' (III, 11) [in the tormented state of mind which has distracted all my thoughts until now! (p. 85)]. The disturbing effect the encounter had on him is described as a form of internal destruction ('zerrissen', 'verstören'), something pulling him apart. Whereas Anselmus's encounter allowed an intimation of wonder, Nathanael's provides '[d]unkle Ahnungen eines gräßlichen mir drohenden Geschicks' (III, 11) [dark forebodings of a hideous, menacing fate (p. 85)]. In this way, his experience can be seen as a direct counterpart to that of Anselmus. Whereas Anselmus's encounter with Serpentina took place under a tree dappled with evening sun, Nathanael's encounter gives him the sense of being covered by dark clouds which no sun can penetrate (III, 11). If Anselmus's experience is one of enlightenment, Nathanael's is one of obscured perception.

Nathanael's obscured perception forms a contrast with the clear vision of his fiancée Clara, whom he increasingly ignores, and instead falls in love with Olimpia. As in 'Der goldne Topf', the experience of falling in love brings with it a form of animistic metamorphosis. In 'Der goldne Topf', it is when Anselmus gazes into Serpentina's eyes that inanimate nature appears to come alive. In 'Der Sandmann' the process of looking into female eyes also sets in motion only a profound affective transformation in the protagonist but also an animistic metamorphosis of the external world. This happens when Nathanael uses glasses that he has been given by Coppola to look at Olimpia:

> Nur die Augen schienen ihm gar seltsam starr und tot. Doch wie er immer schärfer und schärfer durch das Glas hinschaute, war es, als gingen in Olimpias Augen feuchte Mondesstrahlen auf. Es schien, als wenn nun erst die Sehkraft entzündet würde; immer lebendiger und lebendiger flammten die Blicke. (III, 36)
>
> [It was only her eyes that seemed to him strangely fixed and dead. As he peered ever more intently through the glass, however, he thought he saw moist moonbeams shining from Olimpia's eyes. It was as though her power of vision were only now being awakened; her eyes seemed to sparkle more and more vividly (p. 106)]

Unlike Anselmus looking into Serpentina's eyes, Nathanael's animating gaze, which transforms Olimpia's eyes from death-like ('starr und tot') to living ('lebendiger und lebendiger'), has ominous undercurrents. It is mediated through an optical instrument that was given to Nathanael by the dubious figure Coppola, whom Nathanael has linked to the nursery-tale Sandman, who is said to cast sand into children's eyes and make them bleed and pop out. The link to the Sandman suggests an evil process at work upon Nathanael's vision. While Freud reads Nathanael's fear of losing his eyes as a fear of castration, a particular form of violent bodily change that constitutes a threat to identity (XII, 243), for the talented artist Hoffmann, the idea of losing eyes is not merely a bodily threat and a threat to masculine identity, but a psychological threat, a distortion of vision (as the idea of the 'Nachtstücke' suggests) that alters perception and understanding. An interest in optical distortion can be found throughout Hoffmann's work, though not always under such ominous circumstances. For example, in his later tale *Meister Floh*, Hoffmann imagines a lens inserted into the eye that enables the character Peregrinus Tyß to read other people's thoughts (VI, 383). In *Meister Floh*, this optical instrument provides privileged access to hidden inner life. In 'Der Sandmann' an instrument of optical technology seems to provide privileged access to Olimpia's inner life and feeling, but it will become apparent that the animistic transformation is a distortion of reality.

The passage above is also made ominous through the lexis of death ('starr' and 'tot'). In bringing Olimpia's eyes into life through his optically distorted vision, Nathanael is animating something that is not alive. As in 'Der goldne Topf', the process of animistic metamorphosis, as a bringing-to-life of inanimate nature and as animation of the affects, is described through the metaphor of kindling ('entzünden'). However, in the passage above, kindling produces a fire that threatens to go out of control ('immer lebendiger und lebendiger flammten die Blicke') while remaining obsessively centred upon Olimpia.

The image of fire is connected to the possibility that Nathanael fears, that he is subject to the workings of dark forces. The moments that propel Nathanael towards breakdown are all associated with fire: the fire in which his father dies, leaving Nathanael traumatized by the figure Coppelius; the fire that burns down his house, after which Nathanael is moved to a room opposite Olimpia, thereby encouraging his dangerous obsession. Whenever Nathanael feels threatened, he imagines a 'Feuerkreis' [fiery circle]. For example, he writes a poem in which he imagines being thrown into a 'Feuerkreis' by Coppelius, and then trapped forever with his fiancée Clara, who looks at him with dead eyes. Nathanael's passionate rendition of this poem horrifies Clara, who regards it as an act of madness. For Nathanael, however, the intense feelings expressed in the poem are a sign of a profound inner life, which Clara refuses to see (Nathanael calls her a 'lebloses, verdammtes Automat' III, 32 [lifeless, accursed automaton]). Yet Nathanael's need to express intense feelings is also what leads him to become trapped in the 'Feuerkreis' that he fears, which can be read as a circle of enflamed emotion that threatens to take over and make him lose grip on reality. Hoffmann's repeated use of the motifs of hot and cold (or fire and ice) to describe affective states might be read as clichéd style, but they also reveal an insistence on the connection between feeling and sensation, or mind and nature, that is central within *Naturphilosophie*.

The image of the 'Feuerkreis' recurs when Nathanael goes to ask for Olimpia's hand in marriage, and sees her as a lifeless puppet without eyes, and bloody eyes on the ground. At this point Nathanael starts to repeat the word 'Feuerkreis' until he is taken to an asylum. After recovering from this incident, Nathanael is reminded for a third time of the 'Feuerkreis', and this time it leads to his death. When he is at the top of the tower he again looks through the glasses, sees Clara, and starts shouting '*Feuerkreis* dreh dich' (III, 49) [Fiery circle, spin! (p. 118)]. On all of these occasions, the 'Feuerkreis' articulates Nathanael's feeling of being trapped, his perceptual field restricted, and the horrors from the past recurring.

According to the psychology of the day, Nathanael's obsession with the idea that he is subject to dark forces might be seen as a kind of *idée fixe* that leads into madness.[34] Around the late eighteenth century, as Foucault argues in *Madness and Civilisation*, madness was seen as a result of excessively passionate behaviour, as well as the inability to control one's passions.[35] It is no coincidence that in the highly affective literary works of this period madness is a prominent topic. Hoffmann, whose works are filled with characters like Nathanael who become overwhelmed by extreme emotions, was particularly interested in the question of how madness arises. By placing importance on passion as what makes one human, as opposed to an automaton, there is also the danger that when passions go out of control, the integrity of the subject comes under threat.

Nathanael is threatened through his inability to align his feelings with reality. Nathanael intimates Olimpia's true nature through recurrent feelings of horror, but overcomes these by the obsessive passion he feels as he gazes at her through instruments of optical distortion. A further example is when Nathanael first has physical contact with Olimpia, after having used Coppola's glasses to watch Olimpia sing:

> er küßte Olimpias Hand, er neigte sich zu ihrem Munde, eiskalte Lippen begegneten seinen glühenden! — So wie, als er Olimpias kalte Hand berührte, fühlte er sich von innerem Grausen erfaßt, die Legende von der toten Braut ging ihm plötzlich durch den Sinn; aber fest hatte ihn Olimpia an sich gedrückt, und in dem Kuß schienen die Lippen zum Leben zu erwarmen. (III, 40)

> [he kissed Olimpia's hand, he bent down to her mouth, his burning lips met ice-cold ones! Just as he had done on touching Olimpia's cold hand, he felt himself gripped by inward horror, and the legend of the dead bride suddenly flashed through his mind; but Olimpia was clasping him tightly and his kiss seemed to bring warmth and life to her lips (p. 110)]

The short clauses convey the intensity of his passion, and his shock at encountering her cold lips. The allusion to Goethe's poem 'Die Braut von Korinth' (1797), in which the narrator falls in love with a dead bride, adds to the lexis of horror, death, and the uncanny surrounding Olimpia. However, Nathanael overrides his unease with his passion. Indeed, when other people mock Olimpia's dullness, Nathanael thinks of accusing *them* of dullness for failing to recognize Olimpia's depth of soul (her 'tiefes, herrliches Gemüt'). Nathanael claims to be the privileged recipient of Olimpia's loving gaze, which enables him to gain the heightened experience of self that the notion of Romantic love brings with it: 'nur in Olimpias Liebe finde ich mein Selbst wieder' (III, 42) [only in Olimpia's love do I recognize myself (p. 111)]. However, as Freud argues, Nathanael's passion is a narcissistic one (XII, 248). Nathanael's feelings turn inwards, trapping him in the narrow circle of flames that he fears. In this way, 'Der Sandmann' explores the converse side to the passionate, poetic sensibility that transforms reality. Whereas in 'Der goldne Topf' poetic sensibility allows access to a wonderful realm and an intimation of a higher self, in 'Der Sandmann' Nathanael's poetic perception is distorted and leads to a fatal disjunction between feeling and reality.

In Hoffmann's later collection *Die Serapionsbrüder*, Serapion's madness is diagnosed as resulting from a disjunction between feeling and reality. Serapion lives wholly in his fantasy world, occupying a small hut in the woods near B★★★, which he believes to be the Thebian desert. The story of Serapion reveals the danger of the imagination. While imagination can allow access to wonder, it can also lead to delusion and madness. At the end of the tale, the friends discuss Serapion's madness, and Theodor claims that madness results from a 'Misverhältnis des inneren Gemüts mit dem äußeren Leben, welches der reizbare Mensch fühlt' (IV, 38) [disparity between inner feeling and external circumstances experienced by temperamental types]. Intense inner feelings become problematic when misaligned with reality.

The story of Serapion is used to formulate the idea of the 'Serapiontic principle', which scholars frequently claim as central to Hoffmann's poetics: the idea that access to the wonderful realm should be through reality, and that writers must remain aware of the tension between the two realms.[36] But the tale of Serapion is also an account of feeling, and of what happens when inner feeling and outer life are misaligned. While the poetic sensibility with its capacity to transform itself affectively and to transform reality perceptually can allow access to higher meaning, when the passions are based on distorted perception, any disturbance to this inner vision can cause the inward-turning passions to escape from one's control.

Perceptual Metamorphosis: Affective Subjects

In both 'Der goldne Topf' and 'Der Sandmann', metamorphosis happens through perception. As Nathanael animates Olimpia, the boundaries between living and non-living being, and between reality and delusion, become blurred. The disintegration of identity is central throughout 'Der Sandmann', since it revolves upon the uncertainty over the identities of Coppola and Coppelius, with their ominous association with the figure of the Sandman. Such confusion of identity is part of Hoffmann's wider poetics of metamorphosis, of identities breaking down and transforming.

One of the central issues in this tale is whether Coppola is indeed Coppelius, and an evil figure conspiring against Nathanael, or whether Nathanael is suffering from delusions.[37] Since the reader only has access to the incident involving Coppelius and the encounter with Coppola through Nathanael's perspective, it is difficult to get a clear purchase on the possible identity of Coppola and Coppelius. These figures also threaten Nathanael's perception, both through Coppola's glasses, and through Coppelius's Sandman-like threat of pulling out Nathanael's eyes. If, as scholars have argued, eyes are the dominant sense organs of the Enlightenment, representing insight, the loss of eyes is a marker of profound perceptual failure.[38] For Nathanael, the threat of losing his eyes is connected to a childhood encounter with Coppelius in which Coppelius appears as the dreaded Sandman. As Nathanael recounts it, his father pleads with Coppelius not to throw embers into the boy's eyes, and Coppelius relents. However, Coppelius claims that he wants to take Nathanael apart to observe the mechanism of his hand and feet: 'Und damit faßte er mich gewaltig, daß die Gelenke knackten, und schrob mir die Hände ab und die Füße und setzte sie bald hier bald dort wieder ein' (III, 17–18) [And with these words he seized me so hard that my joints made a cracking noise, dislocated my hands and feet, and put them back in various sockets (p. 91)]. The threat represented by Coppelius is not merely the threatened loss of vision, but that of bodily dismemberment and the destruction of the boundary between human and machine. The technologies that make mechanized beings (automata) and optical instruments (magnifying glasses) pose possible threats to individual autonomy. Nathanael's fear is that of being operated upon by forces outside his control, of being treated as an automaton, and in the encounter with Coppelius he perceives this to be literally the case.

The uncertain distinction between Coppola and Coppelius is reinforced by the linguistic similarity of their names, for which Freud suggests an etymological association: 'Zur Ableitung des Namens: *Coppella* = Probiertiegel (die chemischen Operationen, bei denen der Vater verunglückt); *coppo* = Augenhöhle' [*Coppella* = crucible (the chemical operations that caused the father's death); *coppo* = eye-socket] (XII, 241). Whether or not Hoffmann intended these associations, the figures Coppelius and Coppola represent both the loss of vision and the physical transformation of matter. As Kremer has pointed out, both 'Der goldne Topf' and 'Der Sandmann' revolve around the main protagonist's involvement with a figure who is suspected of carrying out transformations.[39] In 'Der goldne Topf' this is the benevolent figure Lindhorst, while in 'Der Sandmann' it is the malevolent figure Coppelius. While Lindhorst gets Anselmus to copy texts, enacting a cabbalistic form of metamorphosis,[40] Coppelius appears to have been involved in alchemical and mechanical experiments designed to transform matter. Indeed, Kremer claims that Nathanael's madness is a direct result of Coppelius's alchemical experiments.[41] By becoming involved with these masters of metamorphosis, the protagonists undergo perceptual and affective transformations, which affect their identities, and result in them becoming subsumed into another realm — Anselmus into the magical and wonderful Atlantis, and Nathanael into a world of dark, manipulative forces.

Nathanael's final breakdown, and the affective transformation that accompanies it, results from the reawakening of the threat of being trapped in the 'Feuerkreis'. Coppelius again prompts this fear, when Clara points him out in the market place as a strange grey bush that seems to be approaching. However, it is only after Nathanael looks through Coppola's spectacles and sees Clara, that an intense affective change becomes apparent in him. Nathanael starts to cry out madly, repeating 'Holzpüppchen dreh dich' [Spin, wooden dolly], and attempts to throw Clara from the tower. This happens on the top of a tower at noon, a time and place where there should be complete visual clarity, without shadows. However, it is at this point that Nathanael's perception is distorted and he finally succumbs to the psychological breakdown that had threatened him throughout.

The seeming paradox of Nathanael's breakdown happening at noon may be resolved if we consider noon, as Nietzsche does, as the time of shortest shadow. Noon, for Nietzsche, is the moment in which object and shadow become one.[42] Oddly, the tower has just been described as casting a giant shadow over the marketplace, and in this sense by going up the tower, Nathanael is entering the source of the shadow. It is also at noon that object and shadow break apart, and one becomes two, and it is at this time that Nathanael breaks down. After entering the shadow, the 'strange grey bush' that is Coppelius returns. Shadows, smoke, and the colour grey are used as motifs to suggest not only obscured perception but also Nathanael's sense that dark forces are operating over him, rendering him akin to an automaton. At the point of noon, Nathanael's dark fears emerge, and he is threatened with splitting apart. According to Alenka Zupančič, Nietzsche's figure of mid-day as that of the shortest shadow is also a concept of a temporal moment in which past and future merge and circularity and timelessness briefly appear.[43] In Hoffmann's tale, Nathanael's descent into madness and final metamorphosis is caused by the reawakening of past fears, and in that sense is not a linear but a cyclical process in which the past cannot be escaped, and the subject becomes trapped as though in a 'Feuerkreis'.

Dystopian Metamorphoses: Affective Conflict and Narrative Control

Nathanael's breakdown is partly a result of his poetic sensibility, particularly his intense emotional fixation, which prevents him from seeing clearly, and encourages a sense of being manipulated by dark forces. The image of the 'Feuerkreis' reflects his intense passions spinning out of control. Underlying the text is a model of the self as fragile and liable to break down under the influence of emotions, which are depicted as threatening, external forces.

The highly emotional central male protagonists of Hoffmann's tales, such as Anselmus and Nathanael, are often contrasted with more prosaic types, such as Veronika and Clara. In many of Hoffmann's texts, a contrast between two female characters is used to represent the dichotomous choice between intense Romantic love or a more restrained model of bourgeois love. While Anselmus attempts to choose between sensuous Serpentina and pragmatic Veronika, Nathanael is attracted by Olimpia's selfless love rather than his fiancée Clara's robust sense of self. Through the male protagonist's choice between two potential love interests, Hoffmann opens up a dichotomy between different emotional styles, either intense passion or pragmatic affection. However, while both Serpentina and Olimpia offer the promise of intense passion, Nathanael mistakenly attributes deep feeling to Olimpia, when she is in fact an automaton. In this sense, Hoffmann depicts intense passion as both seductive but also dangerous, when feelings are not allied to reality. The disjunction between passion and reality can lead to psychological breakdown and physical metamorphosis. The more pragmatic affective behaviour exemplified by Veronika and Clara does not carry the dangerous potential of metamorphosis, but also does not allow for the intimation of wonder, and the access to a higher poetic plane of existence, that intense passion provides.

A sense of the alluring but problematic nature of intense passion can also be identified through the narrative reflection upon the affects of the text. Both 'Der goldne Topf' and 'Der Sandmann' are framed by the external perspective of a first-person narrator. In both tales, the narrator positions himself as a friend of the main protagonist, thereby raising a close emotional tie to the narrative. It is because of his emotional investment in the story and its main protagonist that the narrator intervenes early on in 'Der Sandmann' to explain to the reader his choice to begin the story with letters. The narrator claims that starting with stock phrases such as 'once upon a time', or 'In the small provincial town of S. there lived', would be too mundane, while beginning 'medias in res', with Nathanael's terror at meeting Coppelius, would come across as comical. On one end of the scale is a lack of affect that fails to draw the reader in, and on the other is intense affective expression that needs to appear genuine if the reader's sympathy is to be aroused.

The use of Romantic irony, through drawing attention to the process of writing, is also a way of drawing attention to the affects of the text, and making a case for the inclusion of intense affects, while also guiding the reader towards emotional participation. While the focalization through the main protagonist invites emotional involvement, the narrative frame also makes it possible to stand back from the protagonist's intense affect and thereby achieve a level of irony and reflection.

An attempt to master difficult affects through reflecting upon them can also be sought through the writing of letters. The letters that begin 'Der Sandmann' show Nathanael struggling with his intense reaction to meeting Coppola. However, it is significant that Nathanael's letters do not continue, as he becomes more absorbed in emotional experience than in self-understanding. Nathanael's inward, emotional focus is intensified in reaction against Clara, who undermines Nathanael's emotions both through her letter, and then through her response to his impassioned poem. While Nathanael exemplifies the danger of intense, inward-turning passion, the narrative frame works to position and control the dangerous affects of the narrative, which otherwise threaten to lose touch with external reality, and to overflow, thereby leading to the loss of autonomy and disintegration of identity.

Scherzo: Metamorphosis as Social Satire

Besides humans losing and changing identity, assuming other bodily forms, and inanimate objects coming to life, Hoffmann also writes of animals becoming human. While metamorphosis in Hoffmann's work can articulate desires for a higher self or fears of losing control, as explored above, it is in his animal tales that Hoffmann's talent for satire comes to the fore. A full understanding of Hoffmann's work, and the role of metamorphosis within it, needs to take into account not only wonder and horror, but also humour.

Hoffmann's preface to the *Fantasiestücke in Callots Manier* provides insight into his use of speaking animal figures and animal–human metamorphosis. In the preface, Hoffmann brings his work into contact with that of baroque illustrator Jacques Callot, singling out Callot's animal–human grotesques as worthy of particular praise:

> Die Ironie, welche, indem sie das Menschliche mit seinem ärmlichen Tun und Treiben verhöhnt, wohnt nur in einem tiefen Geiste, und so enthüllen Callots aus Tier und Mensch geschaffene grotesque Gestalten dem ernsten, tiefer eindringenden Beschauer alle die geheimen Andeutungen, die unter dem Schleier der Skurrilität verborgen liegen. (II, 18)
>
> [The irony that mocks the human with its meagre day-to-day affairs, resides only within a deep soul, and so do Callot's grotesques, created from animal and human, reveal to the more serious and more deeply enquiring viewer all of the secret insinuations that lie hidden under the veil of whimsy.]

According to Hoffmann, Callot's animal–human figures satirize human society in a way that is comical, but that also contains a deeper meaning. By characterizing Callot's work in this manner, Hoffmann draws attention to the comic seriousness of animal–human hybrids and metamorphoses that, he implies, might be traced in his own work. This can be explored in particular through two tales from the *Fantasiestücke* in which animals become human — that of the ape Milo, and the dog Berganza.

Entering Human Society: Milo, Berganza, and Critique of Superficial Bildung

The story of Milo is part of the 'Kreisleriana', a collection of opinions, anecdotes, and creative pieces about music by Hoffmann's fictional alter ego Johannes Kreisler, who features in a number of Hoffmann's tales. In one episode ('Nachricht von einem gebildeten jungen Mann' [News from an educated young man]), Kreisler claims to have met an extraordinary young man, and provides the letter in which this individual details his entry into society and his musical success ('Schreiben Milos, eines gebildeten Affen, an seine Freundin Pipi in Nord-Amerika' [Writings of Milo, an educated ape, to his girlfriend Pipi in North America]. Milo's ready acceptance in human society raises questions about the nature of a society in which ape-like copying is praised as musical talent. Milo's understanding of what it is to be human, and his account of how he achieved success in human society, provides the vehicle for Hoffmann's satire.

The satire begins with Milo explaining how his desire to become human began with the imposing sight of a hunter's boots. Milo equates these boots with the 'herrlichen Anlagen zur Wissenschaft und Kunst, die in mir nur geweckt werden durften' (II, 420) [glorious aptitude for science and art, which only needed to be awakened within me], thereby equating the 'higher' attributes of humanity with his materialistic desire for status. Milo runs after the hunter, despite his uncle's warning, and the hunter captures him, so Milo's uncle throws a coconut which hits Milo behind the ear. The ensuing wound, Milo speculates, may have encouraged the growth of new organs, making possible his newfound abilities (II, 421). If this wound is the cause of his transformation, then the transformation is an unintended one like that of Lucius in Apuleius' *Golden Ass*. We might also read the coconut throwing as a form of punishment (though it is not clear if the uncle aimed at the hunter or at Milo), which is a common motive for transformation in classical narratives such as Apuleius's *Golden Ass* or Ovid's *Metamorphoses* as well as in Romantic *Märchen*. It is also significant that Milo's entry into culture starts with violence and a wound, as in Nietzsche's later *Zur Genealogie der Moral*.[44] Human abilities are achieved at a cost, and following a wound, as is also the case in Kafka's story of an ape's assimilation into human society, which I examine in the next chapter.

Although the wound might suggest that Milo's transformation is extraordinary, his ability to act as human is not portrayed as an exceptional achievement, requiring uniquely human skill, but as the result of an ape's ability to mimic or 'ape' others ('nachäffen'). The metaphorical expression 'nachäffen' is played out at a literal level in this tale. Milo claims that by copying human behaviour, it was extremely easy for him to be accepted into society (II, 422). According to Milo, the ape-like impulse to copy is the same as the human urge to acquire culture, or rather, since people do not really care about acquiring culture, to pretend to be cultured (II, 422). The 'wisest' people, Milo claims, have long adopted the principle of copying, and have thereby shown how cultured they are. When a work of art is praised, they attempt to copy it, and when something slightly different results, they claim that this was what they had intended all along (II, 422). The cultured society that Milo speaks of is based on little more than ape-like copying.

Even speaking involves no more than the ability to mimic. An aesthetics professor advises Milo to focus on speaking, rather than thinking:

> Sprechen, sprechen, sprechen müssen Sie lernen, alles übrige findet sich von selbst. Geläufig, gewandt, geschickt sprechen, das ist das ganze Geheimnis. Sie werden selbst erstaunen, wie Ihnen im Sprechen die Gedanken kommen, wie Ihnen die Weisheit aufgeht [. . .] Oft werden Sie sich selbst nicht verstehen: dann befinden Sie sich aber gerade in der wahren Begeisterung, die das Sprechen hervorbringt (II, 423)

> [Speaking, speaking, speaking is what you must learn, everything else happens of its own accord. Speaking with familiarity, urbanity, skill, that is the entire secret. You will be amazed at how thoughts arise while speaking, how wisdom emerges [. . .] often even you won't understand yourself: but that's when you succumb to the true rapture that speaking produces]

Hoffmann's tale engages with a subject of debate popular at the time: the question of how humans acquired language, which Herder had notably discussed in his prize-winning essay of 1772.[45] However, rather than celebrate human language as a unique achievement, Hoffmann satirizes the shallow, thoughtless use of language that the aesthetics professor advocates.

As a newcomer to human society, the figure of Milo allows for reflection upon the qualities considered part of cultured and educated society. These qualities become apparent when Milo forgets his human identity, and reverts to animal urges, for example, when he throws an apple at an official during dinner (II, 428). As a human, Milo is expected to behave respectfully towards those in power. On another occasion, while out walking with friends, Milo suddenly rushes joyfully up a tree, and is later ashamed (II, 427). Shame serves as a marker of his desire to be human. Milo wishes to rid himself of his primal urges, which must be suppressed in order to acquire culture. In this way, Milo's transformation might be read as a comment on the loss of spontaneity and the burden of shame inherent in human society, echoed in Nietzsche's later critique of 'Sklavenmoral' [slave morality] in *Zur Genealogie der Moral* (1887). The irony of Milo's pleasure in becoming educated becomes apparent towards the end of the letter, when Milo encourages the ape Pipi to learn to read. He says that this will enable her to achieve the 'innern Ruhe und Behaglichkeit [. . .], die nur die höchste Kultur erzeugt, wie sie aus dem innern Ingenio und dem Umgang mit weisen, gebildeten Menschen entspringt' (II, 428) [inner peace and comfort [. . .] generated only by the highest culture, as they arise through inner wit and the interaction with wise, educated people]. Milo's claim about achieving inner satisfaction is undercut by the recurrent unease that he mentions suffering.

While Milo embraces his entry into human society, the opposite is the case with the dog Berganza in Hoffmann's 'Nachricht von den neuesten Schicksalen des Hundes Berganza' [News of the latest adventures of the dog Berganza]. The title refers to the fact that the tale is envisioned as a continuation of Cervantes's tale (*El coloquio de los perros*, 1613). The tale mainly consists in a conversation between the artistically minded narrator and the dog Berganza, in which Berganza relates what happened to him since the time of Cervantes's tale. This includes being temporarily transformed into a human.

In contrast to philistine Milo, in Berganza the artistically minded narrator finds a kindred spirit. A conversation springs up between them after the narrator, walking home from a tavern, hears a woeful voice by the river. He is surprised to find that the voice belongs to a dog, but, open to the unexpected, decides to help the dog out by sprinkling some river water upon him, explaining that this is because the dog appeared to be 'ganz auf den Hund gekommen, unerachtet Sie selbst einer scheinen zu wollen belieben' (II, 102) [completely gone to the dogs, notwithstanding the fact that you seem inclined to be one yourself]. A witty repartee begins in which the narrator and Berganza play upon metaphorical expressions about dogs and humans. Berganza replies that he could almost have doubted that the narrator was human, for, 'wahres Mitleiden mit einem Hunde, das wäre gar nicht menschlich' (II, 103) [true sympathy with a dog, that would be quite inhuman]. The narrator, however, assures Berganza that he loves dogs, and they begin a conversation in which they playfully explore stereotypes and reflect upon the nature of dogs and humans.

Through the conversation with Berganza, an alternative view of both dogs and humans becomes possible. As a dog, Berganza has been able to observe human society from the critical position of the outsider, but with privileged access: 'Nun liege ich unbeachtet als Hund unter dem Ofen und Eure innerste Natur, ihr Menschlein! die ihr ohne Scham und Scheu vor mir entblößt, durchschaue ich mit dem Hohn, mit dem tiefen Spott, den Eure ekle leere Aufgedunsenheit verdient' (II, 131) [Now I lie unnoticed, a dog under the oven, and your inner nature, you little people! Which you reveal to me without shame and shyness, I see through it with the contempt, the deep mockery, which your revolting empty bloatedness deserves]. Unlike Milo, who simply mimics human behaviour, Berganza sees through it with the ironic perspective of the artist and outsider. The use of a dog to provide an ironic perspective on human society will be encountered again in the discussion of Kafka's 'Forschungen eines Hundes' [Investigations of a dog] in chapter 2.

Berganza's ability to talk can be traced to a metamorphosis that happened in the course of his exploits since Cervantes's tale. Berganza explains how he encountered some witches (in the forms of a toad and a black cat) stirring a cauldron, possibly alluding to the witches' kitchen in Goethe's *Faust I*.[46] From the cauldron, strange creatures emerge: 'Eidechsen mit albern lachenden Menschengesichtern, spiegelglatte Iltisse, Mäuse mit Rabenköpfe, allerlei widriges Ungeziefer' (II, 110) [lizards with inane, laughing human faces, glassy smooth polecats, mice with raven's heads, all sorts of repugnant creatures]. The witches' magic brings forth hybrid creatures with grotesque combinations of features. Berganza watches the toad jump into the cauldron, which spits fire and water, creating more horrific forms:

> tausend abscheulichen Gebilden, die in Sinne beängstendem, rastlosem Wechsel hervorblitzten und verschwanden. — Da waren es seltsam häßliche Tiere, Menschengesichter nachäffend; da waren es Menschen, in gräßlicher Verzerrung mit der Tiergestalt kämpfend, die ineinander, durcheinander fuhren und, miteinander ringend, sich verzehrten. (II, 112)

> [a thousand abominable figures, that surfaced and disappeared in sense-alarming, restless change. — There were strange, horrible animals, aping human faces; there were humans fighting in ghastly contortions with the animal forms,

which ran into and through one another, and that wrestling with one another, ate each other up.]

In this scene, boundaries between humans and animals become uncertain. Animals mimic humans, and humans fight their animal form. The scene reveals a horror of becoming reduced to the status on an animal, and a fear of animals spitefully assuming human form. Yoko Tawada, the final author examined in this book, claims that Romantic *Märchen* often involve humans being forced to transform into animals, or animals transforming into humans of their own free will.[47] A horror over becoming animal and fear of animals becoming human can be traced in many metamorphosis tales, suggesting a model of animal existence as degrading. While Hoffmann's witch scene depicts horrific animals and the horror of becoming animal, his figure of Berganza offers a counterbalance, as an admirable creature who only becomes human unwittingly.

The blending of boundaries in the passage above is horrifying ('gräßlich') and violent, as animals fight each other, and even consume one another, thereby mixing boundaries yet further. Eating, in particular, may be seen as a process in which boundaries between humans and animals become blurred.[48] While watching the horrific blending of forms, the witch-cat pounces upon Berganza, and after a fight Berganza loses consciousness only to awaken covered in disgusting grease. This magic ointment causes a strange form of transformation:

> ein unbeschreibliches Gefühl durchbebte mein Innres. Es war, als müsse ich aus meinem eignen Körper herausfahren, zuweilen sah ich mich ordentlich als ein zweiter Berganza daliegen, und das war ich wieder selbst, und der Berganza, der den andern unter den Fäusten der Hexen sah, war ich auch, und dieser bellte und knurrte den liegenden an und forderte ihn auf, doch tüchtig hineinzubeißen und mit einem kräftigen Sprunge aus dem Kreise herauszufahren — und der liegende — doch! — was ermüde ich dich mit der Beschreibung eines Zustandes, der, durch höllische Künste hervorgebracht, mich in zwei Berganzas teilte, die miteinander kämpften. (II, 114)

> [an indescribable feeling convulsed my insides. It was as if I must be travelling out of my own body, at the same time I saw myself properly, lying there as a second Berganza, and that was myself again, and the Berganza who saw the other under the clutches of the witches, was also myself, and this one barked and growled at the one lying down and called upon him to bite hard and to get out of the circle with a powerful jump — and the one lying down — but! — why should I bore you with the description of a circumstance, which, brought about by devilish artistry, split me into two Berganzas, who fought with one another.]

Berganza experiences the transformation as an unusual affective state and gains an altered perspective of himself as a result of bodily splitting. Berganza seems to leave his own body, and split in two, with one body lying in the hands of the witches, and the other body trying to free the first. In this way, the metamorphosis causes a conflict between two parts of the self, as though externalizing an inner conflict.

Although Berganza escapes from the witches and becomes one again, the ointment has a lasting effect, and every year on the anniversary of this day, he experiences an agonizing transformation (II, 117). His transformation begins with an unusual appetite for sardine salad and wine and an exhibition of strange behaviour. Berganza starts avoiding fierce dogs and instead kicks small dogs who cannot retaliate. His vision becomes blurred and he is troubled by the strange desire to walk upright in brightly lit rooms, to hold in his tail, to wear perfume, to eat ices, to speak French and say 'mon cher Baron', 'mon petit Comte!'. In this way, Berganza's transformation into a human brings with it disturbing feelings:

> Ja, es ist mir dann entsetzlich ein Hund zu sein, und indem ich schnell wie der Gedanke in einer vermeintlichen Bildung zum Menschen steige, wird mein Zustand immer ängstlicher. Ich schäme mich, jemals an einem warmen Frühlingstage auf der Wiese gesprungen oder mich im Grase gewälzt zu haben. Im härtesten Kampfe werde ich immer bedächtiger und ernsthafter. — Zuletzt bin ich ein Mensch und beherrsche die Natur, die Bäume deshalb wachsen läßt, daß man Tische und Stühle daraus machen kann, und Blumen blühen, daß man sie als Strauß in das Knopfloch stecken kann. Indem ich mich aber so zur höchsten Stufe hinaufschwinge, fühle ich, daß sich eine Stumpfheit und Dummheit meiner bemächtigt, die, immer steigend und steigend, mich zuletzt in eine Ohnmacht wirft. (II, 118)

> [Yes, in such moments it appals me to be a dog, and as I ascend quick as thought to a supposedly educated human condition, my state of mind becomes ever more troubled. I feel shame at ever having jumped around in a meadow on a warm spring day or rolled around in the grass. In the most difficult struggle I become increasingly deliberate and serious. — After all, I am a human, and in control of nature, allowing trees to grow for the purpose of making tables and chairs out of them, and flowers to bloom so that they may be put into a buttonhole as a bouquet. But as I swing myself up to the highest level I feel that a stupor and stupidity is taking possession of me, which, the higher and higher I climb, will eventually render me unconscious.]

Berganza's transformation into a human provides a pointed critique of human society with its supposed learning. As in Milo's tale, human society is the source of negative feelings of anxiety and shame. However, whereas Milo ignores these while striving for the social acclaim that comes with appearing to be educated, the artistically sensitive Berganza is troubled by the anxieties that accompany human pretensions to superiority. Ironically, as Berganza ascends the heights of human *Bildung*, he descends psychologically, becoming stupid, senseless, and eventually completely helpless. For Berganza, becoming human is not something to be celebrated, since it means cruelty, pretentiousness, a rejection of the joys of nature, and the adoption of a utilitarian perspective, in which natural objects are only considered of value in so far as they benefit humans in some practical way.

Machine-Men and Artist-Animals: The Importance of Individuality

Milo's and Berganza's experiences of becoming human reveal some of Hoffmann's problems with contemporary society, in particular the lack of true understanding and feeling, and the pretence of *Bildung* as a way of achieving social status, sought through mimicking those in power. However, the main thrust of his critique concerns the practice of art, and in particular, music, a subject of great concern to Hoffmann.

In Milo's account of his success as a musician, he claims that the whole secret of playing the piano is that of being able to move one's fingers quickly. In the social circles in which he moves, Milo is praised for this mechanical skill. Indeed, Milo's desire to learn the piano was not the result of a love of music, but of a wish to impress others with his skill. Milo's view of music is shown further by the fact that he disdains composition (he leaves the task of composition to his 'inferiors'), although he enjoys the praise that comes from claiming to be a composer (II, 424). Milo even becomes a singing virtuoso despite not having a good voice. Indeed, a good voice is said to be a disadvantage, since a good voice will be ruined after striving for unnaturally wide vocal ranges, but Milo, with his robust voice, can easily achieve a falsetto (II, 425). Through the ridiculous figure of Milo, as an embodiment of ape-like philistinism, Hoffmann provides a critique of music practised as mechanical skill, rather than as expression of genuine feeling.

Hoffmann's satire is reinforced by the short love poem with which Milo finishes his letter, copied from Hamlet. The poem comes across as derivative and clichéd, especially since the exhortation 'Zweifl', ob lügen kann die Wahrheit, | Nur an meiner Liebe nicht!' (II, 428) [Doubt truth to be a liar | But never doubt I love] is undermined by Milo's lack of concern for Pipi earlier in the letter. In Milo, genuine feeling and understanding are absent, and what remains are superficial, mechanical abilities, which ironically are those which society praises. As Günter Wöllner claims, Milo can be read as a form of 'Doppel-Gegensatz' [Opposite-Double] to the real musician Kreisler, who exhibits the musical and personal qualities that Milo lacks.[49]

The critique of unfeeling, mechanical art and behaviour is central throughout Hoffmann's work. In his letters Hoffmann criticizes certain members of society whom he referred to as 'Maschinen-Menschen, die mich umlagern mit platten Gemeinplätzen' [machine men, who surround me with dull platitudes], or elsewhere called 'ästhetischen Cretins mit automatischer Bewegung ohne inneres Leben' [aesthetic cretins with automatic movement that lack inner life].[50] Hoffmann's criticism of such people is played out in his literary satire of those who lack individuality, inner life, and feeling. The description of such people as 'Maschinen-Menschen' might be read as a critique of the idea of mechanical man developed by early modern philosophers such as La Mettrie, with his *L'Homme machine* (1748), and which Romantic writers reacted against by stressing qualities that appear non-mechanistic, such as individual thought and feeling, sensitivity, and creativity. Figures such as animals, puppets, and other non-humans provide the vehicle for such a critique, which is not so much a critique of the non-humans, but of the humans who admire mechanical skills. The figure of Olimpia is another key example. Several pages are devoted to the fact that no-one ('apart from very clever students') had noticed Olimpia's lack of life (II, 46–47). Indeed, people feel betrayed by Spalanzani for concealing the truth. It is only after discovering that Olimpia is an automaton that people claim to have noticed suspicious things about her, such as the fact that she sneezed more than she yawned (said to be a way to conceal the noise of the mechanism). After this, members of the tea-drinking circles start yawning more than ever, and never sneezing in order to refute any suspicion. They also start demanding that their lovers sing less strictly in time and give the impression of being able to think and feel (II, 46–47). By successfully passing as human, both Olimpia and Milo reveal the superficiality of certain social circles.

Hoffmann's critique of the lack of genuine feeling and independent thought is played out in a particularly pointed way through the metamorphic figure in his *Klein Zaches, genannt Zinnober* (1819) [Little Zaches, known as Zinnober]. Zaches is an ugly changeling ('Wechselbalg') who has undergone a magical spell, which means that, even though he speaks rubbish ('Zinnober'), the achievements of others are attributed to him. Zaches has no redeeming qualities or ability of his own, not even Milo's ability to mimic. However, through the effects of the spell he becomes an official of the highest rank ('Minister im Orden des grüngefleckten Tigers mit zwanzig Knöpfen').

Zaches lacks all identity, personality, and inner life, only reflecting that of others. As Detlef Kremer points out, the name 'Zaches' recalls a tick ('Zecke'), which is appropriate since Zaches could be said to be, as Kremer claims, a parasite par excellence.[51] Ernst Loeb compares the tale to Kafka's *Die Verwandlung*, pointing out that both stories explore the consequences of a metamorphosis.[52] However, even before Zaches has the spell cast upon him, he is a changeling, an unwanted creature substituted in place of a human being. In this sense, Zaches already begins as a non-person. The spell does not so much cause a single metamorphosis as constant metamorphosis of Zinnober's personality and identity. The metamorphosis also happens through other characters' perception, since the spell causes others to mistakenly attribute praiseworthy behaviour to Zinnober. However, those whose talents were stolen by Zinnober become outraged, and see Zinnober for what he really is, as merely the changeling Zaches.

Once Zinnober's three magical hairs are pulled out, everyone awakes 'wie aus dem Traum' (III, 627), and the empty figure of Zaches ends up drowning in his chamber pot, thereby undergoing a ridiculous death. The humour of the tale is intentional, as the narrator later suggests: 'Hast du, geliebter Leser! hin und wieder über manches recht im Innern gelächelt, so warst du in *der* Stimmung, wie sie der Schreiber dieser Blätter wünschte' (III, 645) [If you, dear reader! laughed quite heartily from time to time over some of this, then you were in *the* mood that the writer of these pages wished]. Zaches's death is humorous rather than sad, since Zaches lacks a personality with which one might empathize. His death, according to the physician, was a result of the honorary buttons on Zinnober's coat damaging his backbone, and thereby affecting the cerebral system, said to be the seat of consciousness and personality. This caused Zinnober to become obsessed by ideas of sacrificing himself to the service of the state, leading to cessation of consciousness and relinquishing of personality. The physician concludes that Zinnober 'hatte bereits seine Persönlichkeit aufgegeben, war also schon mausetot, als er hineinstürzte in jenes verhängnisvolle Gefäß. — So hatte sein Tod keine physische, wohl aber eine unermeßlich tiefe psychische Ursache' (III, 642) [had already given up his personality, so was already dead as a dormouse when he dropped into that fateful vessel. — thus his death had no physical cause, but an immeasurably deep psychological one].

In the physician's diagnosis we find not only a critique of those who lack inner life, attesting to the Romantic ideal of individuality, but a critique of the psychologically damaging effects of social status and power on the individual. The non-human figures Olimpia, Milo, and Zinnober are all perceived to have musical talent, but in reality they are an automaton, an ape and a changeling, who lack the human qualities of true thought and feeling. Their perceived metamorphosis into humans provides insight into the qualities that Hoffmann considers are core to being fully human.

Humanity and its Depths of Feeling

In Hoffmann's work, tales of metamorphosis allow exploration of what it is to be human by highlighting the difference between those who have individuality and inner depth and those who only copy people's behaviour mechanically. Through metamorphosis, Hoffmann explores the possibility (and impossibility) of attaining the qualities that are essential to being a human and individual. Central to Hoffmann's Romantic ideal of human existence is the idea of possessing interior depths and a particular form of affectivity evidenced by the true Romantic artist. Through his tales of metamorphosis, Hoffmann promotes a particular set of affects as particularly human.

The importance of deep feeling as a marker of the human was firmly established in the early nineteenth century, as the advice given to Milo reveals: 'Reden Sie viel von den Tendenzen des Zeitalters — wie sich das und jenes rein ausspreche — von Tiefe des Gemüts — von gemütvoll und gemütlos u.s.w.' (II, 423) [Keep speaking of the current trends — how such and such should be clearly pronounced — of the depths of feeling — of sensibilities and lack of sensibility etc.]. By repeating fashionable phrases, such as mention of the capacity for feeling ('Gemüt'), Milo will be able to give the impression of being an educated human with an emotional sensibility. Although the word 'Gemüt' has now largely fallen out of fashion, the term was highly popular in the mid-eighteenth to early nineteenth century.[53] The word referred to the part of the mind or soul concerned with feeling, and designated a space of 'innerer Sinn' [inner sense] which was extensively explored after 1800.[54] Hoffmann's use of 'Gemüt' is significant in that it reveals a model of the individual specific to the late Enlightenment and Romantic period. The spatial quality of 'Gemüt' suggests that individuals are invested with a hidden interior space that is potentially endlessly deep, and that provides the individual with meaning and individuality.[55] To have a deep 'Gemüt' was to be a person in the fullest sense.

Hoffmann's satire is not simply directed towards those who fail to demonstrate this depth of feeling, but towards those who, like the ape Milo, falsely profess this quality. Milo's newfound esteem for depth of feeling leads him to develop contempt for his own species, the apes, whose eyes remain dry, thereby lacking the human 'Tiefe des Gemüts' [depths of feeling]. Ironically though, Milo fails to acquire the 'Tiefe des Gemüts' himself, despite his thorough assimilation into human society. Through Milo, Hoffmann criticizes the hypocrisy of those who constantly speak about depths of feeling, but who fail to show it, thereby making the idea of the 'Tiefe des Gemüts' appear ridiculous and insincere.

The tale of Berganza similarly highlights the lack of those superior depths of feeling that humans profess. Berganza, a dog in whom the artistic narrator finds a kindred spirit, argues that his growling and barking are perfectly adequate means of communication, and that it is the human failure to understand rather than a failure on his behalf that is the problem. Indeed, Berganza sees his tail-wagging as a particularly apt means of expressing 'alle Nuancen unseres Wohlgefallens von der leisten Rührung der Lust bis zur ausgelassensten Freude' (II, 104) [all the nuances of our pleasure from being moved most gently to the most frolicsome joy]. Berganza's sensitivity for feeling is what the narrator particularly praises:

> es scheint mir, als verbändest du Verstand mit Gemüt, welches in der Tat eine recht seltne Sache ist. — Versteh' übrigens den Ausdruck Gemüt richtig oder sei vielmehr überzeugt, daß er mir nicht bloß als schales Wort gilt, wie vielen so ganz Gemütlosen, die ihn beständig im Munde führen. (II, 104)
>
> [it seems to me that you combine understanding with feeling, which is indeed a very rare thing. — Do, by the way, understand the term 'feeling' correctly, or do be convinced that it's not a word I use glibly, like so many of those who lack feeling, yet who constantly take the word upon their lips.]

The narrator affirms the value of the capacity to feel against those who make empty claims about their 'Gemüt', but is also willing to grant that Berganza, a dog, possesses this rare quality. As a sensitive, witty soul, Berganza differs from Milo, who lacks feeling and self-awareness. For this reason, the two tales produce their satire in different ways. While Berganza is aware of the shortcomings of human society, and we may laugh with him, Milo is not, and so we laugh at his mimicry of shallow philistinism. Berganza and Milo's differing attitudes towards becoming human are indicative of their contrasting personalities, for while Milo embraces human society, Berganza finds it a torment. For those who possess true feeling, or 'Gemüt', contemporary society is anathema in its shallow pretension to real feeling.

The contrast between those who possess real depths of feeling and those for whom this is mere superficial talk is developed most fully in Hoffmann's late novel *Lebens-Ansichten des Katers Murr* (1819–21), upon which Hoffmann pinned his greatest ambitions.[56] However, rather than use metamorphosis, Hoffmann contrasts the biography of self-satisfied tomcat Murr with the fragments of biography belonging to musician Johannes Kreisler, which Murr used as blotting paper, and which are interspersed non-chronologically throughout. This narrative technique makes Kreisler's genuine artistic sensibility apparent, while allowing humorous articulation of his deep misgivings about the superficiality of bourgeois sentiment.

Although Hoffmann has been criticized for his affective style, with its lack of subtlety and tendency towards extremes, it is important that his style is not considered mere sensationalism. Hoffmann's insistence on feeling reflects a deep conviction in the need for feeling as the basis for art and humanity. Through tales of metamorphosis, Hoffmann explores the contrast between insincere sentiment and true feeling. Metamorphosis functions, moreover, not only as a contrastive device, but as a way of articulating the tension between mundane and higher realms of existence. It is this tension that renders the individual unstable and transformable. To read Hoffmann as himself engaging in insincere, sensationalist sentiment is one of the most unfortunate kinds of misreading. Hoffmann's conviction in the value of feeling can be attributed to Romantic beliefs in the power of feeling to articulate the depths of the inner self. As Charles Taylor argues, the idea that we find the truth within us, and particularly within our feelings, is indispensable to Romanticism.[57] Taylor's view assumes an inexhaustible inner domain, a depth within the subject, and the idea that it is from these inner depths that the subject expresses themselves.[58] Whereas the metamorphoses of 'Der goldne Topf' might be seen as attempts to realize the poetic potential of this inner depth, and those of 'Der Sandmann' as a reaction against the more fearful darkness within, in Hoffmann's animal tales there is a constant tension between those with depth of feeling and those without. While becoming human should involve the attainment of such depths, for Milo, who mimics the superficial humans around him, and for Berganza, with his already deeply poetic sentiment, it does not, and therein lies the irony.

As a late Romantic, Hoffmann wrote during a period of radically changing affective style. In criticizing insincere sentiment and a certain mode of bourgeois affect control, which leads Milo to suppress his joyful animal urges, Hoffmann engages with the changing predicament of his time. As the Romantic age closed, the expression of intense feelings had become increasingly subject to scepticism and concerns over exaggeration and excess, and correspondingly, the term 'Gemüt' began to fall out of fashion.[59] Standing at the end of this period, Hoffmann's work points towards the difficulties with the intense affects of Romanticism, but continues to insist upon the importance of feeling as a means of accessing higher awareness and depth of being. Those who admire Hoffmann's work are often sympathetic to such belief in feeling. As Friedrich Hebbel later claimed, everything that Hoffmann wrote stemmed from an endlessly deep 'Gemüt'.[60] For Hoffmann, whose tales of metamorphosis are used to explore this very quality, this would surely be a great compliment.

Conclusion

In Hoffmann's work, the possibility of metamorphosis is raised through the tensions inherent in the modern individual. Having inner depths of feeling allows for self-realization, but also contains destabilizing potential. Metamorphosis allows for the sublime possibility of realizing the self in a wonderful, poetic realm, but it can also raise the horrific possibility of psychological breakdown. Besides these two extremes, metamorphosis can also be used to explore satirically the tensions between longing for a higher existence and being subject to restrictive social norms.

Hoffmann's work stands at the beginning of a modern way of representing metamorphosis in that the metamorphoses are not positioned as part of the natural world order, but are made possible through the poetic imagination. In 'Der goldne Topf' Anselmus gains awareness of a wonderful realm in which figures take on other forms, and in doing so perceptually enacts an animistic metamorphosis of nature and becomes affectively transformed. In order to perceive the physical transformations of figures and things it is necessary to be in the right kind of affective state, since this is vital to the poetic and artistic capacity.

However, while the Romantic emphasis on affect can lead towards an accentuated sense of self, intense inner emotions can also threaten the self when perception becomes distorted and emotions fail to be aligned with the outside world. This leads to Nathanael losing his sense of autonomy, as his feelings escape from his control. When feelings are regarded as the source of individuality, losing control over feelings mean losing control over the self, and this psychological breakdown may be expressed through images of physical and affective transformation.

Metamorphosis is central in Hoffmann's work because it is part of the poetic capacity for seeing things differently. Metamorphosis can allow one to imagine wonderful, higher possibilities of being, or it can intimate feelings of being subject to dark forces, or it can be used to explore the tensions between the realms of the imagination and the realities of everyday life. As outsiders who gain insight into human society through their metamorphosis, Hoffmann's animal figures provide a critique of philistines who lack depth of feeling. It is this capacity for feeling that is vital for the full realization of individuality, which for Hoffmann is the highest form of existence.

Notes to Chapter 1

1. Ursula Reber, *Formenverschleifung: Zu einer Theorie der Metamorphose* (Paderborn: Fink, 2009), pp. 166–67.
2. The function of the metamorphosis of animal bridegrooms has been discussed in Maria Tatar, *The Hard Facts of the Grimms' Fairy Tales* (Princeton: Princeton University Press, 2003), pp. 156–78; also Gabriela Brunner-Ungricht, *Die Mensch–Tier Verwandlung: Eine Motivgeschichte unter besonderer Berücksichtigung des deutschen Märchens in der ersten Hälfte des 19. Jahrhunderts* (Bern: Land, 1998), pp. 178–89.
3. E.g. Gerhard Neumann reads Hoffmann's texts as 'Erkundungsformen' between fantasy and realism: Gerhard Neumann, 'Romantische Aufklärung: Zu E. T. A. Hoffmanns Wissenschaftspoetik', in *Aufklärung als Form: Beiträge zu einem historischen und aktuellen Problem*, ed. by Helmut Schmiedt and Helmut J. Schneider (Würzburg: Königshausen & Neumann, 1997), p. 106.
4. For example, Ursula Reber claims that Hoffmann and Tieck would be key authors for an exploration of metamorphosis in Romanticism, although her own chapter on Romanticism (in *Formenverschleifung*) deals with Brentano (p. 19).
5. Reber makes the distinction between 'Wandelbarkeit' and 'Verwandlung', with the former being based on contingency and overlapping, and the latter as an essentialist notion involving cohesion. Reber claims that her distinction is similar to Caroline Walker Bynum's distinction between 'hybrid' and 'metamorphosis' (Reber, p. 55). For Bynum, the former belongs to a view of a world that is multiple whereas the latter defines a single process (pp. 29–31).
6. Johann Wolfgang von Goethe, *Sämtliche Werke, Briefe, Tagebücher und Gespräche*, 40 vols (Frankfurt a.M.: Deutscher Klassiker, 1993–2011), XXXIV, 412.
7. Heinrich Heine, *Die Romantische Schule*, in *Sämtliche Schriften*, ed. by Klaus Briegleb, 6 vols (Munich: Deutscher Taschenbuchverlag, 1968–76), III, 440–41.
8. H. M. Brown, *E. T. A. Hoffmann and the Serapiontic Principle: Critique and Creativity* (Rochester, NY: Camden House, 2006), p. 4.
9. Ute Frevert and others, *Gefühlswissen: eine lexikalische Spurensuche in der Moderne* (Frankfurt a.M.: Campus, 2011), p. 20.
10. Johann Gottfried Herder, 'Zum Sinn des Gefühls', in *Schriften zu Philosophie, Literatur und Kunst im Altertum*, ed. by Jürgen Brummack and Martin Bollacher, IV (Frankfurt am Main: Deutscher Klassiker-Verlag, 1994), pp. 233–42 (p. 236).
11. The idea that dualism ('Dualismus'), as the conflict between contrasting elements, can be resolved in duplicity ('Duplizität'), as the recognition of the duality of existence, is most clearly

articulated in Hoffmann's 'Der Einsiedler Serapion'. Serapion, who lives in an imaginary realm, fails to recognize dualism. The recognition of dualism often involves irony or satire and produces humour. Klaus Deterding in particular has called attention to the difference between dualism and duplicity in Hoffmann's work, most recently in his book *E. T. A. Hoffmanns Leben und Werk* (Würzburg: Königshausen & Neumann, 2010), pp. 108–13.

12. E. T. A. Hoffmann, *Sämtliche Werke*, ed. by Wulf Segebrecht and others, 6 vols (Frankfurt a.M.: Deutscher Klassiker, 1985–2004), II, 17. All further references are given after quotations in the text.
13. E. T. A. Hoffmann, *The Golden Pot and Other Tales*, trans. by Ritchie Robertson (Oxford: Oxford University Press, 2008), pp. 4–5. All subsequent references to translations of Hoffmann's 'Der goldne Topf' and 'Der Sandmann' are taken from this edition, and are provided after quotations in the text.
14. Maria M. Tatar, 'Mesmerism, Madness and Death in Hoffmann's "Der goldne Topf"', *Studies in Romanticism*, 14.4 (1975), 365–89 (pp. 369).
15. Ibid., p. 370.
16. Immanuel Kant, *Kritik der Urteilskraft* [1790] (Hamburg: tredition, 2011), Bk II, §29, pp. 121–22.
17. E. T. A. Hoffmann, Letter of 19 Aug. 1813, in *Sämtliche Werke*, I, 292–96 (p. 293).
18. Joseph von Eichendorff, *Sämtliche Gedichte und Versen*, ed. by Hartwig Schultz (Frankfurt a.M.: Deutscher Klassiker, 2006), p. 328.
19. Brunner-Ungricht, *Die Mensch–Tier Verwandlung*, p. 137.
20. Andrew Bowie, 'Friedrich Wilhelm Joseph von Schelling', *The Stanford Encyclopedia of Philosophy* (Winter 2010 Edition), ed. by Edward N. Zalta, http://plato.stanford.edu/archives/win2010/entries/schelling/, accessed 2. Apr. 201.
21. Friedrich Wilhelm Joseph von Schelling, 'Ideen zu einer Philosophie der Natur', in *Schellings Werke: Nach der Original in neuer Anordnung*, ed. by Manfred Schröter, 12 vols (Munich: Beck, 1965), I, 77–350 (p. 706).
22. Brown, p. 34.
23. Tzvetan Todorov, *The Fantastic: A Structural Approach to a Literary Genre*, trans. by Richard Howard (Ithaca: Cornell Paperbacks, 1975), esp. p. 26.
24. E.g. David Sandner, *Fantastic Literature: A Critical Reader* (Westport: Praeger, 2004), p. 4.
25. Detlef Kremer, *Romantische Metamorphosen: E. T. A. Hoffmanns Erzählungen* (Stuttgart: Metzler, 1993), esp. p. 134.
26. Andrew Webber, *The Doppelgänger: Double Visions in German Literature* (Oxford: Clarendon, 1996), p. 118.
27. Bruce Clarke, *Allegories of Writing: The Subject of Metamorphosis* (Albany: State University of New York Press, 1995), p. 2.
28. Detlef Kremer, *E. T. A. Hoffmann: Erzählungen und Romane* (Berlin: Schmidt, 1999), p. 12.
29. Brown, p. 4.
30. Ibid., p. 5.
31. Peter-André Alt, *Begriffsbilder: Studien zur literarischen Allegorie zwischen Opitz und Schiller* (Tübingen: Niemeyer, 1995), p. 3.
32. Kremer, *Romantische Metamorphosen*, p. 201.
33. Rosemary Jackson, *Fantasy: The Literature of Subversion* (London and New York: Routledge, 1981), p. 47.
34. Hoffmann read the works of contemporary physicians Johann Christian Reil and Philippe Pinel, who discussed the *idée fixe*. The narrator of 'Der Einsiedler Serapion' claims to have read these authors as a way of trying to learn about madness (IV, 27).
35. Michel Foucault, *Madness and Civilisation: A History of Insanity in the Age of Reason* (London: Tavistock, 1967), p. 86.
36. The Serapiontic principle has been discussed in particular by Brown.
37. E.g. Maria M. Tatar, 'E. T. A. Hoffmann's "Der Sandmann" Reflection and Romantic Irony', *Modern Language Notes*, 95 (1980), 585–608.
38. E.g. Hans Richard Brittnacher claims: 'Das Auge ist das zentrale Organ der Erkenntnis, Bedingung aufklärerischer Emanzipation' (Brittnacher, *Ästhetik des Horrors: Gespenster, Vampire, Monster, Teufel und künstliche Menschen in der phantastischen Literatur* (Frankfurt a.M.: Suhrkamp, 1994), p. 307).

39. *Romantische Metamorphosen*, p. 154.
40. Ibid., pp. 129–42.
41. Ibid., p. 158.
42. Friedrich Nietzsche, *Götzen-Dämmerung*, in *Sämtliche Werke*, ed. by Giorgio Colli and Mazzino Montinari, 15 vols (Munich: Deutsches Taschenbuch, 1999), vol. III of division XI, p. 72 (section IV, part II of *Götzen-Dämmerung*).
43. Alenka Zupančič, *The Shortest Shadow: Nietzsche's Philosophy of the Two* (Cambridge, MA: MIT Press, 2003), p. 21.
44. Friedrich Nietszche, *Sämtliche Werke*, ed. by Giorgio Colli and Mazzino Montinari, 15 vols (Munich: Deutsches Taschenbuch, 1999), section 6, vol. II 'Zur Genealogie der Moral', 259–430 (III, 13, p. 385).
45. Johann Gottfried Herder, *Abhandlung über den Ursprung der Sprache* (Berlin: Christian Friedrich Voss, 1772).
46. Petra Mayer, 'Hoffmanns poetischer Bullenbeißer — eine Ausgeburt des Grotesken. *Nachricht von den neuesten Schicksalen des Hundes Berganza*', *E. T. A. Hoffmann-Jahrbuch*, 15 (2007), 7–24 (p. 10).
47. Yoko Tawada, *Verwandlungen. Tübinger Poetik-Vorlesungen* (Tübingen: Konkursbuchverlag, 1998), p. 57.
48. Medievalist Joyce E. Salisbury provides an interesting discussion of eating as blurring boundaries between human and animal in her book *The Beast Within: Animals in the Middle Ages* (New York: Routledge, 1994), pp. 34–60, esp. p. 34.
49. Günter Wöllner, *E. T. A. Hoffmann und Franz Kafka: Von der 'fortgeführten Metapher' zum 'sinnlichen Paradox'* (Berne: Haupt, 1971), p. 117.
50. Eberhard Hilscher, 'Hoffmanns poetische Puppenspiele und Menschenmaschinen', *Text + Kritik*, 3. 2 (1992), 20–31 (p. 20).
51. Detlef Kremer, *E. T. A. Hoffmann: Erzählungen und Romane* (Berlin: Schmidt, 1999), p. 105.
52. Ernst Loeb, 'Bedeutungswandel der Metamorphose bei Franz Kafka und E. T. A. Hoffmann: Ein Vergleich', *The German Quarterly*, 35.1 (1962), 47–59 (p. 47).
53. Frevert, pp. 20–24.
54. Monique Scheer, 'Topographien des Gefühls', in Ute Frevert and others, *Gefühlswissen: eine lexicalische Spurensuche in der Moderne* (Frankfurt a.M.: Campus, 2011), pp. 41–64 (p. 43).
55. Ibid., p. 55.
56. In 1821 Hoffmann wrote to his friend Hitzig: 'Was ich jetzt bin und sein kann, wird *pro primo* der Kater [. . .] zeigen' (VI, 202).
57. Charles Taylor, *Sources of the Self: The Making of Modern Identity* (Cambridge, MA: Harvard University Press, 1989), pp. 368–69.
58. Ibid., p. 390. Holly Watkins explores the idea of depth in connection with Hoffmann's view of music in *Metaphors of Depth in German Musical Thought: From E. T. A. Hoffmann to Arnold Schoenberg* (Cambridge: Cambridge University Press, 2011).
59. Scheer, p. 56.
60. Friedrich Hebbel, 'Tagebuch 9. Januar 1842', *Werke*, IV, ed. by Gerhard Fricke, Werner Keller, and Karl Pörnbacher (Munich: Hanser, 1966), p. 458.

CHAPTER 2

Being Animal:
Kafka and the Wordless World

Metamorphosis and Modernism

The use of metamorphosis to explore the tensions of the individual continues into the modernist aesthetic of the early twentieth century, with increased emphasis on the physical and psychological experience of metamorphosis. Indeed, the work of late Romantic E. T. A. Hoffmann has been seen as a precursor to psychological modernism.[1] As Charles Taylor argues in his history of modern identity, modernism can be characterized both by a new inwardness (exemplified by the development of stream-of-consciousness writing), exploring new recesses of feeling and celebrating subjectivity, but also by a de-centring or destabilizing of the subject. That is, Taylor identifies the seeming paradox of both a subjective and anti-subjectivist thrust in modernism, though he argues that these stem from the same source.[2]

These two features can provide insight into the configuration of metamorphosis in modernist literature. First, metamorphosis texts may reflect the turn towards the subject by emphasizing individual perception. Late-nineteenth century empiricist psychology anchored knowledge of the world in sense perception, to the extent that 'the only reality was that of our consciousness'.[3] Judith Ryan links the psychology of this period to modernist literature, which emphasizes subjective perception.[4] This means that we might expect modernist literature to treat metamorphosis as a subjective process, focusing on individual experience. While Hoffmann's Romantic texts opened up the possibility of hesitating over the reality of the metamorphosis, there can be no hesitation as to whether a metamorphosis is real if the only reality is that of our consciousness. As long as the protagonist experiences it as such, the fact of the metamorphosis having happened is not subject to doubt.

The other aspect of modernism identified by Taylor is the anti-subjectivist thrust, which might be connected to empirical psychology locating the self not in the body as an objectively existing entity but in fragile individual consciousness.

According to Ryan, the new psychologies of this period gave rise to a 'sense of dissolution and fragmentation' in modernist literature.[5] Such understanding of the self raises the possibility that modernist literary representations of metamorphosis may depict the bodily change as peripheral, while inner thoughts and feelings are central. Moreover, consciousness itself might be subject to fragmentation, with Freudian psychoanalysis popularizing the idea of the unconscious and the different parts of a self ('Es', 'Ich', and 'Über-ich'). While the Romantic texts of the previous chapter used metamorphosis as a way of accessing a higher or deeper self, modernist metamorphoses may reflect new topographies of the self.

The rapidly changing social environment plays a part in the new configurations of the self in this period. Industrialization and technological advances meant a reconfigured urban landscape that threatened to encroach into the inner realms of the individual. The encroachment of urban life is reflected in modernist literature, for example in the opening of Rilke's *Die Aufzeichnungen des Malte Laurids Brigge* (1910) [The Notebooks of Malte Laurids Brigge], in which the narrator claims that he cannot sleep with the window open, because 'Elektrische Bahnen rasen läutend durch meine Stube. Automobile gehen über mich her' [Electric trolleys race clanging through my room. Automobiles rush over me].[6] The disappearing contours between external world and inner self give rise to a loss of agency, which modernist literature explores through individuals who appear helplessly subjected to forces beyond their control, and a literary style focusing on fragmentary impressions (often described as 'Aufzeichnungen'). According to this model, metamorphosis is likely to be externally imposed rather than actively chosen. Examining the process of metamorphosis in the texts of this chapter may thus be used to provide insight into configurations of self and identity in this period.

While metamorphoses between man and machine become prominent in the modernist period, in response to concerns that the individual is being replaced by technology,[7] I focus on humans changing into animals and vice versa. In doing so, I take into account the impact of theories of evolution, which claim the existence of metamorphosis, as a change from one species to another, over a long-term scale. The introduction of evolutionary theory brings with it with new scientific and literary interests in animal perspectives and in human–animal difference. The work of Franz Kafka is particularly important in this respect. As well as writing from animal perspectives, Kafka uses metamorphosis as subject matter and as literary process. As Monika Schmitz-Emans claims: 'Verwandlungen sind Kafkas Kernmotiv und zugleich das prägende Gestaltungsprinzip seiner Texte' [Transformations are Kafka's core motif as well as the defining formation principle of his texts].[8]

Like Hoffmann, Kafka's literary writing stood in tension with his work as a lawyer. The conflict between bourgeois reality and poetic fulfilment has been highlighted in both writers' work,[9] even though Hoffmann is not considered to have directly influenced Kafka.[10] The central importance of metamorphosis in the work of both Hoffmann and Kafka, however, may be linked to the sense of split self, engendered in part by their social circumstances. Born into a middle-class Jewish family in Prague, Kafka wrote in German, the language of social respectability, though he could also speak Czech, read French and Greek, and became interested in

Yiddish after attending a Yiddish theatre in 1911. However, his sense of being cut off from his Jewish heritage and the insecurities he faced surrounding social mobility might be traced in his use of the perspectives of outsider figures in his work. These include animals and those who are exiled or cut off, such as the protagonist of *Der Verschollene* [The Man Who Disappeared], the novel Kafka had been writing when he started *Die Verwandlung*. The difficulties with identity throughout Kafka's work can be related to Kafka's use of metamorphosis, as a process of taking on a different identity.

Understandably, for an author who has been placed amongst the greatest writers of the twentieth century, scholarship on Kafka is vast. Indeed, it is even possible to trace movements within literary scholarship through the changing approaches to Kafka's texts. While this chapter has the advantage of drawing on such wide scholarship, thereby highlighting key approaches to Kafka's use of metamorphosis, it also situates Kafka's writing within a wider context of metamorphosis literature. I also focus upon the affective construction of the self in Kafka's narratives of changing bodies and identities. While the affective turn has been accompanied by increased attention to the affects of Kafka's work (notably, Stanley Corngold's *Complex Pleasure: Forms of Feeling in German Literature*, which devotes a chapter to 'Rapture in Exile' in *Der Verschollene*),[11] this chapter relates the forms of affect in Kafka's texts to his depiction of changing identities and bodies.

This chapter focuses on *Die Verwandlung* (written 1912, published 1915), which has become one of the most well-known stories of bodily transformation in literature. I situate the text within the context of Kafka's other texts written from animal perspectives. Particular attention is given to 'Ein Bericht für eine Akademie' (first published 1917 in the magazine *Der Jude*, and in 1920 included in Kafka's collection *Ein Landarzt*), a story of an ape being accepted into human society. After considering issues of style, form, and affect in the presentation of the metamorphosis in the first part of *Die Verwandlung*, I turn what it means to become animal in the second part of *Die Verwandlung* as well as in 'Ein Bericht für eine Akademie'. I then address what it means to lose human language and to become open to music and to hitherto supressed affective experience, focusing on the last part of *Die Verwandlung*. I thereby aim to provide insight into the affects at the heart of Kafka's texts, and shed light upon why metamorphosis plays such an important role within Kafka's work.

Extraordinary Change

The Shock of Transformation

Kafka begins *Die Verwandlung* with what is now one of the most famous opening lines in literary history: 'Als Gregor Samsa eines Morgens aus unruhigen Träumen erwachte, fand er sich in seinem Bette zu einem ungeheueren Ungeziefer verwandelt'[12] [As Gregor Samsa woke one morning from uneasy dreams, he found himself transformed into some kind of monstrous vermin].[13] Whereas Hoffmann's writing followed the Serapiontic principle of progressing to the strange and wonderful via the real, everyday world, here an extraordinary metamorphosis happens in the midst of the everyday. The story thus begins with a shock that may be both comic and disturbing, a characteristic and compelling combination in Kafka's work. While the situation is outright absurd, the threefold repetition of the prefix 'un-' emphasizes the deeply negative nature of the change. If we follow Freud's analysis of the prefix 'un-' in his essay on the uncanny ('Das Unheimliche'), which refers to Hoffmann's 'Der Sandmann' as an example, then we might read 'un-' as a suggestion of the repressed aspects of Gregor's psyche that are brought to the fore through the metamorphosis. Freud claims that the uncanny ('unheimlich') is not simply that which is not familiar ('heimlich'), but an unsettling mixture of somehow familiar but not quite, hinting at that which has been repressed (XII, 259). As in Hoffmann's texts, the metamorphosis seems to bring to the fore aspects of the individual that are absent from everyday life.

Rather than providing further details about the process of transformation, the narrative proceeds with a detailed description of Gregor's perception of his new body:

> Er lag auf seinem panzerartig harten Rücken und sah, wenn er den Kopf ein wenig hob, seinen gewölbten, braunen, von bogenförmigen Versteifung geteilten Bauch, auf dessen Höhe sich die Bettdecke, zum gänzlichen Niedergleiten bereit, kaum noch erhalten konnte. Seine vielen, im Vergleich zu seinem sonstigen Umfang kläglich dünnen Beine flimmerten ihm hilflos vor den Augen. (I, 115)
>
> [He lay on his hard, armour-like back, and if he lifted his head a little, he could see his curved brown abdomen, divided by arch-shaped ridges, and domed so high that the bedspread, on the brink of slipping off, could hardly stay put. His many legs, miserably thin in comparison with his size otherwise, flickered helplessly before his eyes. (p. 29)]

Gregor is not shown to react emotionally to the transformation. Rather, the narrative is focalized through his impassive perspective as he views his body, which is conveyed with illusory precision. The accumulation of adjectives describing Gregor's torso ('panzerartig', 'hart', 'gewölbt', 'braun', 'bogenförmig', 'geteilt') give an impression of a beetle, but only in the most general of terms. The description mainly serves to convey the encumbered and vulnerable nature of his body, with its stiff back and pathetic legs ('kläglich', 'dünn', and 'hilflos'). That Gregor's bedcover is about to fall off his belly comically suggests the incongruity between his insect-like body and the ordinary bed in which he is lying, and hints at the unsustainability of the whole situation.

Within the opening paragraph there is no explanation of why the transformation has happened, nor is one ever suggested or even sought. In this respect, the transformation differs not only from classical stories of transformations, which are often enacted by gods for specific reasons, but also from many Romantic *Märchen*, in which transformations serve some narrative or moral purpose within a magical context. In Kafka's story, however, the transformation is simply an inexplicable occurrence to which Gregor is helplessly subjected. For Kafka, whose daily work at the 'Arbeiter-Versicherungs-Anstalt' [Workers' Accident Insurance Institute] meant dealing with cases involving accidents in the workplace, thoughts about the numerous ways in which bodies may be injured, damaged, and deformed must have been constantly present. Indeed, many of Kafka's stories reveal a preoccupation with bodily disfigurement, most notoriously perhaps in the torture machine of *In der Strafkolonie* [In the Penal Colony]. The fact that Kafka considered including *In der Strafkolonie* together with *Das Urteil* [The Judgement] and *Die Verwandlung* in a collection entitled *Strafen* [Punishments] suggests that we might interpret the transformation in *Die Verwandlung* as a punishment. However, while transformations as punishment are common in myth and *Märchen*, it is not clear what Gregor would be being punished for (in the other two stories the reason for the punishment is also obscure). For this reason, writer Yoko Tawada, whose work I explore in chapter 4, speaks of *Die Verwandlung* as having a 'hole in the text', and speculates upon the possible reasons for Gregor's punishment.[14] Although many metamorphosis stories are stories of people being helplessly subjected to unwanted bodily change, *Die Verwandlung* demonstrates a particularly radical loss of agency because of the lack of explanation. There is not even a search for cause or meaning, since neither Gregor nor his family ask why he has become an 'Ungeziefer'. As Dieter Hasselblatt claims, Kafka's prose tends to be 'initiofugal'.[15] That is, it unfolds from the initial premise set out at the beginning. Thus *Die Verwandlung* explores the consequences of the transformation, but does not look backwards for a cause.

Although the transformation is extraordinary, we are not invited to read it as a delusion. The narrator rules out this possibility: '"Was ist mit mir geschehen?" dachte er. Es war kein Traum' (I, 115) ["What has happened to me?" he thought. It was not a dream (p. 29)]. Unlike Hoffmann's Romantic protagonists, Gregor does not hesitate over whether the transformation is real or not, but experiences it as a real-life occurrence. While hesitation over reality is a defining feature of fantastic literature, according to Todorov, the lack of hesitation in Kafka's text suggests that the text is not fantastic, or represents a different kind of fantastic literature. Todorov claimed the later, by describing *Die Verwandlung* as symptomatic of a new type of literature that he called a 'generalized fantastic which swallows up the entire world of the book and the reader along with it'.[16] Other scholars have also called for Kafka's work to be considered within a broad tradition of fantastic writing.[17] However, whereas Romantic texts often position the extraordinary in tension with the everyday, with protagonists hesitating between the two possible frames of reference, in *Die Verwandlung*, the extraordinary is to be read as real, literal fact, with little uncertainty as to what has happened.

There are, however, some indications that Gregor is unsure whether to trust his own experience. Although he does not consider the possibility that he is deluded, he does wonder whether his family will also perceive him to be transformed:

> er war begierig zu erfahren, was die anderen, die jetzt so nach ihm verlangten, bei seinem Anblick sagen würden. Würden sie erschrecken, dann hatte Gregor keine Verantwortung mehr und konnte ruhig sein. Würden sie aber alles ruhig hinnehmen, dann hatte er keinen Grund sich aufzuregen, und konnte, wenn er sich beeilte, um acht Uhr tatsächlich auf dem Bahnhof sein. (I, 130)

> [he was eager to learn what the others, who were asking for him now so much, would say at the sight of him. If they were terrified, then Gregor no longer bore

the responsibility and could be at peace. But if they took it all calmly, then he
too had no cause to get upset, and could, if he hurried, really be at the station
at eight o'clock. (p. 37)]

The passage above suggests that Gregor intends to base his assessment of himself on the reaction of his family. His identity, as horrific creature or as ordinary person, is constructed through the eyes of others. For Gregor, his own bodily evidence is not enough. Rather, he expects his family to provide his identity for him. Thus, the reality of the metamorphosis is not only based on Gregor's perception, but also on the perception of his family. By allowing his family's reaction to determine the reality of the metamorphosis, Gregor can happily avoid responsibility, should his appearance shock them. Or, if they accept him as normal, he can rid himself of anxiety and resume everyday activity.

The presentation of an extraordinary event as matter-of-fact reality is already present in Kafka's early works. An example is the story 'Unglücklichsein' [Unhappiness] (published 1913), in which the narrator takes an intriguing attitude towards being confronted with a ghost:

> 'Was soll ich machen?' sagte ich, 'jetzt habe ich ein Gespenst im Zimmer gehabt.' 'Sie sagen das mit der gleichen Unzufriedenheit, wie wenn Sie ein Haar in der Suppe gefunden hätten.' 'Sie spaßen. Aber merken Sie sich, ein Gespenst ist ein Gespenst.' 'Sehr wahr. Aber wie, wenn man überhaupt nicht an Gespenster glaubt?' 'Ja meinen Sie denn, ich glaube an Gespenster? Was hilft mir aber dieses Nichtglauben?' 'Sehr einfach. Sie müssen eben keine Angst mehr haben, wenn ein Gespenst wirklich zu Ihnen kommt.' 'Ja, aber das ist doch die nebensächliche Angst. Die eigentliche Angst ist die Angst vor der Ursache der Erscheinung. Und diese Angst bleibt. Die habe ich geradezu großartig in mir.' (I, 38–39)
>
> ['What am I to do' I said. 'I've just had a ghost in my room.'
> 'You say that with the same dissatisfaction as you would if you'd found a hair in your soup.'
> 'You're joking. But just remember: a ghost is a ghost.'
> 'Very true. But what if one doesn't believe in ghosts at all?'
> 'Do you think I believe in ghosts, then? But what good is this not believing to me?'
> 'Very simple. Just don't be afraid any more if a ghost really turns up.'
> 'Yes, but that's the lesser fear, after all. The real fear is the cause of the apparition. And that fear sticks. I have it in me on a truly grand scale.' (p. 18)]

Even though the narrator does not believe in ghosts, he still has to deal with the fact that a ghost has been in his room. Not believing in ghosts may dispel the fear of the ghost itself, but a fundamental fear remains, which is the fear of what has caused him to see a ghost. The word 'Erscheinung' [apparition] allows for either a psychological or supernatural explanation of the ghost's presence. As in *Die Verwandlung*, the extraordinary situation is both comic and fearful in its irrationality. One might argue, adapting Winfried Menninghaus's claim that Kafka's stories work to neutralize disgust, that Kafka's writing neutralizes the fear that would normally be associated with supernatural occurrences.[18] Since Kafka has his protagonists experience such occurrences as unhesitatingly real, the story comes across partly as ridiculous. However, fear of the inexplicable remains, albeit below the surface. Yet although the narrator of 'Unglücklichsein' is afraid of what caused the ghost, he does not want his neighbour to take the ghost away. This might be because the ghost is a past self or the narrator's alter ego,[19] but it might also be read as a comment on the necessity of the strange, and of literature itself as a way of uncovering the strange, monstrous, and shocking that lies within.

Like the narrator of 'Unglücklichsein', Gregor's reaction to the transformation is one of mild surprise and inconvenience. After initially wondering what has happened to him, Gregor is tempted to ignore the problem: 'Wie wäre es, wenn ich noch ein wenig weiterschliefe und alle Narrheiten vergäße' [What if I went on sleeping for a while and forgot all these idiocies (p. 27)]. However, despite attempting to turn onto his side to sleep, and to think only about the strenuous nature of his job, Gregor is eventually forced to confront his new bodily state as inescapable reality. However, how do we interpret a literary text in which such a bizarre and shocking event is taken as reality? And what can we make of the fact that Gregor has become an 'Ungeziefer'? Is the metamorphosis a metaphor for something else?

Metamorphosis and Metaphor

Many discussions of Kafka's metamorphosis revolve around the question of what it means to become an 'Ungeziefer'. The term is not a scientific one, designating a specific animal, but connotes a creature that is unwanted and repulsive (often translated as 'vermin'), and was used as an insult.[20] The description of Gregor as an 'Ungeziefer' corresponds to the way in which Gregor's bodily form is never entirely clear. The initial description of Gregor's body serves more to emphasize his vulnerability than to provide classification (the words used to describe his legs include 'kläglich', 'flimmerten', and 'hilflos'). This ambiguity is not, however, an invitation to uncover precisely what creature Gregor has become, and to approach the text 'in the manner of a criminal detective', as attempted by one scholar.[21] Rather, we are to read Gregor precisely as an 'Ungeziefer', that is, as a repulsive creature, whose precise physical nature is left vague. Kafka did not want an illustration of an insect on the front cover of the book, since 'Ungeziefer' is an affectively laden concept rather than a scientifically defined entity.[22] Scholars have often noted the rich metaphorical potential that the semantic ambiguity of 'Ungeziefer' provides.[23]

Because the term 'Ungeziefer' can be used in reference to both humans and animals, several scholars have regarded the transformation as a way of taking the figurative or metaphorical use of 'Ungeziefer' (as an insult) and making it literal. Günther Anders argued along these lines in 1947, when he claimed that Kafka takes his point of departure from the figurative nature ('Bildcharakter') of language, and from taking metaphors literally ('beim Wort').[24] More recently, however, the idea of the metamorphosis as a literalization of metaphor has come under intense scrutiny, most notably by Stanley Corngold.[25] Corngold takes Anders's claims as a starting point, but also draws upon Walter Sokel's investigation of Kafka's metamorphosis serving as 'extended metaphor'. Sokel claims that 'extended metaphors, metaphoric visualizations of emotional situations, uprooted from any explanatory context' are characteristic of Expressionist prose'.[26] In his later work, Sokel develops a more advanced position, in which he claims that Kafka's poetics do not originate in metaphor, as a process of transforming reality, but in counter-metamorphosis, in which a metaphor is turned back into reality. Despite the sophisticated arguments made by scholars who see Kafka's metamorphosis as a reversal of the metaphorical use of language, Corngold and Wagner fundamentally object to ideas that Gregor Samsa is a metaphor come alive, calling this an 'exemplary interpretative error'.[27]

Corngold's main argument for why this is an error is that Gregor has not truly become an insect, but something in-between insect and human. Corngold writes that if the metaphor was literalized then we would have 'not an indefinite monster, but simply a bug. Indeed, the continuing alteration of Gregor's body suggests ongoing metamorphosis, the *process* of literalization in various directions and not its end state'.[28] Gregor's insect characteristics seem to develop as the story progresses. However, this need not mean that Gregor is becoming more like an insect, but rather that Gregor is discovering his physical nature. For example, it is not clear that Gregor's voice deteriorates. Instead we might read Gregor as initially believing incorrectly that he is speaking. Nevertheless, there is no full literalization of the term 'Ungeziefer'. As Corngold and Wagner put it, Gregor is 'not a true beetle, but a shifting social construction'.[29] Gregor does not literally become a beetle. However, if we understand the 'literal' sense of 'Ungeziefer' not as meaning a beetle, but precisely as a shifting social construct, there may be room for the idea that a process of literalization is at work.

To do so means understanding 'Ungeziefer' as a term connoting repulsiveness, rather than regarding the term as a metaphor, in which animal characteristics are transferred onto humans. This interpretation draws support from the fact that Kafka was critical of metaphors, once writing:

> Die Metaphern sind eines in dem vielen, was mich am Schreiben verzweifeln lässt. Die Unselbstständigkeit des Schreibens, die Abhängigkeit von dem Dienstmädchen, das einheizt, von der Katze, die sich am Ofen wärmt, selbst vom armen alten Menschen, der sich wärmt. Alles dies sind selbstständige, eigengesetzlichen Verrichtungen, nur das Schreiben ist hilflos, wohnt nicht in sich selbst, ist Spaß und Verzweiflung.[30]
>
> [Metaphors are one of the many things that make me despair of writing. Writing's lack of independence of the world, its dependence on the maid who tends the fire, the cat warming itself by the stove; it is even dependent on the poor old human being warming himself by the stove. All these are independent activities ruled by their own laws; only writing is helpless, cannot live in itself, is a joke and a despair.][31]

Accordingly Kafka's work might be read not as an attempt to create metaphor, but as a radical engagement with the situation of being dependent, played out in Gregor's helpless situation. Moreover, one problem that Kafka had with metaphor is its failure to capture feeling: 'Zwischen tatsächliches Gefühl und vergleichende Beschreibung ist wie ein Brett eine zusammenhanglose Voraussetzung eingelegt' [An incoherent assumption is thrust like a board between the actual feeling and the metaphor of the description].[32] Rather than using comparative description or metaphor to express Gregor's situation, Gregor lives his condition as 'Ungeziefer', and so we must read what happens within the text without assuming that his condition is a metaphor for something that lies outside the text.

Through the metamorphosis therefore, Gregor has become an 'Ungeziefer' in the fullest sense of the word, and his family treat him as such through their horror, disgust, and anger. It is significant that they never ask about the transformation itself, nor do they inquire into its cause or into the possibility of its reversal. This is because the story is not about a human becoming an insect. It is about Gregor's existence as an 'Ungeziefer', an abject body. If humans can be vermin, then the parents may be shocked to find that their son is vermin, but this is not beyond the realms of possibility. The process at work is not the literalization of metaphor, but the elision of the distinction between 'Ungeziefer' as an insult for an undesirable person, and 'Ungeziefer' as a repulsive physical creature. This process happens during Gregor's uneasy dreams, for it is during sleep that distinctions become uncertain.

If the idea of the story was to explore what it means to become a beetle, then the question arises why Gregor does not discover his wings and fly out of the window, a point made by Vladimir Nabokov, ardent entomologist as well as novelist and lecturer.[33] However, the possibility does not arise, because the story is not about becoming a beetle, but about being an 'Ungeziefer'. As an abject creature, Gregor's presence within the family becomes increasingly undesirable, and the situation can only be alleviated by Gregor's death. Corngold describes the source of the metamorphosis not as the metaphor of 'Ungeziefer' but as a 'radical aesthetic intention'. That is, the metamorphosis is not simply an experiment in language-play, but an attempt to represent the predicament of an 'Ungeziefer'.[34] The substance of the narrative is comprised from Gregor's experience of being an 'Ungeziefer', and his gradual psychological transformation as he deals with his new bodily situation.

Feeling the Way: Becoming Animal as Literary Practice

One would expect that after having been transformed, Gregor's new bodily state would command his full attention. However, he remains preoccupied by his daily concerns. While he is reflecting upon the strains of working as a commercial traveller, his thoughts linguistically point to his new state as he considers the 'Geschäftsdiener' [chief clerk] as being a 'Kreatur des Chefs, ohne Rückgrat und Verstand' (I, 194) [the boss's creature, stupid and spineless (p. 31)]. While the entomological lexis raised by 'creature' and 'spineless' reminds us of his bodily physicality, Gregor is unaware of the irony of the expression. The humour of the situation is brought out by Gregor's refusal to acknowledge his physical change. His avoidance becomes increasingly unsustainable, however, as his parents begin banging on the door in an effort to get him to go to work. Once Gregor's physical state becomes apparent Gregor is forced to acknowledge it.

The focus of the story is thus neither the events leading up to the transformation, nor the process of transformation itself, but rather, it is Gregor's adjustment to his new physical state, and the effect that this new state has, most importantly, upon his family, and secondly, upon himself. The metamorphosis provides a means of exploring an alternative existence as a non-human creature. Like Hoffmann, Kafka narrates several of his stories from animal perspectives (as in 'Forschungen eines Hundes' [Investigations of a Dog] or 'Josefine, die Sängerin' [Josephine the Singer]) or from the perspectives of figures who become animal (*Die Verwandlung*) or stop being animal ('Ein Bericht für eine Akademie'). Kafka even writes about creatures who are neither human nor animal, such as Odradek in 'Die Sorge des Hausvaters' [The Cares of a Family Man], who appears somewhat like a flat, star-shaped bobbin standing upon two sticks (v, 282).

In imagining such alternative existences, Kafka's work provides a prime example of the mimetic capacity, which according to Walter Benjamin is at the heart of literature. Benjamin observes the mimetic capacity in children, who not only play at being people and animals, but even windmills or trains.[35] More recently, the concept of a mimetic capacity has been supported by the discovery of mirror neurons, which suggest that observation of an activity is neurologically closely connected to active participation.[36] What makes Kafka's literary work striking is the extent and intensity with which this process of identifying with radically different perspectives is carried out. The fact that Kafka preferred to write in a single sitting, as he did when writing 'Das Urteil', suggests that emotionally inhabiting the protagonist's perspective, and maintaining the integrity and continuity of feeling, was paramount.

Kafka's use of metamorphosis to explore alternative existences might be considered as a form of escapism, especially if we consider the insect metamorphosis in his earlier story 'Hochzeitsvorbereitungen auf dem Lande' [Wedding Preparations in the Country]. In this story, the protagonist Raban imagines his body going out on social errands while his real self ('wahres Ich') stays in bed in the form of a giant cockchafer ('Maikäfer'). The split self has been read as a childish fantasy of avoiding unpleasant tasks.[37] A similar reading of *Die Verwandlung* would suggest that Gregor's transformation is a way of escaping his strenuous daily life, and that his existence as an 'Ungeziefer' is his real self.[38] However, whereas Raban's bodily form as cockchafer could be read positively, recalling a line from the beginning of Goethe's *Die Leiden des jungen Werthers* [The Sorrows of Young Werther],[39] Gregor's transformation has caused him to become an abject creature. Between Raban and Gregor, Kafka's depiction of metamorphosis has shifted, which might be related to changing cultural attitudes towards cockchafers after the plague of cockchafers in the summer of 1911, which destroyed vast areas of European farmland.[40] Though Gregor is not a cockchafer specifically, his partially cockchafer-like form supports the designation of him as an 'Ungeziefer'. The story may even be structured with the temporal sequence of the cockchafer life-cycle in mind, since Gregor awakes from sleeping (cockchafers lie dormant in the earth for several years before hatching), lives only a few weeks like the cockchafer, and dies soon after having pressed himself onto a picture of a woman in furs, just as cockchafers die after mating in the summer.

In adopting the close experiential perspective of the protagonist, Kafka writes without a pre-existing structure. Indeed, he claimed to write as if in a tunnel, without knowing how the story will turn out.[41] Kafka's many unfinished works attest to this practice. Kafka's concentration on his protagonists' inner perspectives is reinforced spatially in the enclosed spaces in which his figures find themselves, as in Gregor Samsa's failure to move beyond the four walls of his small 'Menschenzimmer' [human being's room]. Similarly in *Der Bau* [The Burrow], Kafka's most radical exploration of self-enclosure, the animal narrator is intent upon fortifying his underground dwelling against intruders. Kafka's writing thus aims at accessing an inner, subjective space. However, it also reveals the impossibility of inhabiting a completely enclosed space of interior subjectivity, and suggests that the Romantic use of metamorphosis to access a higher or deeper self is misguided.

The process of inhabiting an interior world means not only complete concentration and withdrawal, but focus upon feeling. According to Walter Sokel, Kafka insisted upon the presence of the original feeling that inspired the writing, and felt that any word in excess of that feeling would falsify the work. In striving for what he called 'truth', Kafka's writing required, as Sokel argues, a 'direct outflow' and 'unmediated vision of the inner self', going beyond the romantic and existential cult of authenticity to achieve the greatest possible closeness between the feelings of character and author.[42] However, after *Das Urteil* Kafka realized that his writing was not a vehicle of truth, but the opposite, since the passages that he considered best were scenes of dying, in which Kafka masked his pleasure of writing them, so that they seem deeply sad and moving.[43] Writing is inevitably duplicitous, since the writer and protagonist cannot fully merge together. Though the act of metamorphosis, as an act of imagining oneself into another perspective, is central to Kafka's writing, it is not sustainable. Despite aiming to identify closely with his protagonists, what Kafka in fact produced might be read, as Ritchie Robertson argues, as 'exercises in sustained irony, designed to induce a fine balance in the reader between emotional participation, and the poise of superior knowledge'.[44]

Kafka's emphasis on immediacy and truthfulness of feeling coincides with the distrust of language that he shared with authors of the *Sprachkrise* [Language Crisis].[45] The idea that language is an inadequate means of representing experience is part of the new concern with inner subjectivity and affective experience. Hofmannsthal's 'Chandos letter' of 1902 provides an example of how the inability to use language coincides with the unexpected surfacing of intense feelings provoked by everyday things. The narrator attempts to describe the affective moments which leave him without words: 'es ist ja etwas völlig Unbenanntes, und auch wohl kaum Benennbares, das in solchen Augenblicken, irgendeine Erscheinung meiner alltäglichen Umgebung mit einer überschwellenden Flut höheren Lebens wie ein Gefäß erfüllend, mir sich ankündet' [it is something completely unnamed, and indeed barely nameable that is revealed to me in such moments, filling like a vessel anything appearing within my daily environment with an overflowing flood of higher life].[46] The narrator's sense of higher life is provoked in particular by intense identification with other beings. For example, the narrator recalls having asked for rat poison to be put in the cellars, and starts to picture the dying rats with great affective intensity. The feeling experienced, he claims, was not pity, but an 'ungeheures Anteilnehmen, ein Hinüberfließen in jene Geschöpfe' [monstrous participation, an overflowing into such creatures] (p. 51). Human language becomes difficult as writers seek to inhabit non-human existences, even that of abject vermin.

The use of non-human perspectives in modernist literature coincides with increasing scientific interest in understanding animal perspectives. Of particular significance is the work of biologist Jakob von Uexküll with his 1909 exploration of the *Umwelt und Innenwelt der Tiere* [Surrounding and Interior World of Animals] (as well as his later *Streifzüge durch die Umwelten von Tieren und Menschen* in 1934 [A Foray into the Worlds of Animals and Humans]). Uexküll investigated the 'Umwelt' of different organisms, which is their subjective perceptual environment, as opposed to an 'Umgebung' as an objective environment. Kafka's focalization through Gregor's perspective reflects the emphasis on subjective experience and the idea that objective access to the world is not possible. Kafka's animal figures also allow for an alternative perspective on human society. For example, the poetically inclined dog narrator of Kafka's 'Forschungen eines Hundes' [Investigations of a Dog] is used similarly to Hoffmann's dog Berganza, discussed in the previous chapter, to observe and offer an alternative interpretation of human behaviour. However, Kafka's tale goes further than Hoffmann's in emphasizing the dog's subjective perspective by removing humans from the dog's perspective. For Kafka's dog narrator, food appears to drop from the sky, and small dogs, 'Lufthunde' [aerial dogs], appear to remain in the air (presumably carried by their owners). Kafka's animal texts highlight the limited perceptual field of the individual. This does not mean that the stories deal with individual concerns that are of limited general interest. On the contrary, the animal outsiders are particularly apt for offering an alternative view of human existence, and highlighting its more deplorable aspects.

Animal Existence

Animal Bodies: Disgusting Desires

Why write from the perspective of an animal? Within the field of animal studies, a central claim is that animals should be important not just for what they mean to humans but for what they are in themselves.[47] Accordingly, some of those who approach Kafka's work through animal studies have argued that Kafka is sympathetic to the project of comprehending animal perspectives.[48] Yet for others, such as Theodor Adorno, Kafka's writing is not so much about animals as about the animality of humans.[49] Following the latter view, animal protagonists could be seen as a way of exploring specific aspects of human existence. Certainly in *Die Verwandlung*, where Gregor is not a specific animal, we might read the story as exploring the human condition of being vermin. Despite his physical change, Gregor maintains psychological continuity with his human life; indeed, to such a degree that he initially ignores his transformation and worries about being absent from work. Comically, the unheard-of situation is not the transformation but the idea of not working, and having to call in sick, which seems 'äußerst peinlich und verdächtig' (I, 118) [extremely embarrassing and suspicious (p. 31)]. Gregor's work will help reduce his parents' debt ('Schuld', I, 117), while the idea of not working evokes considerable guilt (another meaning of 'Schuld').

Despite his negative feelings, Gregor experiences an unusual sense of physical health in his new animal state: 'Gregor fühlte sich tatsächlich, abgesehen von einer nach dem langen Schlaf wirklich überflüssigen Schläfrigkeit, ganz wohl und hatte sogar einen besonders kräftigen Hunger' (I, 119) [In fact, apart from feeling quite unnecessarily sleepy after such a long lie-in, Gregor felt perfectly well, and even particularly hungry (p. 31)]. The metamorphosis brings Gregor's bodily needs to the fore, and even changes his taste. When Grete brings him a glass of milk, he finds he cannot stand the taste of it, and prefers an overripe cheese that he had previously declared inedible: '"Sollte ich jetzt weniger Feingefühl haben?"' dachte er und saugte schon gierig an dem Käse, zu dem es ihn vor allen anderen Speisen sofort und nachdrücklich gezogen hatte' (I, 148) ['Might I have become less sensitive?' He thought, already greedily sucking at the cheese, which had immediately, and insistently, attracted him ahead of all the other food on offer (p. 46)]. Instead of his former favourite drink of milk, with its connotations of infancy, innocence, and purity, he now prefers foods considered disgusting by human standards. His acute hunger can also be seen as part of his repulsiveness, since, for Kafka, voracious appetite is often associated with undesirable animal drives. His story 'Ein Hungerkünstler' [A Hunger Artist] is a prime example of the rejection of animal appetite. The hunger artist enjoys going without food, though as his feats of ascetic self-denial go out of favour, the crowds ignore the hunger artist in favour of the strong vitality of the beast of prey (at the end a 'Raubtier' [carnivore] moves into the cage once occupied by the hunger artist, (VI, 349)). As an animal, Gregor experiences a vigorous and uncouth appetite, but since he continues to think as a human, he questions his loss of 'Feingefühl' [sensitivity]. Gregor ultimately rejects his animal vitality as he sacrifices himself for his family. As in 'Ein Hungerkünstler' the story ends with self-destructive asceticism being replaced by animal vitality, as represented not by Gregor but by Grete, who alights from the tram to the countryside ('ins Freie') and stretches her young body (I, 200).

The contrast between human asceticism and the vitality of the animal body is prominent in the work of Nietzsche, which made a strong impression upon Kafka.[50] In *Zur Genealogie der Moral* (1887) Nietzsche uses the image of the beast of prey ('Raubtier') as an affirmation of vitality and power, which he associates with early aristocratic races.[51] This mode of being is contrasted with that of certain present-day humans whom Nietzsche describes as priests or ascetics, and even refers to as parasites or weeds. Indeed he describes the psychology of such character types as that of a 'Sumpfboden' [swamp] containing the 'Würmer der Rach- und Nachgefühle' [worms of vengeance and resentment].[52] While Gregor's existence as 'Ungeziefer' seems to exemplify Nietzsche's idea of the unhealthy ascetic, Gregor also exhibits the powerful animal drives of the carnivore. The metamorphosis could thus be seen as dramatizing the conflict between animal vitality and human asceticism. Gregor's turn towards the latter is a result of his family's influence, in particular after the apple thrown by his father lodges in his back and rots. After this, Gregor becomes associated with sickness and rotting, decaying, polluted matter.

Gregor's transformation brings not only increased bodily drives, but also a discovery of new bodily pleasures.[53] The unrealized sexual desires of Gregor's previous life are intimated by the picture of the lady in fur which hangs on Gregor's wall. Later, Gregor attempts to prevent his sister from removing the picture:

> da sah er an der im übrigen schon leeren Wand auffallend das Bild der in lauter Pelzwerk gekleideten Dame hängen, kroch eilends hinauf und preßte sich an das Glas, das ihn festhielt und seinem heißen Bauch wohltat. (I, 165)
>
> [hanging on the wall, which was otherwise bare, he was struck by the picture of the lady dressed in nothing but fur. He crawled up to it hurriedly and pressed himself against the glass, which held him fast, and did his burning stomach good] (pp. 55–56)

By attaching himself to the picture, Gregor expresses physical desire for the woman as well as opposition towards his sister: 'Er saß auf seinem Bild und gab es nicht her. Lieber wollte er Grete ins Gesicht springen' (I, 166) [He was sitting on the picture and he wasn't giving it up. He would rather make a leap for Grete's face. (p. 56)]. His action enrages her: '"Du, Gregor!" rief die Schwester mit erhobener Faust' (166) ['Gregor!' his sister called, raising her fist with a compelling look (p. 56)]. Her response has been read as an expression of sexual jealousy, in conjunction with a link between Gregor's name and Hartmann von Aue's *Gregorius* (c. 1190), in which Gregorius has incestuous union with his sister.[54] Yet it could also be read as repulsion towards Gregor's display of sexuality.

The use of metamorphosis to explore unrealized sexual urges is suggested by the link between the picture in Gregor's room and the 1870 novel *Venus im Pelz* [Venus in Furs] by Leopold von Sacher-Masoch. In Sacher-Masoch's novel, the central character Gregor becomes the slave and lover of Wanda, a figure of animalistic sexuality, who is shown in a picture as a Venus in furs. The allusion to *Venus im Pelz* suggests a link between the masochistic desires of Sacher-Masoch's Gregor, and the latent sexuality and submissive character of Kafka's Gregor. Following this intertextual link, the transformation may even be regarded as a masochistic fantasy, a pleasure in being degraded and repelled. Through becoming vermin, Gregor indulges a desire to be crushed (his father's feet appear intimidatingly large) and to submit passively to the cruelty and repulsion of his family (Gregor accepts his sister's decision that he should be got rid of).[55] As an animal, Gregor's socially unacceptable desires become manifest, and he is rejected by his family.

Central to the story is the way in which Gregor's family view him as an object of repulsion. They express this in different ways: the father is angry, the mother faints, and the sister, despite being the only one to enter Gregor's room and provide him with food, picks up the bowl of milk that Gregor has touched using a rag, and appears relieved when Gregor remains under the settee. While the term 'Ungeziefer' connotes something repulsive, scholars have argued that the disgusting is not an objectively existing category, but is something that challenges accepted categories or offends against a sense of order.[56] Gregor does not physically belong in the human, family environment in which he is enclosed. The transformation itself is also offensive in the way it challenges the distinction between human and animal.

If the disgusting involves unwanted substances trespassing bodily boundaries, such as the rotten food that Gregor eats, this includes the sticky secretions that Gregor emits. These have been linked to nocturnal emissions, suggesting Gregor's repressed sexuality coming to the fore.[57] His bodily fluids can also be seen as a sign of his alterity and non-human, insect-like nature. When he is cut he oozes a brown liquid, a colour which suggests rot and decay. The use of the word 'Flüssigkeit' [fluid], as Ritchie Robertson has argued, also makes Gregor seem more like a machine.[58] Images of disgusting, monstrous bodies are strongly anchored in literature of this period, connected in particular to disgust at the modern industrial city and its workers, where the body is in tension with the modern order.[59] Representations of disgusting bodies assert a boundary between primitive monstrosity and the modern, healthy and productive body.[60]

As an animal, Gregor's existence is incompatible with that of his family, a problem that becomes increasingly pronounced. Gregor is frequently referred to as a 'Tier', which instates a human–animal binary, and places Gregor firmly on the non-human, animal side. This side is incompatible with human life: 'ein Zusammenleben von Menschen mit einem solchen Tier [ist] nicht möglich' (I, 191) [it's not possible for human beings to live with a beast like that (p. 69)]. As Gregor's body becomes increasingly unwelcome his sister is finally led to assert: 'wir müssen versuchen, es loszuwerden' (I, 189) [we must try to get rid of it (p. 69)]. In the impersonal pronoun 'es' Gregor has indisputably become a non-human, no longer a valued family member, but an unwanted pest. As an animal, Gregor makes visible bodily desires that should remain repressed. As Adorno and Horkheimer put it, there is both a sadness and consolation in animals, for they remind us of nature that has been overcome by civilization and stand in place of what has been repressed in the self.[61] The uncovering of repressed animality is not welcome, however, in Gregor's family. Through expressing socially unacceptable desires, Gregor could even be seen as reverting to a lower state of animality. In the next section I consider whether the metamorphosis involves a regression to a past state, or a break into something new.

Metamorphosis and Evolution: Models of Temporality

As a sudden and extreme change that disrupts linear temporality, metamorphosis bears an affinity to short prose forms, such as the novella, which revolve around what Goethe called an 'unerhörte Begebenheit' [unheard-of incident], a single event causing profound change. Gregor's metamorphosis causes an irreparable break with his former life, in the process possibly reversing temporality. His animal existence may be read as a regression to a state of early infancy, since he is initially confined to lying on the bed. Later he is able to crawl around the room, but is dependent upon his sister to bring him food, and is unable to communicate verbally. Gregor is in a childlike position of vulnerability and dependence. Gregor's perspective could also be seen as childlike, something that has been claimed as a common feature of Kafka's protagonists.[62]

Gregor's transformation also places him at the bottom of a hierarchical model of evolution, which places humans at the top, and insects at the bottom of all animal species. In this sense, the transformation might be read as a regression to a past state both at the individual level and at a species level. At the time of Kafka's writing, the theory of evolution had become relatively established, but debate still existed, particularly concerning the question of progress. To some thinkers, Darwin's model of evolution seemed to suggest that animals progressively adapt and thereby move from a state low on the evolutionary scale to the pinnacle of evolution, humanity. While Darwin's model drew attention to the commonality between humans and other species, his work does not rule out a Christian privileging of the human above other species. Against the hierarchical model of evolution, biologist Jakob von Uexküll argued that animals are already perfectly adapted to their own environment, rather than being in a state of progression up the evolutionary ladder.[63] Following Uexküll, Gregor's transformation into an insect might be read as a subversion of the idea of hierarchical progress.

The temporal model of the metamorphosis in *Die Verwandlung* might be considered alongside that of Kafka's 'Bericht für eine Akademie' (1917), which deals with a transformation in the opposite direction, from ape to human. Like Hoffmann's tale of the ape Milo, discussed in the previous chapter, Kafka's 'Bericht' can be read as a satire on human society and the idea of human superiority. Like Milo, Kafka's ape Rotpeter does not transform physically, but becomes human through achieving human abilities that have a base, vulgar quality to them. Kafka's ape has reached (albeit with much effort, unlike the ease with which Milo managed it) 'die Durchschnittsbildung eines Europäers' [the average educational level of a European],[64] an achievement which he downplays: 'Das wäre an sich vielleicht gar nichts, ist aber insofern doch etwas, als es mir aus den Käfig half und mir diesen besonderen Ausweg, diesen Menschenausweg verschaffte' (VI, 312) [That would in itself perhaps be nothing, but it is still something insofar as it did help me out of the cage, and made this particular way out available to me, this human way out (p. 45)]. As in Hoffmann, becoming human is not something to be celebrated. The metamorphosis serves to mock human pretentions to superiority. However, whereas Milo is a figure of ridicule, unable to see the hollowness of the society into which he 'ascends', seduced by power and status, Rotpeter becomes human through painful necessity, as the only way to avoid remaining trapped in a cage. Unlike Milo, who is proud of his acceptance into human society and success as a musician, Rotpeter is not satisfied with his new life and the 'almost unsurpassable success' of his performances, but he does not complain. Rotpeter chose the life of the entertainer over the only other option he felt he had, to be a circus animal, but he does not attempt to pass judgement on human existence. He ends by stressing that he only wishes to report his experience: 'Im übrigen will ich keines Menschen Urteil, ich will nur Kenntnisse verbreiten, ich berichte nur, auch Ihnen, hohe Herren von der Akademie, habe ich nur berichtet' (VI, 313) [I am not asking for a judgment from any human, my only wish is to make these insights more widely known; I am simply reporting; to you too, honoured gentlemen of the academy, I have been simply making a report (p. 45)]

The critique of human society in both Hoffmann's and Kafka's ape stories works by stressing the questionable value of human abilities. While Milo takes superficial society people as his role models, Rotpeter learns by copying the coarse behaviour of the sailors on board the ship. Thus Rotpeter learns first to spit, and then to spit into people's faces, though unlike the sailors, Rotpeter licks his face clean afterwards. He also learns to smoke and to drink schnapps, although the smell revolts him. In order to become human, therefore, he must conquer his disgust. Whereas in *Die Verwandlung* disgust is associated with animality, in the 'Bericht', it is human customs that are disgusting.

In both Hoffmann and Kafka's ape stories, entry into human society begins with a wound. Rotpeter is shot twice; once in the cheek, which leaves behind a large red scar (causing him to be called Rotpeter, as distinct from Peter, another ape), and the second bullet hits him beneath the hips. The second wound is particularly bad, and results in a permanent limp. Rotpeter is ready to reveal this wound to anyone, and show what is no more than a scar surrounded by fur. The wound might be read as a form of castration, suggesting that becoming human involves the loss of sexuality.

Rotpeter's transformation might also be read as a critique of the faith in the inevitability of human progress that was characteristic of the positivist outlook of previous decades. As a human, Rotpeter's existence is not an improvement, but the result of a forced change, or 'vorwärtsgepeitschte Entwicklung' [forwardly driven development] which leads to him feeling trapped in the 'Menschenwelt' [human world]. He envisions his past as a hole that has become so small that he can no longer go back through it. Only a breeze on the heels reminds him of his past, a corporeal trace that lingers on a vulnerable body part (if we associate the heels with Achilles' heel). As in *Die Verwandlung*, to be animal is to be vulnerable, and this remains within human existence even if it has become almost unnoticeable.

Rotpeter's rapid transition from ape to human contrasts with models of gradual evolution, and brings temporality into question. Although the transition happened within a period that can be counted in weeks, Rotpeter experienced it as though corresponding to the long evolutionary process by which our ape-like ancestors became human. Rotpeter claims that he is no longer able to report on his life as an ape since he is irremediably separated from that past: 'Nahezu fünf Jahre trennen mich vom Affentum, eine Zeit, kurz vielleicht am Kalender gemessen, unendlich lang aber durchzugallopieren.' (VI, 299) [Almost five years separate me from the estate of apedom, a short time perhaps measured by the calendar, but infinitely long to gallop through as I have done (pp. 37–38)]. The speeding up of time can be compared to the modern condition in which technological advances made it possible to speed between places that would previously have required far longer travelling time.[65] Rotpeter enacts this transformation by learning assiduously and 'rücksichtslos' [mercilessly]. He jumps between teachers in different rooms, enjoying the 'Eindringen der Wissensstrahlen von allen Seiten' [penetration of the awakening brain from all sides by the radiance of knowledge (p. 45)]. At the same time, his teachers risk becoming apelike as they deal with him. Rotpeter claims that he was only able to make this progress by not showing 'Rücksicht' ['consideration' or literally 'looking backwards'], a word whose significance has been discussed in relation to *Die Verwandlung*, in which Gregor gradually stops showing 'Rücksicht'.[66] By relinquishing his past Rotpeter is able to move forward, and yet this means that he is unable to judge what he has lost from his animal state. As in theories of evolution, change happens out of necessity, but, Kafka's text suggests that this may not mean progress or improvement.

Rotpeter accomplishes in a lifetime the equivalent of the evolutionary transition from pre-human apelike ancestor to present day human. In this sense, Kafka's story parallels the popular scientific idea, promoted by Ernst Haekel, that ontogeny recapitulates phylogeny, in other words, that the development of the individual parallels the development of a species as a whole. Kafka appears to have supported this theory. In 1913 he wrote in his diary of the 'vollständig[e], immer wieder aufzufindended[e] Gemeinsamkeit gesamt- und einzelmenschlicher Entwicklung. Selbst in den verschlossensten Gefühlen des einzelnen' [complete harmony [. . .] between the development of mankind as a whole and of the individual man. Even in the most secret emotions of the individual].[67] The second sentence is significant, for in Kafka's work, becoming human also involves an affective change. Whereas animality is associated with the uninhibited expression of bodily desires and emotions, being human means a suppression of these urges and the acquisition of social emotions such as shame and disgust of those who contravene social norms.

Rotpeter's condition is made clearer when he speaks of returning home to a half-broken-in female ape, whose company he can only enjoy at night, for in the daytime he sees in her the confusion of the performing ape, which he cannot stand. As a performing ape, Rotpeter is successful, but to be so he must relinquish his animal past, and accept the impossibility of full integration into human society. Indeed, one of the main ways in which this story has been read, influenced by Kafka's friend Max Brod, is as a story of Jewish assimilation into society.[68] Despite abandoning his past, true assimilation appears impossible for Rotpeter. While this reading may not do justice to the many possible ways of interpreting the story it is biographically important, and helps emphasize how human–animal metamorphosis can be a way of exploring social pressures. As in Hoffmann's texts, becoming human allows for a critique of human society. In Kafka's story the target of the critique is not the lack of feeling inherent in society, but the sense of another existence that has been lost in the forcible process of becoming human.

Trapped Animals and the Impossibility of Freedom

In *Die Verwandlung* and the 'Bericht', existence as an animal in a human world is characterized by a feeling of being trapped. The first description of Gregor's post-metamorphic body is of lying on a 'panzerartig harten Rücken' (I, 115) [hard, armour-like back (p. 29)]. The word 'panzerartig' (armour-like) implies that his hard outer body is a form of protection. The parts that are not enclosed are vulnerable (his legs are 'hilflos', and he discovers that 'der untere Teil seines Körpers augenblicklich vielleicht der empfindlichste war'). Gregor is not only enclosed within his body, but is forced to remain within his room, a 'human being's room'. Although we may read his confinement as unwanted, we may also read it as protective.

Gregor's transformation at first seems to offer him the possibility of escaping the job that he dislikes. Although he is concerned about not working, he discovers pleasure and humour in his new situation. He experiences getting out of bed as a game (I, 123) and smiles to imagine calling his father and the maid to help him out of bed, a scene reminiscent of the slapstick comedy in the films that Kafka liked to watch.[69] Gregor reflects that if his appearance is shocking, he will no longer need to work. Seen in this light, the transformation can be seen as an 'Ausweg' [escape route], a way of avoiding work. Ultimately, however, Gregor's animal existence does not lead to a positive alternative, but is, as Ulf Abraham puts it, the 'Ausweg, den es nicht gibt' [escape route that does not exist].[70]

The search for an 'Ausweg' is central in Kafka's 'Bericht'. After the ape is captured he is put into a cage which is too small to stand in and too narrow to sit in. He is forced to adopt an uncomfortable crouching position, with the bars pressing into his flesh. He feels that he has no way out: 'In alledem aber doch nur das eine Gefühl: kein Ausweg'. The need to have a means of escape is crucial, and it is for this reason that he takes the only way out available to him, the 'Menschenausweg' [human way out]. He stresses that becoming human was not a way of gaining freedom, but only an 'Ausweg':

> Ich habe Angst, daß man nicht genau versteht, was ich unter Ausweg verstehe [. . .] Ich sage absichtlich nicht Freiheit. Ich meine nicht dieses große Gefühl von Freiheit nach allen Seiten. Als Affe kannte ich es vielleicht und ich habe Menschen kennengelernt, die sich danach sehnen. (VI, 304)
>
> [I am afraid that you will not understand exactly what I mean by a way out [. . .] I deliberately do not say freedom. I do not mean this great feeling of freedom on all sides. Perhaps as an ape I may have known it, and I may have been acquainted with humans who yearn for it.] (p. 40)

Becoming human is only a way to avoid remaining trapped, but will not lead to freedom. Rotpeter suggests that freedom is not possible for humans, but perhaps for animals, though he can no longer remember what it was like to be animal.

The idea of animals having the capacity for a more free and unbounded state of being resonates with much literary writing of the early twentieth century. Around the same time as Kafka wrote *Die Verwandlung*, Rainer Maria Rilke explored the condition of the animal in his first of his *Duineser Elegien* [*Duino Elegies*] in which he writes:

> [. . .] die findigen Tiere merken es schon,
> daß wir nicht sehr verläßlich zu Haus sind
> in der gedeuteten Welt [. . .] (II, 201)
>
> [the knowing animals are aware | that we are not really at home | in the interpreted world]

For Rilke, animals possess an intuitive understanding that humans lack. In these lines, an in-the-moment animal mode of existence ('findig') is posited against the interpreted world of human existence ('gedeutet'). For humans, the animal mode of existence is foreclosed, just as it is foreclosed to Rotpeter, who is unable to return to his former animal state, and also to Gregor, who is unable to fully access it. As humans, these figures remain trapped by social demands and anxieties, forced to suppress their animal impulses. They are unable to attain freedom because of the confines of humanity, and the fears over the non-humanity that animals represent. If animal existence appears degraded, as in the existence of a performing ape or a vermin, then that is because humans force them to be so. Trapped in a cage or a human being's room, animals are unable to thrive.

For Deleuze and Guattari the search for a way out is one of Kafka's main themes, exemplified through his animal figures:

> According to Kafka, the animal is the object *par excellence* of the story: to try to find a way out, to trace a line of escape [. . .] We would say that for Kafka, the animal essence is the way out, the line of escape, even if it takes place in place [sic], or in a cage. *A line of escape and not freedom.*[71]

While both Gregor's and Rotpeter's transformations could be read as a search for a way out, for Rotpeter, relinquishing animal essence is necessary in order to escape. Deleuze and Guattari also claim that all of Kafka's figures are intent upon a way out, yet Walter Sokel argues that Deleuze and Guattari downplay the self-punishing aspect of Kafka's work.[72] Indeed texts such as 'Ein Hungerkünstler' (1922) offer a very different view of being in a cage from that in the 'Bericht'. The hunger artist is not looking for a way out, but wants to remain in the cage as a way of withdrawing from the world. Being caged is not so much a positive 'escape' from the world, as a self-punishing ascetic retreat.

An ascetic desire to withdraw from life, including withdrawing from eating and from moving around freely, is also apparent in *Die Verwandlung*. Kafka does not pursue the possibility that Gregor might discover his wings and fly out of the window. By ignoring his potential and subjecting himself to others, Gregor recalls the protagonist of Kafka's parable 'Vor dem Gesetz', who waits years for permission to go through a door and gain entry to the law, without considering just walking through the doorway. Gregor's complete subordination to his father and his familial obedience mean that his dead-ended trajectory is set from even before the transformation. After the transformation, when Gregor can no longer continue as provider for the family, he remains compliant with his family's wishes, and does not protest when his sister decides that he should be got rid of. Even when he is locked into his room by his sister, who is relieved to see the back of him, his last thoughts are of tenderness for his family: 'An seine Familie dachte er mit Rührung und Liebe zurück. Seine Meinung darüber, dass er verschwinden müsse, war womöglich noch entschiedener, als die seiner Schwester' (I, 193) [He thought back on his family with tenderness and love. His own opinion that he should vanish was, if possible, even more determined than his sister's (p. 71)].

Like the hunger artist, Gregor ends his life in willing imprisonment. Gregor's withdrawal into his room and the hunger artist's withdrawal into his cage are paralleled by the withdrawal from their own bodies. Both end, after long hunger, as bare husks. The hunger artist is swept away along with the straw of his cage, and replaced by a panther, while Gregor's flat, dried up body is unceremoniously pronounced dead by the cleaning lady. This is not a search for a way out, but a retreat from the world, just as the animal protagonist of *Der Bau* builds his burrow as a way of blocking out the world as much as possible. Metamorphosis provides the possibility of a way out to those who desire it, but ultimately leads to only another cage, a cage such as Gregor's 'human being's room' or the gilded cage of the performing ape. In his 'er' fragments Kafka writes: 'Als Gefangener enden

— das wäre eines Lebens Ziel. Aber es war ein Gitterkäfig' [To end as a prisoner — that could be a life's ambition. But it was a barred cage that he was in].[73] The fantasy of being trapped belongs to the desire to withdraw from the world as fully as possible.

Languages of Affect

Animal Voicelessness and Human Language

In Kafka's work, being an animal in a human world also means being linguistically confined. The loss of voice that typically comes with transforming into an animal is an important feature of metamorphosis in classical myth, such as Ovid's tale of Io, in which Io as heifer tells her father of her transformation through her sad eyes and by marking her name in the sand. Though links between Ovid and Kafka have been discussed,[74] Gregor differs from Io in not attempting to assert his identity. Instead Gregor quickly resigns himself to being seen solely as an unpleasant animal, despite maintaining human consciousness.

Gregor's physical transformation is coupled with a change in voice, though not a complete loss of voice. Kafka takes great care to express precisely what this change involves, after Gregor attempts to answer his mother's knock on the door:

> Gregor erschrak, als er seine antwortende Stimme hörte, die wohl unverkennbar seine frühere war, in die sich aber, wie von unten her, ein nicht zu unterdrückendes, schmerzliches Piepsen mischte, das die Worte förmlich nur im ersten Augenblick in ihrer Deutlichkeit beließ, um sie im Nachklang derart zu zerstören, dass man nicht wusste, ob man recht gehört hatte. (I, 119)

> [Gregor was startled when he heard his own voice in reply; no doubt, it was unmistakably his previous voice, but merging into it as though from low down came an uncontrollable, painful squealing which allowed his words to remain articulate literally for only a moment, then stifled them so much as they died away that you couldn't tell if you'd heard them properly (p. 31)]

In this complex, multi-claused sentence, Gregor's voice is described as recognizably the same, suggesting that Gregor is still himself in some sense. However, a new element has been introduced that prevents successful communication. This 'Piepsen' [squealing], a kind of raw, non-human sound, is painful and not under his control. The idea of the sound coming as though from low down suggests a repressed element coming to the fore. The squealing sound causes confusion, making words appear clear at first, but then leads to uncertainty. The illusory precision in both the description of Gregor's body and in Gregor's voice emphasize that the transformation is not so much about scientifically exploring animal existence, but about physically experiencing uncertainties over identity.

The change in Gregor's voice is something that he wishes to conceal from his parents. He responds briefly to his mother with 'Ja, ja, danke Mutter, ich stehe schon auf' (I, 119) [Yes, yes, thank you mother, I'm just getting up (p. 31)] and is relieved when his answer appears to satisfy her. In speaking to his father Gregor attempts to make his voice as inconspicuous as possible by speaking carefully with pauses between the words. His attempt to conceal his vocal impediment, and with it his physical change, suggests that he experiences the change as shameful, and as something that ought to remain hidden. Gregor's behaviour also reveals a desire to contradict the physical evidence of his transformation. He tells himself that the change in his voice is nothing more than a cold ('Verkühlung', I, 121), a frequent problem for commercial travellers. In his article 'Samsa war Reisender' John Zilcosky points out an important difference between Gregor and Raban, who has never travelled: while Raban's transformation is a positive one, Gregor's transformation is unwanted, and appears to be linked to his health-threatening occupation.[75] The fact that Gregor links his vocal change to frequent travelling raises a link between travel and metamorphosis. Being constantly on the move may destabilize identities.

In *Die Verwandlung*, the degradation and alienation from the human world involved in becoming animal is reinforced by the inability to communicate. From the beginning, there is no indication that Gregor's family or the company officer understands him, even though Gregor interprets their behaviour as meaning that they understand. The fact that they stop banging on the door or become angry does not provide evidence that they have understood Gregor. Once they have seen Gregor as an 'Ungeziefer', both Gregor and his family stop attempting to communicate with one another through verbal language. The first sign of this is the father shooing Gregor back into the room with a hissing sound (I, 141). From this point onwards, the possibility of human communication is ruled out. That Gregor's family regard him as a mute animal that lacks understanding is exemplified by the father's later assumption: 'wenn er uns verstünde [. . .] Aber so — ' (I, 190) ['If he understood us,' the father repeated [. . .] 'But as it is — ' (p. 69)]. Gregor does not attempt to correct his father's view, suggesting that he has either internalized his position as an uncomprehending animal, or has given up hope of being able to show his family that he is still himself mentally.

Kafka's animal perspectives engage with the state of being exiled within the community, unable to communicate successfully. For Kafka, the impossibility of genuine communication is often linked to the situation of the animal. In a letter to his then fiancée Felice Bauer, written a few months after *Die Verwandlung*, Kafka writes of his fear over their relationship, which leaves him feeling like a mute animal:

> Meine eigentliche Furcht — es kann wohl nichts Schlimmeres gesagt und angehört werden — ist die, daß ich Dich niemals werde besitzen können. Daß ich im günstigen Falle darauf beschränkt bleiben werde, wie ein besinnungslos treuer Hund Deine zerstreut mir überlassene Hand zu küssen, was kein Liebeszeichen sein wird, sondern nur ein Zeichen der Verzweiflung des zur Stummheit und ewigen Entfernung verurteilten Tieres.[76]
>
> [My real fear — perhaps no worse can be said or heard — is the fear of never being able to possess you. That at best I will remain confined, like a senseless, faithful dog, to kissing the hand that you have absent-mindedly left out for me, which will not be a sign of love, but only a sign of despair in the animal, sentenced to muteness and eternal distance.]

Kafka's fear of never being able to possess Felice reveals a desire to be fully acknowledged, attested also by the volume of letters that Kafka sent to Felice, despite the short time spent physically together. The comparison to a being a dog is a way of articulating a sense of not being fully understood, and of being treated indifferently and condescendingly, thereby being condemned to muteness and distance. Under these conditions, genuine love seems impossible. Kafka uses animal existence to highlight his own fears of being unable to make himself fully understood, and to connect truly with another person.

The communicative gap that Kafka explores can be linked to the crisis of language at the beginning of the twentieth century. A profound disillusionment with the possibilities of communication through language marks Kafka's earliest letters.[77] Kafka's disillusionment with language is experienced, however, as a personal predicament: the 'Brief an den Vater' [Letter to His Father] begins by calling attention to Kafka's difficulty in communicating (VI, 143). Through writing, Kafka attempts to overcome these difficulties. However, for Gregor, the possibility of writing does not arise, despite the model provided by Ovid's Io, who writes her name using her hooves. Unlike Io, Gregor fails to assert his identity, instead allowing himself to be defined by his family.

Being without language means being trapped. For the ape Rotpeter, speaking is a way of way of escaping his animal confinement. Right after demonstratively drinking a whole bottle of Schnapps in front of the men, Rotpeter spontaneously breaks out into language: 'weil ich nicht anders konnte, weil es mich drängte, weil mir die Sinne rauschten, kurz und gut "Hallo!" ausrief, in Menschenlaut ausbrach, mit diesem Ruf in die Menschengemeinschaft sprang' (VI, 310) [because I couldn't help it, because I had an urge to, because my senses were intoxicated, in short, when I called out "Halloo!", breaking into human sounds, and with this call made the leap into the human community (p. 44)]. As in the 'Bericht' as a whole, Rotpeter downplays his 'achievement'. The acquisition of language comes not through conscious effort, but as an unintended effect of intoxication. His first word marks Rotpeter's 'leap' into human society, and is the key moment of his transformation. The idea of a leap from a non-linguistic to a linguistic state is based on the idea of language as a key marker of the difference between humans and animals. The theory of evolution raised the question of how human language developed, which became the subject of significant debate around the late nineteenth century. Often language was seen as marking the start of being human, as in Haeckel's bestselling *Die Welträtsel* [The World Riddle] of 1899. Haeckel attempts to explain human origin by developing the idea of an ape-man who is in between ape and man, but without language.[78] Only once he acquires language does the ape-man become a man. Similarly, in Kafka, the possibility of being human, yet lacking language, does not come into question. Once Gregor gives up attempting to speak, he accepts his family's designation of him as an animal. The idea that one cannot be human without language is deeply ingrained in this period. For example, philogist Helmut Steinthal, writing in 1881, claims: 'die Sprache ist dem menschlichen Wesen so notwendig und natürlich, dass ohne sie der Mensch weder wirklich existiert, noch als wirklich existieren gedacht werden kann. Der Mensch hat entweder Sprache oder ist gar nicht' [language is so necessary and natural for mankind that it neither properly exists without man, nor can it be thought of as properly existing. Man either has language or is not man].[79]

As an animal, Gregor is unable to communicate with humans. Even though Gregor feels able to speak, the company officer describes Gregor's voice as a 'Tierstimme' [animal voice]. Several of Kafka's animal figures, such as Josefine and the dog in 'Forschungen eines Hundes', fail to be understood by the other creatures around them. Like Hoffmann's tale of the dog Berganza, Kafka's 'Forschungen eines Hundes' inverts the relationship between human and dog, with the dog observing human society and perceiving humans as linguistically impoverished. Kafka's dog narrator describes humans as 'arme, geringe, stumme, nur auf gewisse Schreie eingeschränkte Wesen' (VI, 486) [poor, paltry, and silent, restricted to certain cries (p. 121)]. Both Hoffmann and Kafka use dog protagonists not to remind us that animals are without language, but to suggest that humans are unable to communicate successfully. The gap between human and animal communication is largely due to human failure to understand. As an animal, Gregor is condemned to be misunderstood, but in his mute state, other possibilities of communication may open up, if only he pays attention to them.

Animal Nourishment: Music as Affective Language

As Gregor becomes increasingly withdrawn, neglected by his family, and suffering from the festering apple lodged in his back, his need for nourishment becomes more pronounced. The arrival of the lodgers makes Gregor's diminished capacities particularly apparent. The family's eagerness to oblige the lodgers, who provide for them financially, contrasts to their treatment of Gregor, who is thereby faced with a new reminder of his inadequacy. Gregor's unfulfilled appetite is exacerbated by the sound of the lodgers chewing, which emphasizes that they, unlike Gregor, have the teeth that are necessary for eating: '"Ich habe ja Appetit", sagte sich Gregor sorgenvoll, "aber nicht auf diese Dinge. Wie sich diese Zimmerherren nähren, und ich komme um!"' (I, 183) ['I do have an appetite,' said Gregor sorrowfully to himself, 'but not for these things. How these gentlemen feed themselves, and I perish!' (p. 65)]. Gregor's hunger is part of a general dissatisfaction and desire for something that remains unspecified.

Gregor's longing for unknown food overrides his consideration towards his family and wish to spare them the sight of his shameful body, and drives him to creep towards the room where his sister is playing the violin. While the lodgers turn away from Grete as if disappointed, Gregor is moved by Grete's playing. Indeed, the music even seems to point the way towards the nourishment that Gregor longs for: 'War er ein Tier, da ihn Musik so ergriff? Ihm war, als zeige sich ihm der Weg zu der ersehnten unbekannten Nahrung' (I, 185) [Was he a beast, that music should move him like this? He felt as if the way to the unknown nourishment he longed for was being revealed (p. 66)]. Nourishment might be understood here not simply as food, but as emotional nourishment or well-being. The word 'Nahrung' has been used in this way in Goethe's *Die Leiden des jungen Werthers* (1774) when Werther exclaims early on: 'man möchte zum Maikäfer werden, um in dem Meer von Wohlgerüchen herumzuschweben, und alle seiner Nahrung darinne finden zu können' (XIII, 10) [one could wish to be a cockchafer, floating in a sea of wonderful scents and finding all one's nourishment there].[80] However, whereas Werther imagines insect existence as a blissful, nourished state, Gregor lacks nourishment.

Although Gregor was previously unmusical, he now feels deeply moved by music. It seems that animal existence has provided him with musical sensitivity. Corngold describes the sentence 'War er ein Tier, da ihn Musik so ergriff?' as 'Kafka's 'unfathomable sentence', in which 'paradox echoes jarringly without end'.[81] The paradox, Corngold explains, results from the discrepancy between the vermin's body and its cravings and the other sort of nourishment for which Gregor yearns. However, Corngold finds coherence in the idea of the 'Ungeziefer', as a word without physical significance, seeking divine nourishment in music, the language of signs without significance.[82] The idea that an animal being moved by music is unfathomable and paradoxical has its basis in depictions of animal existence as degrading and crude, as initially appears to be the case in *Die Verwandlung*. The question 'War er ein Tier, da ihn die Musik so ergriff?' has also been problematic because it can be read in two contrasting ways: either Gregor is questioning whether he is really an animal, or he is using his new-found feelings to confirm that he must be an animal.

Following the first reading, Barry Murnane uses the question 'war er ein Tier' to ask whether Gregor has really become an animal, or only metaphorically, and considers whether the work is, to use Corngold's terms, only 'low fantastic literature' or 'high classical modernism'.[83] However, Murnane does not address the issue of why being moved by music would prompt questioning on whether Gregor is an animal. Is it because animals cannot be moved by music, or because they can? Sokel bases his reading on the idea that animals are unmusical, claiming that Grete's playing 'reminds Gregor of his humanity, his community with his sister, his family, his oneness with his species'.[84] Sokel's reading emphasizes music as communal spirit, drawing on Nietzsche's Dionysian concept of music. A sense of communality through music is important elsewhere in Kafka's works (such as in 'Josefine, die Sängerin' or in 'Forschungen eines Hundes'). However, this sense of communality and the ability to be moved by music is not a sign of humanity, but of animality.

Indeed, the alternative way of reading the question is to read Gregor's musical sensitivity as confirming his animal nature. Gregor's musical longing is allied to his new corporeal drives, as suggested by the way in which his musical enrapture turns to protectiveness for his sister and then to a semi-erotic fantasy of possession. In 1920, Kafka wrote of the strength he possessed in being unmusical, which might be read as a claim to have supressed his unwanted animality.[85] Kafka claimed to have directed all his energy towards writing, which means neglecting the pleasures of sex, eating, drinking, and philosophical reflection on music.[86] The mental capacity for writing is, on this account, opposed to the bodily capacity for musical contemplation. While Romantic writers, such as Hoffmann, used music to become aware of a higher self, Kafka links music to corporeality, and to bodily desires which are both base but also of vital importance.

As an animal, Gregor becomes aware of the corporeally affective potential of music. In Kafka's works it is not music as such that is powerful, but the affects that it evokes. Thus, in some of his stories it is not clear whether there even is any music, or whether the effect is actually being produced by silence. For example, in the short, enigmatic text 'Das Schweigen der Sirenen' [The Silence of the Sirens] (1917) Kafka adapts Homer's story of Odysseus sailing past the sirens, and claims that Odysseus took the 'childish precaution' of putting wax in his ears, 'childish' because it would not have stopped their song. In Kafka's story, Odysseus is saved because the sirens were not singing. Instead of seducing him, the sirens are themselves seduced by Odysseus's happiness at believing himself to be overcoming them. However, in a final twist, Kafka considers the idea that Odysseus knew that the sirens were silent and was only pretending to believe them to be singing. In this story, the seductive power of music is replaced by the mere idea of music and its power. Silence can have the same effect as music if treated as such.

A similar concept of music and its affective power is apparent in Kafka's 'Forschungen eines Hundes' (1922). The dog narrator recollects a defining incident in his youth in which he encountered seven music artists:

> Sie redeten nicht, sie sangen nicht, sie schwiegen im allgemeinen fast mit einer großen Verbissenheit, aber aus dem leeren Raum zauberten sie die Musik empor. Alles war Musik, das Heben und Niedersetzen ihrer Füße, bestimmte Wendungen des Kopfes, ihr Laufen und ihr Ruhen, die Stellungen, die sie zueinander einnahmen, die regelmäßigen Verbindungen, die sie miteinander eingingen. (VI, 490)
>
> [They didn't talk, they didn't sing, they were generally silent, almost doggedly so, yet by their magic they conjured up music out of empty space. All was music, the way they lifted and placed their feet, the way they turned their heads with a certain motion, their running and resting, the attitudes they took up towards each other, the patterned movements they made with one another. (p. 123)]

In this passage, music is not in sound, but in affective body language, movement and gesture, a corporeal, felt experience rather than an auditory quality. The dog's desire to learn more about music suggests the importance of music within Kafka's work, but not so much in terms of the sound created, but in its affective potential. Understood in this manner, music and silence can be one.

The affective potential of music is especially apparent in Kafka's last story, 'Josefine, die Sängerin, oder Das Volk der Mäuse' [Josephine, the Singer or The Mouse-People] (written in 1924, while Kafka was severely ill). Josefine embodies the power of music: 'Wer sie nicht gehört hat, kennt nicht die Macht des Gesangs' (VI, 651) [If you haven't heard her, you do not know the power of song (p. 65)]. However, the mice people are not musical, and it is not even clear whether what Josefine does is music. In fact her singing may just be whistling ('Pfeifen'), and not even a whistling that goes beyond ordinary mouse whistling. We might want to read Josefine's whistling as symbolic, though as Michael Minden argues, 'pfeifen is not used to convey a meaning, but to prevent one congealing'.[87] Josefine's power has nothing to do with the sound she makes, but with the affects she creates. These affects help to bind the community, even while the raw ingredients, the sounds, or the words in a work of literature, may not differ from everyday means of expression.

Although metamorphosis might be considered a 'morbid subject', when considering the loss of language, losing language also raises the positive possibility of a non-verbal language of affect.[88] Such affective language is experienced corporeally, and is therefore closely linked to animal existence. Kafka's literature seeks access to this affective state, which may even be regarded as recalling the pre-linguistic state of infancy. Indeed, Gabriele Schwab argues that literature is a way of searching for the non-representational experience that we had before language, and which, in literature, is captured in mood. The mood of a literary work, Schwab claims, pertains to the 'inner core' of a person.[89] For Kafka, literature opens the way towards an expression of intensely corporeal and even animalistic drives, which would otherwise remain hidden. In a letter of 1904, Kafka claimed that 'ein Buch muss die Axt sein für das gefrorene Meer in uns' [a book should be the axe for the frozen sea within us].[90] For Kafka, literature is an attempt to recover something that remains deep within. To do so involves violence and difficulty. Kafka does not think of melting a way through the ice, but of penetrating it. The animal within will not be released but will remain forever distant, elusive, seductive, and abject at the same time.

The Animal Origin of Emotion

To understand the connection between animal existence and emotion in Kafka's work, it is worth considering the historical link between these two concepts. Emotion has been positioned in opposition to rationality since antiquity, with the former associated with the body and with animals, and the latter associated with the mind and with humans.[91] By the late nineteenth century, the idea of feelings originating in the animal body was deeply ingrained. H. G. Wells's 1896 novel *The Island of Doctor Moreau* provides an apt example. In this novel, the doctor attempts to make humans out of animals, but has trouble with something concealed in the seat of the emotions. He notices 'cravings, instincts and desires that harm humanity, a strange hidden reservoir to burst forth suddenly and inundate the whole being with anger, hate or fear'.[92] Doctor Moreau wants to get rid of these feelings and thereby purge the animal from his creations. The elusive, but violent feelings that he uncovers belong to animals and not to humans. This is a very different concept of feeling from the Romantic view of feelings as markers of the human, of 'higher' awareness and artistic ability, which I examined in the previous chapter.

The contrasting attitude towards feelings between the Romantic and modernist texts I examined points to a deep ambivalence over the value of emotion that begins around the end of the Romantic period. To capture the ennobling and degrading nature of emotions, a distinction is introduced between 'Gefühl' and 'Empfindung', where humans have the former, and animals the latter. 'Empfindung' was considered to be a form of feeling that is sensual and in the moment, lacking the capacity to reflect and consider, unlike the more rational 'Gefühl'.[93] With the advance of physiology in the late nineteenth century, the concept of drives ('Triebe') also entered discourse surrounding emotions. Drives are pre-conscious passions that motivate us to act, with the further distinction between 'blinde Triebe' [blind drives] and 'geistige Triebe' [mental drives]. The former is a drive to fulfil basic needs, desires, or instincts, including eating, drinking, moving, and sex. These are drives that animals have, whereas the latter are ascribed to humans and considered 'higher', although they have their basis in the lower.

The idea of blind drives as animal qualities is apparent in Kafka's work. The trajectory of texts such as *Die Verwandlung* or 'Ein Hungerkünstler' is towards getting rid of animal drives and becoming ascetic. However, the protagonists' aim is self-destructive. Animal drives are necessary for life, and can be both pleasurable and repulsive. Indeed, Gregor's greatest pleasures, such as his excitement over eating rotten food and crawling upon the walls, arise from his animal nature. It is only as an animal that Gregor can indulge in the pleasures of blind drives. Walter Benjamin claimed that for Kafka, animals are placeholders for the forgotten ('Behältnisse des Vergessenen'). What is forgotten above all, Benjamin claims, is the body.[94] Animal existence means confronting the bodily sensations and affects that are repressed in human society.

The ambivalent status of animals in Kafka's texts is connected to the ambivalent status of emotion in Kafka's work. Kafka claimed that he lacked feeling, and at worst, feared it.[95] He particularly admired Flaubert's fiction, with its dispassionate narrators. By focusing on writing, Kafka may be neglecting bodily functions and sensations, but these come back into his writing and in the metamorphoses into figures, often animals, that embody this fascinating and repulsive side of humanity. Kafka's writing cannot be said to be lacking in affect, therefore. However, it does not display affects upon the surface in Romantic fashion but, rather, affects are found beneath the surface in 'das gefrorene Meer in uns' [the frozen sea within us].[96] Although Kafka's narrators do not attempt to draw in the reader with direct entreaties and impassioned rhetoric, as in Hoffmann's texts, Kafka's writing is aimed at truth of feeling. Indeed, the affective complexity and depth has been central to the success of Kafka's literature.

The opposition between feeling and rationality, and between humans and animals, had become subject to dispute by the time Kafka was writing. In particular, the introduction of evolutionary theory affected the ways in which the difference between humans and animals was conceived. Questions about whether animals have feelings, and what these feelings might be like, were also raised. Darwin's major work *The Expression of Emotions in Man and Animals* (1872) attests to the importance of understanding human–animal similarity and difference through emotion. As in *On the Origin of Species* (1859), Darwin's aim was to investigate human origins, but he does so by comparing expressions of emotion in humans and animals and considering possible evolutionary origins. Darwin claims that many human emotions are innate rather than learnt, and that there is a commonality between humans and the 'lower animals', although the display of emotions can also be related to specific bodily make-up. As well as undermining strict distinctions between human and animal, Darwin's work also helps to challenge racial prejudice by showing that the same emotional expressions are exhibited by people throughout the world. After Darwin, animal drives and emotions could be understood as being within humans.[97]

Kafka's adoption of animal perspectives can be seen as part of the dismantling of hierarchies and as an engagement with the perspectives of outsiders and figures that are often degraded, such the 'Ungeziefer', the performing ape, the stray dog, the mouse or mole. While Kafka allies animals with 'lower emotions' or 'blind drives', his animal figures are also highly rational and intelligent. Kafka uses animals not simply as a way of exploring non-human perspectives, but as a means of exploring what lies within the human. In particular, this means exploring recesses of feeling that even today continue to be considered animalistic. For example, contemporary philosopher Martha Nussbaum asks whether emotions are 'animal energies' or 'suffused with intelligence'?'[98] While philosophers now challenge the opposition between emotion and rationality, Nussbaum's question still presupposes a link between animal nature and what she calls energy (suggesting something similar to an irrational 'blind drive'). In Kafka's work, becoming animal is a way of reaching the raw, affective existence hidden within the human.

Conclusion

Kafka's *Die Verwandlung* has become a paradigm tale of metamorphosis. Yet unlike mythic metamorphoses, the transformation does not fulfil an obvious purpose, but rather conveys a sense of helpless subjection. The metamorphosis remains a lacuna within the text, resisting explanation, a single, shocking event in the midst of the everyday. Reading through Gregor's perspective, we cannot doubt the fact of the transformation, and must turn our attention to what it means to have become an abject vermin. The process of feeling oneself into another existence is fundamental to Kafka's poetics, and allows exploration of the abject, animal, and affective body. By withdrawing into the inner spaces of marginalized figures, Kafka aims to capture the unmediated experience of another subjectivity.

In *Die Verwandlung*, becoming animal means a vital experience of bodily sensations such as hunger and sexual desire, which are considered repulsive by the human Gregor. Gregor's new physical state might be read as a regression to an earlier state of both individual and species development. In this sense, metamorphosis undermines the idea of linear progress, as well as the hierarchy between humans and animals. For Rotpeter, becoming human is not an achievement, but a necessity. Kafka's metamorphoses are forced processes, which seem to offer a way out, but lead only to another cage. Although being caged can be desirable, such ascetic withdrawal and suppression of animal vitality is ultimately self-destructive.

For Kafka, becoming animal is a way of exploring the vulnerable, non-linguistic realms of the human. Without language, Kafka's figures remain exiled. However, being without language makes room for music, understood not just as sound but as affect. When Kafka speaks of the frozen seas within us, he means the corporeal and affective experience that remains unexpressed in human society. If animals occupy an ambiguous status within Kafka's work, as both desirable and repulsive, this may be traced to the ambiguous status of affect itself. While Kafka's texts do not display affect openly on the surface, the inner spaces — spaces of uneasy dreams and strange metamorphoses — are where the frozen seas crack, and suppressed conflicts come to the surface. The need for metamorphosis is a need to uncover one's forgotten animal nature, and to give voice to the conflicted self within.

Notes to Chapter 2

1. Mark Spilka, 'Kafka's Sources for *The Metamorphosis*', *Comparative Literature*, 11 (1959), 289–307 (p. 290); Ernst Loeb similarly argues that Hoffmann is a pioneer of psychological realism: 'Bedeutungswandel der Metamorphose bei Franz Kafka und E. T. A. Hoffmann: Ein Vergleich', *The German Quarterly*, 35.1 (1962), pp. 47–59 (p. 47).
2. Charles Taylor, *Sources of the Self: The Making of Modern Identity* (Cambridge, MA: Harvard University Press, 1989), p. 456.
3. Judith Ryan, *The Vanishing Subject: Early Psychology and Literary Modernism* (Chicago: University of Chicago Press, 1991), p. 2.
4. Ibid.
5. Ibid., p. 4.
6. Rainer Maria Rilke, *Werke: Kommentierte Ausgabe in vier Bänden*, ed. by Manfred Engel, Ulrich Fülleborn, Horst Nalewski, and August Stahl (Leipzig: Insel Verlag, 1996), III, 453.
7. Andreas Huyssen discusses the invasion of technology into the body as manifested in modernist art works (*After the Great Divide: Modernism, Mass Culture, Postmodernism* (Bloomington, IN: Indiana University Press, 1986), p. 11.
8. Monika Schmitz-Emans, *Poetiken der Verwandlung* (Innsbruck: Studienverlag, 2008), p. 160.
9. Günter Wöllner claims that Hoffmann's contrast between bourgeois and poetic soul was in Kafka a 'Grunderfahrung, über deren Abgrund sich kein errerichbarer Himmel mehr wölbt' (*E. T. A. Hoffmann und Franz Kafka: Von der 'fortgeführten Metapher' zum 'sinnlichen Paradox'* (Berne: Haupt, 1971), p. 54.
10. Jürgen Born's *Kafkas Bibliothek: Ein beschreibendes Verzeichnis* (Frankfurt a.M.: Fischer, 1990) lists nothing by Hoffmann.
11. Stanley Corngold, *Complex Pleasure: Forms of Feeling in German Literature* (Stanford: Stanford University Press, 1998).
12. Franz Kafka, *Gesammelte Werke*, Kritische Ausgabe, 12 vols, ed. by Hans-Gerd Koch (Frankfurt a.M.: Fischer, 1994), I, 115. Further references to Kafka's work are taken from this edition, unless otherwise indicated, and are given after quotations in the text. The reference refers to the volume and page.
13. Franz Kafka, *The Metamorphosis and Other Stories*, trans. by Joyce Crick (Oxford: Oxford University Press, 2009), p. 29. English translations of *Die Verwandlung* and 'Unglücklichsein' are taken from this edition, and are given after quotations in the text.
14. Yoko Tawada, *Verwandlungen*. Tübinger Poetik-Vorlesungen (Tübingen: Konkursbuchverlag, 1998), p. 56.
15. Dieter Hasselblatt, *Zauber und Logik: Eine Kafka-Studie* (Cologne: Verlag Wissenschaft und Politik, 1964), p. 49.
16. Tzvetan Todorov, *The Fantastic: A Structural Approach to a Literary Genre*, trans. by Richard Howard (Ithaca: Cornell Paperbacks, 1975), p. 174.
17. In particular, Peter Cersowsky, *Phantastische Literatur im ersten Viertel des 20. Jahrhunderts: Untersuchungen zum Strukturwandel des Genres, seinen geistesgeschichtlichen Voraussetzungen und zur Tradition der 'schwarzen Romantik' insbesondere bei Gustav Mayrink, Alfred Kubin und Franz Kafka* (Munich: Fink, 1983), p. 186.
18. Winfried Menninghaus argues that Kafka's art consists in rendering the intensely disgusting content of his stories almost completely 'unsichtbar' and 'unfühlbar' (Winfried Menninghaus, *Ekel: Theorie und Geschichte einer starken Empfindung* (Frankfurt a.M.: Suhrkamp, 1999), p. 333.
19. Peter-André Alt, *Franz Kafka. Der ewige Sohn. Eine Biographie* (Munich: Beck, 2005), p. 254.
20. Kafka would have been familiar with the use of 'Ungeziefer' as an insult. For example, his father refers to Kafka's friend Yitshak Löwy, the Yiddish actor, as an 'Ungeziefer': Sander Gilman, *Franz Kafka* (London: Reaktion, 2005), p. 54.
21. David Gallagher, *Metamorphosis: Transformations of the Body and the Influence of Ovid's Metamorphoses*

on *Germanic Literature of the Nineteenth and Twentieth Centuries* (Amsterdam and New York: Rodopi, 2009), p. 129.

22. Kafka writes to his publisher: 'ich will [. . .] nur aus meiner natürlich besseren Kenntnis der Geschichte heraus bitten. Das Insekt selbst kann nicht gezeichnet werden' (*Briefe*, 3 vols, ed. by Hans-Gerd Koch (Frankfurt a.M.: Fischer, 1999–2005), II, 145).

23. Barry Murnane, 'Ungeheuere Arbeiter: Moderne Monstrosität am Beispiel von Gregor Samsa', in *Monster: Zur ästhetischen Verfassung eines Grenzbewohners*, ed. by Roland Borgards, Christiane Holm, and Günter Oesterle (Würzburg: Königshausen & Neumann, 2009), pp. 289–308 (p. 294).

24. Günther Anders, *Kafka — Pro und Contra* (Munich: Beck, 1951), pp. 40–41.

25. Corngold develops his argument extensively in 'The Metamorphosis: Metamorphosis of the Metaphor', in *Franz Kafka: The Necessity of Form* (Ithaca, NY: Cornell University Press, 1988). He also discusses metamorphosis and metaphor in other works, most recently, in the chapter 'Thirteen Ways of Looking at a Vermin', in *Franz Kafka: The Ghosts in the Machine*, co-authored with Benno Wagner (Evanston: Northwestern University Press, 2011), pp. 57–74.

26. Walter H. Sokel, *The Writer in Extremis: Expressionism in Twentieth-Century Literature* (Stanford: Stanford University Press, 1959), pp. 46–47.

27. Corngold and Wagner, *Ghosts in the Machine*, p. 57.

28. Corngold, *Necessity of Form*, p. 56.

29. Ibid., p. 57.

30. Franz Kafka, *Tagebücher*, ed. by Hans-Gerd Koch, Michael Müller, and Malcolm Pasley (Frankfurt a.M.: Fischer, 1990), p. 875.

31. Franz Kafka, *The Diaries of Franz Kafka, 1914–1923*, trans. by Martin Greenberg (with the assistance of Hannah Arendt) (New York: Schocken, 1949), pp. 200–01.

32. *Tagebücher*, p. 326; Franz Kafka, *The Diaries of Franz Kafka, 1910–1913*, trans. by Joseph Kresh (New York: Schocken, 1948), p. 201.

33. Vladimir Nabokov, *Lectures on Literature*, ed. by Fredson Bowers (San Diego, New York, and London: Harcourt, 1982), p. 259.

34. Stanley Corngold, *Franz Kafka: The Necessity of Form* (Ithaca, NY: Cornell University Press, 1988), p. 57.

35. Walter Benjamin, 'Über das mimetische Vermögen', *Gesammelte Schriften*, VII.2: *Nachträge*, ed. by Rolf Tiedemann and Hermann Schweppenhäuser (Frankfurt a.M.: Suhrkamp, 1989), pp. 791–92 (p. 792).

36. Gerhard Lauer, 'Spiegelneuronen: Über den Grund des Wohlgefallens an der Nachahmung', *Rücken der Kulturen*, ed. by Karl Eibl, Katja Mellmann, and Rüdiger Zymner (Paderborn: Mentis, 2007), pp. 137–63.

37. Walter H. Sokel, *The Myth of Power and the Self: Essays on Franz Kafka* (Detroit: Wayne State University Press, 2002), p. 76.

38. Comparisons between 'Hochzeitsvorbereitungen auf dem Lande' and *Die Verwandlung* have been made. E.g. Friedmann Harzer, *Erzählte Verwandlung: Eine Poetik epischer Metamorphosen (Ovid, Kafka, Ransmayr)* (Tübingen: Niemeyer, 2000), pp. 109–10; Sokel, *The Myth of Power and the Self*, p. 73.

39. The passage runs: 'man möchte zum Maienkäfer werden, um in den Meer von Wohlgerüchen herumzuschweben, und alle seine Nahrung darinne finden zu können'. Johann Wolfgang von Goethe, *Sämtliche Werke, Briefe, Tagebücher und Gespräche*, 40 vols (Frankfurt a.M.: Deutscher Klassiker, 1993–2011), XIII, 10.

40. Gisbert Zimmermann, 'Maikäfer in Deutschland: geliebt und gehasst. Ein Beitrag zur Kulturgeschichte und Geschichte der Bekämpfung', *Journal für Kulturpflanzen*, 62.5 (2010), 157–72 (p. 167).

41. Max Brod, *Über Franz Kafka* (Frankfurt a.M.: Fischer, 1966), p. 349.

42. Sokel, *The Myth of Power and the Self*, pp. 72–75.

43. Ibid., p. 77.

44. Ritchie Robertson, *Kafka: Judaism, Politics, and Literature* (Oxford: Clarendon, 1985), p. 5.

45. Sokel, *The Myth of Power and the Self*, p. 77.

46. Hugo von Hofmannsthal, *Erfundene Gespräche und Briefe*, ed. by Ellen Ritter, in *Sämtliche Werke*.

Kritische Ausgabe, 40 vols, ed. by Rudolf Hirsch and Heinz Otto Burger (Frankfurt a.M.: Fischer, 1991), XXXI, 50.
47. Philip Armstrong, *What Animals Mean in the Fiction of Modernity* (London: Routledge, 2008), p. 2.
48. E.g. Marc Lucht and Donna Yari, eds, *Kafka's Creatures: Animals, Hybrids and other Fantastic Beings* (Lanham: Lexington, 2010).
49. Adorno discusses Kafka in 'Aufzeichnungen zu Kafka', in *Gesammelte Schriften*, ed. by Rolf Tiedemann, X.1: *Prisms* (Frankfurt a.M.: Suhrkamp, 1997), pp. 254–87. Adorno's view on Kafka and animals is discussed by Christina Gerhardt in 'The Ethics of Animals in Adorno and Kafka', *New German Critique*, 33.1 (2006), 159–79 (esp. p. 169).
50. Walter H. Sokel, 'Nietzsche and Kafka: The Dionysian Connection', in *Kafka for the Twenty-First Century*, ed. by Stanley Corngold and Ruth V. Gross (Rochester, NY: Camden House, 2011), pp. 64–74 (p. 64).
51. Book II, Section 11, pp. 325–29. Subsequent references also refer to the book, section, and page.
52. Ibid., III, 14, pp. 386–87.
53. Discussed in the chapter 'Sliding down the Evolutionary Ladder? Aesthetic Autonomy in The Metamorphosis', in Mark Anderson, *Kafka's Clothes: Ornament and Aestheticism in the Habsburg Fin de Siècle* (Oxford: Clarendon, 1992), pp. 123–44.
54. Patrick Bridgwater, *Kafka, Gothic and Fairytale* (Amsterdam and New York: Rodopi, 2003), p. 167.
55. May Berenbaum discusses the apparently common masochistic fantasy of being an insect crushed by a shoe (a fetishist known as a 'crush-freak'): Berenbaum, 'Fatal Attraction', in *Insect Lives*, ed. by Erich Hoyt and Ted Schultz (New York: John Wiley & Sons, 1999), pp. 219–22 (p. 221).
56. Mary Douglas, *Purity and Danger: An Analysis of Concepts of Pollution and Taboo* [1966] (Abingdon: Routledge Classics, 2007).
57. Elizabeth Boa, *Kafka: Gender, Class and Race in the Letters and Fictions* (Oxford: Clarendon Press, 1996), p. 111.
58. Robertson, *Kafka*, pp. 81–82.
59. Murnane, p. 296.
60. Ibid., p. 307.
61. Theodor Adorno and Max Horkheimer, *Dialektik der Aufklärung* (Frankfurt a.M.: Fischer, 1986), pp. 262–71.
62. Peter Höfle, 'Einleitung', *Einfach Kafka* (Frankfurt a.M.: Suhrkamp, 2008), pp. 7–16 (p. 9).
63. Jakob von Uexküll, *Umwelt und Innenwelt der Tiere* (Berlin: Springer, 1909), p. 4.
64. Translations of Kafka's 'Bericht für eine Akademie' are taken from Franz Kafka, *A Hunger Artist and Other Stories*, trans. by Joyce Crick (Oxford: Oxford University Press, 2012).
65. Zilcosky discusses Kafka's trepidation towards mechanized means of rapid transport in his chapter '"Samsa war Reisender": Trains, Trauma, and the Unreadable Body', in *Kafka for the Twenty-First Century*, ed. by Stanley Corngold and Ruth V. Gross (Rochester, NY: Camden House, 2011), pp. 179–97 (p. 179).
66. Corngold, *The Necessity of Form*, p. 60.
67. *Tagebücher*, 605; *Diaries 1910–1913*, p. 317.
68. Schmitz-Emans summarizes the ways in which Kafka has been read through Judaism in her book *Franz Kafka. Epoche — Werk — Wirkung* (Munich: C. H. Beck, 2010), pp. 203–04.
69. Kafka's interest in film has been discussed by Peter-André Alt in his book *Kafka und der Film: Über kinematographisches Erzählen* (Munich: Beck, 2009).
70. Ulf Abraham, *Franz Kafka: Die Verwandlung* (Frankfurt a.M.: Moritz Diesterweg, 1993), p. 43.
71. Gilles Deleuze and Pierre Félix Guattari, *Kafka: Towards a Minor Literature* (Minneapolis: University of Minnesota Press, 1986), pp. 34–35.
72. Walter H. Sokel, 'Towards the Myth [Festrede]', *Journal of the Kafka Society of America*, 22 (1998), 7–15 (p. 12).
73. *Tagebücher*, p. 849; Franz Kafka, *Aphorisms* (New York: Schocken, 2015).
74. E.g. Theodore Ziolkowski, *Ovid and the Moderns* (Ithaca, NY: Cornell University Press, 2005), pp. 79–82.

75. Ibid., p. 181.
76. Franz Kafka, *Briefe an Felice und andere Korrespondenz aus der Verlobungszeit*, ed. by Erich Heller and Jürgen Born (Frankfurt a.M.: Fischer, 1976, repr. 2003), p. 352.
77. Sokel, *The Myth of Power and the Self*, p. 65.
78. Ernst Haeckel, *Die Welträtsel* [1899] (Norderstedt: Books on Demand, 2008), p. 93.
79. Heymann Steinthal, *Abriss der Sprachwissenschaft*, Part 1: *Die Sprache im Allgemeinen*, vol. 1: *Einleitung in die Psychologie und Sprachwissenschaft* (Berlin: Olms, 1881), p. 355.
80. Johann Wolfgang von Goethe, *The Sorrows of Young Werther*, trans. by Michael Hulse (London: Penguin, 1989), p. 26.
81. *The Necessity of Form*, p. 77.
82. Ibid., pp. 76–77.
83. Murnane, p. 289.
84. Sokel, 'Nietzsche and Kafka', p. 69.
85. Franz Kafka, *Briefe an Milena*, ed. Jürgen Born and Michael Müller (Frankfurt a.M.: Fischer, 1983), p. 122.
86. Franz Kafka, *Tagebücher in der Fassung der Handschrift*, ed. by Michael Müller (Frankfurt a.M.: Fischer, 1983), p. 341.
87. Michael Minden, 'Kafka's "Josefine, die Sängerin oder Das Volk der Mäuse"', *German Life and Letters*, 62.3 (2009), 297–310 (p. 305).
88. Irving Massey, *The Gaping Pig: Literature and Metamorphosis* (Berkeley, Los Angeles, and London: University of California Press, 1976), p. 1.
89. Gabriele Schwab, 'Words and Moods: The Transference of Literary Knowledge', *SubStance*, 26.3 (1997), 107–27 (pp. 114–17).
90. *Briefe*, 1, 36.
91. Pascal Eitler, 'Der "Ursprung" der Gefühle — reizbare Menschen und reizbare Tiere', *Gefühlswissen: eine lexikalische Spurensuche in der Moderne*, ed. by Ute Frevert and others (Frankfurt a.M.: Campus, 2011), pp. 93–120 (p. 96).
92. H. G. Wells, *The Island of Doctor Moreau* (Toronto: Broadview, 2009), p. 130.
93. Eitler, pp. 97–100.
94. Walter Benjamin, *Benjamin über Kafka: Texte, Briefzeugnisse, Aufzeichnunen*, ed. by Hermann Schweppenhäuser (Frankfurt a.M.: Suhrkamp, 1981), p. 30.
95. This claim is made without direct reference by Corngold and Wagner, in *Franz Kafka: The Ghosts in the Machine*, p. 98.
96. *Briefe*, 1, 36.
97. Brittnacher, p. 194.
98. Martha Nussbaum, *Upheavals of Thought: The Intelligence of Emotions* (Cambridge: Cambridge University Press, 2003), p. 1.

CHAPTER 3

Cocooned from the Past: Temporal Subversion in Marie Luise Kaschnitz and Jenny Erpenbeck

Metamorphosis and Socio-Political Change

What part does metamorphosis play in late twentieth-century German literature? It might be supposed that the radical regime changes of this period lead to a focus on pressing social and political concerns, and a disregard for fanciful narratives of metamorphosis. Yet it has also been claimed that periods of political instability and radical social change are particularly conducive to stories of metamorphosis.[1] To examine the connection between metamorphosis and radical social change, this chapter analyses two texts positioned around key *Wendezeiten*, or transitional periods, in late twentieth-century Germany, namely the founding of West Germany in the late 1940s, and the dissolution of East Germany in the early 1990s.

The first text, Marie Luise Kaschnitz's 'Das dicke Kind' [The Fat Child] (first published in 1951) comes from the earliest of her four short-story collections, also entitled *Das dicke Kind* (1952). Kaschnitz (1901–74) wrote stories, poetry, novels, and radio plays since her youth, but is best known for the short story collections published between 1950 and 1970.[2] Much of Kaschnitz's work is autobiographical, drawing on childhood experiences and sibling relationships, and a married life spent in Rome as well as in Germany, besides frequent stays in France, Italy, and Greece with her archaeologist husband. Kaschnitz's story 'Das dicke Kind' exemplifies one of the major themes of her work: the ways in which we deal with difficult episodes in our past, and work towards establishing our identity. Although Kaschnitz's work often draws on her own childhood, her experience of living through wartime Germany also shaped her interest in difficult pasts and in profound, metamorphic change.

The second text I examine is the novella *Geschichte vom alten Kind* [Story of the Old Child] (1999), the literary debut of Jenny Erpenbeck (1967–), a theatre director and writer brought up in East Berlin in a family of writers.[3] Many of her works deal with historical change, for example, *Dinge, die verschwinden* [Things that Disappear]

(2009), and *Heimsuchung* [Visitation] (2008), a novel dealing with the inhabitants of a Berlin house through the Third Reich until past reunification. *Geschichte vom alten Kind* narrates the story of a girl in a children's home, whose identity is not what it seems. As in Kaschnitz's story, Erpenbeck's novella explores an individual's difficult past through the use of a child who eventually undergoes a metamorphosis.

Whereas the previous chapter explored animal–human metamorphosis, these texts involve a metamorphosis in which the transition from childhood to adulthood is configured as an extraordinary, radical change. The metamorphosis simultaneously reveals the child's identity and brings to light a buried past. Both texts have been used in school curricula,[4] though the texts do not just deal with the transition from childhood to adulthood but, most strikingly, they both foreground the narrator's intense aversion towards the child. Both texts position the child figures as abject, objects of fascination as well as repulsion. For psychoanalytic theorist Julia Kristeva, abjection points towards a repressed aspect of the psyche, something that is pushed away from the self in the process of self-formation.[5] This chapter explores the characterization of the child as abject as a key to understanding the later metamorphosis. It also examines the texts' different ways of dealing with difficult pasts and their challenge to personal identity. In doing so, the chapter investigates the extent to which the major social and political changes of late twentieth-century Germany may inform explorations of the individual process of metamorphosis.

Marie Luise Kaschnitz, 'Das dicke Kind'

Kaschnitz's first short story collection, *Das dicke Kind und andere Geschichten*, was published in 1952, although 'Das dicke Kind' itself had been published in 1951, and may have been written as early as 1946.[6] Biographer Elsbeth Pulver claims that 'Das dicke Kind' reveals Kaschnitz's development of an individual voice and style as a short story writer.[7] The story deals with the encounter between the narrator and a child who appears oddly familiar, and towards whom the narrator feels an inexplicable aversion. The uncertainty over the child's identity is resolved in a climactic scene which makes use of the motif of butterfly metamorphosis.

An Abject Encounter

The short story was a popular literary form in post-war Germany, particularly amongst authors who wanted to distance their work from the ideological novels of the Nazi era.[8] Kaschnitz found the short story to be a 'sehr gemäßes Ausdrucksmittel unserer Zeit' [very apt means of expression for our time], admiring in particular the open-endedness of the short story and the inner unity required of its sparse prose.[9] The short story typically has a time scale of no more than a few hours, as is the case in 'Das dicke Kind', which deals with the events of a single afternoon. It has been argued that the short story often focuses on a single episode in which something unexpected disturbs an otherwise ordinary life, a moment which Klaus Doderer has termed a 'Schicksalsbruch' [change of fate] or 'Störung' [disruption].[10] 'Das dicke Kind' begins with a disruption through the unexpected arrival into the narrator's house of a fat child. The encounter between child and narrator forms the basis of the narrative tension, generated from the narrator's complex feelings towards the child.

Kaschnitz's prose is characteristically structured around an encounter between two people, which Elsbeth Pulver argues is not simply one of many features of Kaschnitz's work but the key trigger for the action within her stories and a source of change.[11] In 'Das dicke Kind' the encounter between child and narrator acts as trigger for the later metamorphosis. The encounter begins when the narrator turns round from her desk and sees the child in her room. The child's presence can be explained by the fact that the narrator has started lending books to neighbourhood children, and by the possibility that her recent visitor may have left the door open. However, these explanations do little to dispel the surprise and unease caused by the child's presence. The 'Störung' with which the story begins is an affective disturbance. The narrator's sense of unease centres upon the child, a girl of around twelve years wearing an old-fashioned loden coat and carrying ice-skates, who seems 'bekannt aber nicht richtig bekannt' [familiar, but not really familiar]. The mixture of familiarity and unfamiliarity is characteristic of the uncanny, which for Freud was a sign of something that has been repressed.[12] Following Freud's interpretation of the uncanny, we may read the narrator's attempt to understand her feelings towards the child as an attempt to retrieve what has been repressed.

The unexpected appearance of the child might be compared to Kafka's 'Unglücklichsein' [unhappiness], in which the unhappy narrator is visited by a child ghost. In both stories, the narrator is in a state of tension over wanting the child to stay, as if the child's presence fulfils some important need, and feeling aggravated about the child's presence. Kafka's narrator complains mildly to his neighbour about the child ghost, whereas the child of 'Das dicke Kind' is the source of much stronger negative affects as well as fascination. The narrator starts asking the child questions and offers her the sandwiches she had just prepared, which the child accepts with an almost hurt surprise that the offer has only just occurred to the narrator. The narrator's feelings towards the child are revealed as she observes the child eating:

> Es machte sich daran, die Brote eins nach dem anderen zu verzehren, und es tat das auf eine besondere Weise, über die ich mir erst später Rechenschaft gab. Dann saß es wieder da und ließ seine trägen, kalten Blicke im Zimmer herumwandern, und es lag etwas in seinem Wesen, das mich mit Ärger und Abneigung erfüllte. Ja gewiß, ich habe dieses Kind von Anfang an gehaßt. Alles an ihm hat mich abgestoßen, seine trägen Glieder, sein hübsches, fettes Gesicht, seine Art zu sprechen, die zugleich schläfrig und anmaßend war. Und obwohl ich mich entschlossen hatte, ihm zuliebe meinen Spaziergang aufzugeben, behandelte ich es doch keineswegs freundlich, sondern grausam und kalt. (pp. 28–29)
>
> [She began eating her sandwiches one after the other, and did so in a particular manner, which I only called into account later. Then she sat there and allowed her lethargic, cold gaze to wander over the room, and there was something in her being that filled me with annoyance and aversion. Yes, for sure, I hated this child from the beginning. Everything about her repulsed me, her lethargic limbs, her pretty, fat face, her way of speaking, which was both sleepy and

> insolent. And although I had decided to give up my walk for her, I didn't treat her at all kindly, but was cruel and cold.]

An important feature of the story is its retrospective narration, signalled by phrases like 'über die ich mir erst später Rechenschaft gab' [which I only called into account later]. As a whole, the story can be read as a way of making sense of feelings that were not understood initially, but can later be identified and explained.

In particular, the narrator focuses on her intensely negative feelings towards the child, including annoyance, aversion, hatred, and revulsion. In the passage above, these feelings are expressed in a cumulative series of unrounded open vowels: 'Ärger', 'Abneigung', 'von Anfang an gehaßt', 'Alles an ihm hat mich abgestoßen'. The same sounds predominate in the description of the child, with 'Dann saß es wieder da', and in the adjectives 'träge' (twice), 'kalt', 'schläfrig', and 'anmaßend'. The assonance opens up a link between the child and the narrator, thereby prefiguring the later revelation of the child's identity. Moreover, the behavioural characteristics of emotional 'coldness' that the narrator despises in the child are also what she notes in herself ('kalt' is used for both the child and the narrator). Likewise the child's reaction to not having been offered the food sooner could be compared with the narrator's feeling of vindictiveness ('Rachsucht') towards the child (p. 30).

More than the reflection on the individual feelings themselves, it is the intensity of feeling that forms the main source of narrative reflection. The narrator's overwhelming hatred of the child appears out of proportion with the child's neutral behaviour. As the narrator remarks: 'Es wuchs etwas in mir auf, ein Grauen, das mit der Erscheinung des Kindes in gar keinem Verhältnis stand' (p. 29) [something rose up within me, a horror, which was in complete disproportion with the appearance of the child]. The verb 'aufwachsen' [rise up] suggests that the narrator is overwhelmed by her feelings rather than in control of them. In this sense, the feelings function as external disruptions, which demand analysis. The word 'aufwachsen' also semantically suggests growing or maturation processes, which are central in the story. The growing horror triggered by the child will, however, be contrasted by a growing awareness that allows the narrator to make sense of her initial feelings. At this stage in the story, the narrator is disturbed by her unexpected emotions, and feels 'ein sonderbares Gefühl der Peinigung [. . .] so, wie wenn man etwas erraten sollte, und errät es nicht, und ehe man es nicht erraten hat, kann nichts mehr werden, wie es vorher war' (p. 29) [a strange feeling of torment [. . .] as when you have to guess something, but you can't guess it, and until you're able to guess it, nothing can be as it was before]. The sense of being not quite able to identify a crucial feature which would explain her feelings causes temporal continuity to be put on hold. She cannot go on as before, and in order to move forwards, a radical change is necessary, which must come in the form of a realization or metamorphosis.

Because of her need to understand her puzzling feelings, the narrator does not act upon her inclination to push the child out of the door like a 'lästiges Tier' [annoying animal], but instead asks more questions. The push-and-pull dynamic at work here is characteristic of abjection, an affect directed towards an unwanted other. The other is not one regarded with indifference, but is one to which one has strong ties, a fascination as well as repulsion. The feeling of disgust has also been characterized in this way;[13] however, unlike disgust, abjection has a basis in a repressed aspect of the self, and has been regarded as central to the formation of the self. For Julia Kristeva, the abject other is an object of primal repression. Kristeva writes of abjection as a 'massive and sudden emergence of uncanniness, which, familiar as it might have been in an opaque and forgotten life, now harries me as radically separate, loathsome'.[14] In linking the abject with the uncanny, Kristeva suggests that the characteristically uncanny mixture of familiar and unfamiliar turns to abjection when experienced as intense affect. If the uncanny points towards something that has been repressed, so too does the abject. However, with abjection, the object of repression is also an object of loathing. Kristeva's characterization of abjection aptly describes the situation in 'Das dicke Kind', which begins with an eruption of the uncanny and a growing loathing of the other, a child who may have once been familiar, but whose identity is not yet clear. The encounter with the child thus triggers affects that indicate a repressed and as yet unrecognized aspect of the narrator's psyche. Since abjection suggests the presence of the repressed, it can be part of a narrative of self-formation, in which an abject other is formed as an attempt to establish oneself against that which one is not. In this story, a process of self-understanding is central, played out through the narrator's fascination with the abject child, which continues when the child gets up to leave, and the narrator follows, claiming: 'ich muss doch sehen, wie diese Raupe Schlittschuh läuft' (p. 31) [I have to see how this caterpillar skates].

Caterpillar Existence

The caterpillar motif not only prefigures the later metamorphosis, but also contributes to the child's characterization as abject and animal-like. The comparison of the child to a caterpillar is introduced for the first time while the narrator is observing the child in her room:

> Ich weiß nicht, sagte das Kind, und wie es dasaß in seinem haarigen Lodenmantel, glich es einer fetten Raupe, und wie eine Raupe hatte es auch gegessen, und wie eine Raupe witterte es jetzt wieder herum.
> Jetzt bekommst du nichts mehr, dachte ich, von einer sonderbaren Rachsucht erfüllt. Aber dann ging ich doch hinaus und holte Brot und Wurst, und das Kind starrte darauf mit seinem dumpfen Gesicht, und dann fing es an zu essen, wie eine Raupe frißt, langsam und stetig, wie aus einem inneren Zwang heraus, und ich betrachtete es feindlich und stumm. (p. 30)
>
> [I don't know, said the child, and as she sat there in her hairy loden coat, she looked like a fat caterpillar, and, like a caterpillar, she had eaten, and, like a caterpillar, she now cast about the room again.
> Now you're not getting any more, I thought, filled with a strange vindictiveness. But then I did go out and got bread and sausage, and the child stared at them with a dull face, and then she began to eat, like a caterpillar eats, slowly and steadily, as though from an inner compulsion, and I watched her silently and with hostility.]

The threefold repetition of 'wie eine Raupe' [like a caterpillar] in the first sentence stresses the comparison. The image of the caterpillar is provoked both by the child's fatness and by her hairy loden coat, and contains elements of both the comic and the grotesque. This is corroborated by other animal allusions in the text: she is called a 'seltsame Kröte' [strange frog] and a 'lästiges Tier' [annoying animal]. Through these comparisons the child is relegated to the status of an animal, and specifically to animals considered odd, annoying, or repulsive.

The caterpillar simile is also used to convey the child's manner of eating and behaving. The child behaves apathetically, as suggested by her answering the narrator's questions with 'ich weiß nicht' [I don't know], and her 'dumpfe[s] Gesicht' [dull face] referred to in the passage above. The child's lack of expression links her to a caterpillar. When she eats she does so slowly and as though through an inner compulsion, a form of behaviour that suggests animal instinct as well as lack of emotion. The caterpillar comparison stems in particular from the child's compulsion to eat, which both repels the narrator, but also compels her to want to feed the child. The narrator refers negatively to the child's fatness, elsewhere describing her as a 'Fettkloß' (p. 31) [lump of lard].

The link made in the passage above between fatness and apathetic behaviour is a long-standing one in European culture. In his cultural history of obesity, Sander Gilman examines the association between fatness and apathy, citing Dickens's fat boy Joe, from *The Pickwick Papers*, as a well-known example. Gilman notes two forms of fatness in Dickens: 'fat-cheery' and 'fat-bloated', of which Joe exemplifies the latter.[15] Joe is regularly described as falling asleep, snoring monotonously, and has a vacant and inscrutable countenance. According to Gilman, Dickens's Joe provided a model for medical understandings of obesity, for example in the diagnosis of obesity as an endocrine abnormality, and in the later creation of the 'Pickwick syndrome' in the mid-twentieth century, a form of sleep apnoea connected to obesity.[16] Although 'Das dicke Kind' draws upon the image of the fat and lethargic child popularized by Dickens's Joe, Kaschnitz's child is not an endearing figure of ridicule, but is an object of aversion. The narrator's repulsion towards the child's fatness and compulsion to eat is also a repulsion towards her lethargic behaviour.

By positioning the child as abject, the story marks a change from Kaschnitz's early more idealized versions of childhood in her poetry, and the beginning of what critics have claimed as a more critical approach to childhood.[17] In 'Das dicke Kind', the child is not viewed with nostalgia, and in this sense it goes against a cultural model of childhood as an idealized state, which can be traced back to the Romantic period. In Germany, figures such as Goethe's Mignon (from *Wilhelm Meisters Lehrjahre*) helped to promote an idealized image of childhood innocence and purity.[18] According to Nikola Roßbach, Kaschnitz's tendency to de-romanticize childhood became more pronounced during the 1950s, when she also began to thematize and problematize the process of remembering.[19] In 'Das dicke Kind', the encounter with the child is also a process of remembering. This happens through a technique that Roßbach calls the 'Vergegenwärtigung des Vergangenen' [presencing of the past]. The narrator confronts her past through the living body of the child, whose appearance functions like the unexpected return of a repressed and uncomfortable memory. According to Roßbach, the technique of encountering the past in the present is used in a number of Kaschnitz's autobiographical childhood texts as an extreme form of reconstructive remembrance.[20] The emotional investment in the encounter with the child derives particular power from its association with Kaschnitz's own biography. Kaschnitz claimed that the child in the story was herself, and that she considered the story to be her strongest, because of its cruelty, which was only possible because the object of this cruelty was herself.[21]

The narrator's overwhelmingly negative impression of the child means that she fails to notice aspects of the child that diverge from the apathetic image that she has constructed, and which might provide insight into the child's character and identity. For example, the child says that she does not care if the narrator calls her 'Dicke' [fatty]. However, the child's expression suggests that she does care: 'ich glaube mich jetzt zu erinnern, daß sein Gesicht sich in diesem Augenblick schmerzlich verzog. Aber ich achtete nicht darauf' (p. 28) [I think I now remember that her face crumpled up at this point. But I paid no attention to it]. It is only later that the narrator realizes the existence of these feelings. By claiming not to care what others call her, and telling the narrator only the name which others have given her, the child fails to lay claim to her identity. As well as lacking a proper name, the child lacks gender identity, since she is referred to throughout as 'das Kind' [the child] and with the neuter pronoun 'es'. Although this pronominal use can be read as grammatical agreement with 'das Kind', it would be grammatically possible to switch to 'sie' [she] in many instances. Instead, 'es' is used strategically to emphasize the child as not yet having come into gendered adulthood. By contrast, the child's older sister is referred to as 'sie'. Through the use of 'es' the twelve-year-old is positioned as a child, prior to puberty and to prior to her later metamorphosis.

In focusing on the child's fatness and apathetic expression the narrator fails to recognize the child's feelings. For example, the child becomes more animated when speaking about her sister. The child characterizes her sister as a polar opposite of herself, as someone who is slim and daring, who sits outside in a thunderstorm, sings her own made-up songs, jumps from the highest diving board and swims far out (p. 31). In contrast the child says that she does none of these things and is afraid. When she speaks of her sister, her face expresses pain and sadness: 'wieder erschien auf seinem Gesicht ein Ausdruck von Schmerz und Trauer, und wieder beachtete ich ihn nicht' (p. 30) [an expression of pain and sadness appeared on her face again, and again I paid no attention]. The child's distress reveals an emotional investment in her identity, despite her apathetic surface. The disjunction between a surface lack of affect and hidden emotional investment was also at stake in chapter 2. In his book *Immune Erzähler* (2007) [Immune Narrators], Martin von Koppenfels identifies the disjunction between inner and outer affect as a characteristic of early twentieth-century modern literature.[22] Koppenfels discusses the emotional style in literature of this period in relation to Freud's theory of affect.[23] The idea of a disjunction between surface emotion, as conveyed through the narrative, and unstated inner concerns that are only hinted at, might be linked to Freud's model of the unconscious with its repressed experiences. On this account, affects might be seen as providing links to the repressed experiences of the past. In Kaschnitz's story, the child's flashes of intense affect not only reveal the child's inner concerns, but also the narrator's forgotten or repressed past.

The narrator's repulsion towards the child is brought out further with the comparison between the child's manner of eating and the splashing of a lake, an acoustic association that prefigures the later scene of metamorphosis:

> Ich setzte mich wieder an meiner Arbeit, aber dann hörte ich das Kind hinter mir schmatzen, und dieses Geräusch glich dem trägen Schmatzen eines schwarzen Weihers irgendwo im Walde, es brachte mir alles wässerig Dumpfe, alles Schwere und Trübe der Menschennatur zum Bewusstsein und verstimmte mich sehr. (p. 30)

> [I sat down to my work again, but then I heard the child smacking her lips behind me, and this noise sounded like the lethargic splashing of a black pond somewhere in the forest, it made me aware of all the watery dreariness, all the heaviness and turbidity in human nature, and lowered my mood a great deal.]

The noise of 'schmatzen' [smacking] summons up in the narrator a sense of dullness and lethargy ('träge', 'dumpf', 'schwer', 'trüb') that she finds intensely depressing. Water is associated throughout with the child, who is described at the start and end of the story as having 'wasserhelle[n] Augen' [pale, watery eyes], and also claims to have been born in Aquarius. While these associations do not necessarily convey the bleakness that water conjures up in this passage, they provide a link that becomes significant in the scene of metamorphosis on the frozen lake, when the child is in danger of being pulled under by the 'Wassermann' (p. 34) [Aquarius]. Water imagery often has an ambiguous status in literature, both as potentially deadly and as life-giving. In the passage above, the narrator associates the splashing sound with a black pond, an image which might be compared to the mythical black waters of Lethe, the river of forgetfulness and oblivion. The image also prefigures what happens next on the frozen lake, which is both a scene of metamorphosis and a breaking of the narrator's forgetfulness.

Metamorphosis: Crisis and Rebirth

The metamorphosis functions as a turning point and moment of self-realization. After the child leaves, the narrator follows her to an isolated lake surrounded by dark forests. Now a spectator only, the narrator watches the child skate clumsily towards a place on the ice where her sister had been waving, calling her and skating in circles. When the child crosses a darker patch of ice where her sister had been it breaks under her heavier weight. In this sense, the crisis is born out of the child's physical state, through the fatness that marks her difference from her sister. The terrifying nature of this accident is modulated by the narrator's interventions in which she explains ('ich muss gleich sagen', p. 34 [I have to say straight away]) that the situation is not life-threatening, because the ice freezes in two layers, and the child has only fallen through the first one. The narrator's lack of shock suggests a familiarity with the scene that is not merely occasioned by the retrospective narration, but also by a superior knowledge. This knowledge also prevents the narrator from intervening. As she watches the child standing in the ice, frightened to death, the narrator claims: 'ich spürte gar nichts dabei, nicht das geringste Erbarmen und rührte mich nicht' (p. 34) [I felt nothing during this, not the least compassion, and I didn't make a move]. The narrator's lack of emotion parallels the lack of emotional expression observed earlier in the child, thereby linking the two figures as well as suggesting the narrator's extreme rejection of the child through her failure to empathize.

However, the next paragraph reveals a sudden change. The child suddenly raises her head, and in the moonshine the narrator recognizes a change of expression in the child's face:

> Es waren dieselben Züge und doch nicht dieselben, aufgerissen waren sie von Willen und Leidenschaft, als ob sie nun, im Angesicht des Todes, alles Leben tränken, alles glühende Leben der Welt. Ja, das glaubte ich wohl, daß der Tod nahe und dies das letzte sei, und beugte mich über das Geländer und blickte in das weiße Antlitz unter mir, und wie ein Spiegelbild sah es mir entgegen aus der schwarzen Flut. (p. 34)

> [They were the same characteristics, and yet not the same, they were torn open with will and passion, as if they now, in face of death, were drinking in all the life, all the glowing life of the world. Yes, that's what I believed, that death was near and that this was the end, and I bent over the railings and looked down at the white countenance below me, and like a mirror image I saw it facing me out of the black tides.]

The child's affective transformation, revealed in her change of expression, is the first indication of what will later be described as a metamorphosis. Affectively the transformation is a radical one, in which apathy is replaced by intense passion ('Willen und Leidenschaft'). In the passage above, the short clauses and repetition ('alles Leben tränken, alles glühende Leben der Welt') give a sense of urgency and impassioned focus on the present. The situation is presented as a life-or-death crisis, with the repeated use of 'Tod' and 'Leben'. The contrast between white (the child's coat) and black (the water) underscores the sense of oppositional forces. The white figure on the lake also appears to the narrator like her mirror image, a form of doubling which brings the narrative closer to the revelation of the child's identity. Discussing this story, Lisa Tyler relies on the claim by Elizabeth Abel that the use of the double in writing by women is less likely to represent a threat, and more likely to be used to define a self.[24] Kaschnitz's story supports this claim in that the doubling of child and narrator is part of a process of self-recognition. The description of the figure on the lake can also be read as an allusion to the Greek myth of Narcissus, with white being a common colour of the Narcissus flower. In the myth, Narcissus gazes into a lake and becomes captivated by his own reflection. Around this point it may start to become apparent that the narrator and child are the same person, although this will not be confirmed until the end of the story.

The child's struggle to pull herself out of the lake by holding onto a stake of wood at the end of the jetty is described using the motif of insect metamorphosis:

> Sein Körper war zu schwer, und seine Finger bluteten, und es fiel wieder zurück, aber nur, um wieder von neuem zu beginnen. Und das war ein langer Kampf, ein schreckliches Ringen um Befreiung und Verwandlung, wie das Aufbrechen einer Schale oder eines Gespinstes, dem ich da zusah, und jetzt hätte ich dem Kinde helfen mögen, aber ich wußte, ich brauche ihm nicht mehr zu helfen — ich hatte es erkannt ... (p. 35)

> [Her body was too heavy and her fingers were bleeding, and she fell back, but only to begin again from the start. And it was a long fight, a terrible struggle for liberation and transformation, like the breaking open of a shell or a cocoon, that I was watching, and now I should have been able to help the child, but I knew that I didn't need to help her any more — I had recognised her . . .]

The painful and persistent effort required to escape from the ice is compared to the process of breaking out of a shell or cocoon. It is thus both a metamorphosis and a birth, the beginning of a new identity. Since antiquity, caterpillar–butterfly metamorphosis has been regarded as a form of death and rebirth. Ancient Greek tombs, for example, frequently depicted butterflies as a symbol of the soul's transition to the afterlife. In this sense, the butterfly may be used to represent the intermediate state between life and death, and is thus a symbol that holds particular resonance in the context of wartime Europe. One of the writers who most frequently drew upon the butterfly motif was Nelly Sachs, a German-Jewish poet in exile during the war. For Sachs, metamorphosis provided a sense of hope amidst reports of countless deaths, a hope of moving from the troubled earthly realm towards a place of limitlessness. In the passage above, the idea of metamorphosis is also one of escape ('Befreiung') precipitated by a crisis. The child is escaping from the cold and dark water, associated with death, and at the same time undergoing a radical affective change.

Although the story is one of personal experience, we might also consider reading the long struggle ('langer Kampf', 'schreckliches Ringen um Befreiung und Verwandlung') as informed by the struggle of the war years from which Kaschnitz has only just emerged. While Kaschnitz describes this time as terrible, she also claims it as having a transformative effect on her character. For example, she explained why she did not emigrate by saying:

> falls es mir gelänge, diese schauerliche Epoche [. . .] lebendig zu überstehen, würde ich dadurch viel für meine geistige und menschliche Entwicklung gewonnen haben, daß ich reicher an Wissen und Leben daraus hervorginge, als wenn ich aus den Logen und Parterreplätzen des Auslands der deutschen Tragödie zuschaute.[25]

> [[I knew that] if I managed to survive this ghastly period [. . .], I would have achieved much for my mental and human development, in that I would emerge richer in knowledge and life than if I had watched the German tragedy from the loge and first-floor seating abroad.]

The idea that the crisis of war has a transformative effect on the individual is paralleled by the representation of metamorphosis as struggle, affective transformation, and finally escape. Kaschnitz believed that wartime experience had a profound effect upon the individual. In the essays she published at the end of the Second World War in the journal *Die Wandlung* [The Change] Kaschnitz begins by saying that we need to relearn how to say 'Ich'.[26] Elsbeth Pulver interprets this remark as a response to the years of *Gleichschaltung*, the doctrinal thinking of the Nazi times. But the need for new, individual identity can also be more broadly seen as a response to crisis. Dirk Göttsche argues that it is particularly in her later works that Kaschnitz emphasizes the fleeting nature of the 'Ich'. According to Göttsche, Kaschnitz's work puts into practice the process later described by Deleuze: 'ein Individuum erwirbt erst wirklich einen Eigennamen, wenn es die strengste Depersonalisierung hinter sich hat, wenn es sich den Vielheiten öffnet, die es von einem Ende zum anderen Ende durchziehenden Intensitäten, die es durchlaufen' [an individual only really acquires a personal name after undergoing the strictest depersonalization, after becoming open to the multiplicities running through it, the intensities that traverse it from one end to the other].[27] In this story, it is only after an intensely affective, life-threatening process that the child recognises her own strength, and that the narrator recognises the child as herself.

Perhaps more fittingly than the comparison to Deleuze's model of the individual, Kaschnitz's story might be seen as a Hegelian type of narrative of the emergence of the self. For Hegel, self-consciousness is only made possible through being recognised by another subject. The process of self-recognition through recognition of the other can be identified in Kaschnitz's story in that the recognition of the child's identity is also a recognition of the narrator's own identity. In his *Phänomenologie des Geistes* [Phenomenology of Spirit] of 1807, Hegel describes the process of the development of self-consciousness as a life-or-death struggle, as both consciousnesses struggle to negate the other and establish themselves.[28] The struggle in Kaschnitz's story, with its references to life and death, might be seen as recalling the conflict that is central to Hegel's narrative of the emergence of self-consciousness. The process of self-recognition also finds shape in the description of the child as mirror-image, a visualization of self-recognition that plays a role in many psychoanalytical accounts of the emergence of the self, such as Lacan's notion of the mirror-stage.[29] In this way, we might read Kaschnitz's narrative as an account of the formation of the self through the psychological struggle of the child and narrator.

A second locus of psychological struggle lies in the relationship between the child and her sister. Sibling rivalry is central in many of Kaschnitz's stories. In 'Das dicke Kind' it is the younger sister who, in a life-or-death situation, turns out to have the mental strength and resolution to survive. This is also the case in Kaschnitz's 'Lupinen' [Lupins] (first published in 1966), in which the younger sister manages to jump off a moving train to escape deportation to a concentration camp, while the older sister remains on the train despite having managed the same feat as a child. Both tales suggest that transformation, and even reversal of roles, is possible. The trajectory from a state of fearfulness, hurt, and uncertainty to a state of self-possession and resolve underlies the relationship dynamic in both tales.

The development of a new identity also parallels the bodily and psychological transition from child to adult, as represented in the child being on the brink of puberty. For the child, the move towards new identity involves a realization of inner strength. According to Lisa Tyler, the message of the story is that 'Kaschnitz's heroine must realise the strength and resourcefulness she possessed even as an unattractive child'.[30] While, contrary to what Tyler claims, being physically unattractive is not part of the story, since the narrator speaks of 'sein hübsches, fettes Gesicht' (p. 29) [her pretty, fat face], the story does involve coming to terms with disliked personal characteristics. Because of the strength of her aversion, the narrator fails to recognize the child's qualities as her own, while the child fails to recognize her inner strength. The self-critical story 'Das dicke Kind' can thus be read as an assertion of the need to recognize even the more unattractive aspects of one's past. The story's core message has broader application if we link it to Kaschnitz's view of history. Unlike a number of her contemporaries, Kaschnitz did not regard the end of the war as a *Stunde Null*, a new start in which one should put the past behind oneself.[31] Nor did Kaschnitz feel that the end of war should bring exoneration from guilt. Rather, the crisis of wartime Germany made all the more pressing the need for self-reflection, even, and perhaps especially, when that self comes across unfavourably.

The metamorphosis is a double one in that the child's metamorphic self-realization is paralleled by the narrator's realization, her recognition of the child as herself. The recognition can also be considered a form of metamorphosis in the sense that it brings about a radical psychological change. Marina Warner comments on this constellation: 'some kinds of metamorphosis play a crucial part in anagnorisis, or recognition, the reversal fundamental to narrative form, and so govern narrative satisfaction'.[32] In 'Das dicke Kind', the motif of metamorphosis used in conjunction with the process of anagnorisis marks a turning point in the story. It is while observing what she describes as a metamorphosis that the narrator says: 'ich hatte es erkannt' [I had recognized her]. The process of recognition is only complete in the final line, however, after the narrator has returned home to find on her desk a photograph of herself as a child: 'in einem weißen Wollkleid mit Stehkragen, mit hellen, wäßrigen Augen und sehr dick' (p. 35) [in a white woollen dress with a stand-up collar, with pale, watery eyes, and very fat]. Elsbeth Pulver has commented on the satisfying roundness of this much-anthologized narrative.[33] The final twist allows for a third realization, that of the reader, who now has access to what the narrator has already realized: that the child is the narrator herself. The photograph acts as a physical, affective tie that forms the link between present and past.

Although the tale may be read as a move towards self-understanding, the end is left open. It is not clear whether the narrator's feelings towards her past self have changed, but she has recognized herself. If we read the thawing of the lake ('Tauwetter') in connection with the description of the narrator and child as emotionally cold, then we may read the metamorphosis as causing a thawing of feeling. In this sense the story is essentially optimistic, opening up the possibility that the undesirable and repressed aspects of the past can be, if not accepted, then at least recognized, and that in this process of recognition there is also the potential for change.

Jenny Erpenbeck, *Geschichte vom alten Kind*

Geschichte vom alten Kind was Jenny Erpenbeck's bestselling debut novella, published in 1999 and written when Erpenbeck was around thirty. The text has a basis in a real incident in which Erpenbeck's grandmother, the writer Hedda Zinner, received a letter from a teenage girl, whom she visited in hospital and befriended, and later discovered from the doctor that the girl was a 31-year-old woman.[34] Erpenbeck, a theatre director, conducted research for the book by returning to school for a month and passing herself off as a seventeen-year-old.[35] The novella centres on a girl who is found on the street and taken to a children's home, where she hopes to remain. The impossibility of her project is eventually brought to a head and she is taken to hospital where she is forced to undergo a radical bodily transformation. The novella was written in the decade following the fall of the Berlin wall, and has been read as an allegory of the GDR as closed institution, and as reflecting a reluctance to accept a unified future. But as Nancy Nobile claims, although the GDR allusions are fairly conspicuous and sometimes verging on caricature, reading the tale as a straightforward allegory of the GDR does not unlock all the mysteries of this enigmatic narrative.[36]

Temporal Constriction and Narrative Blockage

The title *Geschichte vom alten Kind* suggests the paradoxical situation (that of the 'old child') that makes up the 'seltsames, unerhörtes Ereignis' [strange unheard-of incident] that Goethe considered central to the novella. Although the text has been variously referred to as a story, tale, fable, or parable, Nancy Nobile points out that the text shows the distinguishing features of a novella.[37] The text is shorter than a novel, and is structured around a single incident, without subplots and with only one main character. However, it is longer than a typical short story, with more extensively developed action. Whereas Kaschnitz's short story recounts the events of an afternoon, Erpenbeck's tale takes place over several weeks, beginning with a child being found on the street, and ending with a metamorphosis in which her identity is revealed. The text hints throughout at the child's undisclosed identity, and in this way, builds narrative tension leading up to the metamorphosis.

As in 'Das dicke Kind', Erpenbeck's novella begins with a girl turning up apparently from nowhere, and posing an inscrutable riddle. However, whereas Kaschnitz's text is structured around a personal encounter between the narrator and the girl, Erpenbeck's text is narrated through an omniscient narrator. As in the famous case of Kasper Hauser, an unknown child is found on the street in circumstances that reveal little about her identity or past: 'Als man es gefunden hat, stand es Nachts auf einer Straße, mit einem leeren Eimer in der Hand, auf einer Geschäftsstraße, und hat nichts gesagt' (p. 5) [When they found her, she was standing on the street with an empty bucket in one hand, on a street lined with shops, and didn't say a word].[38] The empty bucket provides little with which to identify the girl, and instead functions as a way of emphasizing the sense of lack, the lack of insight into the girl's identity. When questioned by the police, she is able to give her age, fourteen, after which the police switch from addressing her as 'Sie' to 'du' (p. 5).

However, the girl apparently remembers nothing else: 'Das Mädchen konnte sich einfach nicht daran erinnern, es konnte sich an den Anfang nicht erinnern. Es war ganz und gar Waise, und alles, was es hatte und kannte, war der leere Eimer' (p. 5) [The girl simply could not remember, she couldn't remember the beginning. She was an orphan through and through, and all she had, all she knew was the empty bucket (p. 5)]. The repeated reference to the bucket again adverts to its emptiness, and brings this into connection with the girl's inability to remember, stressed through the repetition of 'nicht erinnern'. The girl's lack of memory means a lack of beginning to the narrative, for there is no explanation about how the girl ended up in this situation. Like the bucket, the girl's past is empty, so much so that the narrator claims that the girl is 'derart von Nichts umgeben, daß seiner Existenz von Anfang an etwas Unglaubliches anhaftete' (p. 5) [so surrounded by nothingness that there seemed, from the beginning, to be something implausible about her very existence (p. 6)]. The association with the unbelievable ('Unglaubliches') has the effect of opening up the possibility that the girl's existence should not be believed, that her identity is not what it seems. As in Kaschnitz's story the narrator suggests that there is something uncanny about the girl. However, whereas in 'Das dicke Kind' the uncanny is a result of the narrator's sensation of unplaceable familiarity, in *Die Geschichte vom alten Kind*, it seems that the narrator knows the child's hidden identity, but is withholding the information from the reader. Erpenbeck claimed that she wanted her character to be like a block, a cryptic and closed unit, and that she also wanted to write the book itself like a 'Block, wo man als Leser immer draußen bleibt' [block, where the reader is always on the outside].[39] The narrator's withholding of information is one means of creating this block.

The nothingness that is said to surround the child extends to the description of her physical form, which seems indistinct. Her body is described as 'wie aus einem Stück gehauen, weder ist eine Erhebung dort, wo die Brüste sein müßten, noch eine Einbuchtung in Höhe der Taille' (p. 5) [appears to have been hewn from a single block of wood, there is neither a swelling where the breasts should be, nor an indentation at the waist (p. 6)]. Her formlessness means a lack of womanly characteristics. Having described the girl, the narrator claims that the girl still fails to make a convincing impression ('dennoch macht das Mädchen keinen überzeugenden Eindrück', p. 5). The word 'überzeugend' can mean unimpressive, but also unconvincing, thereby suggesting that the girl is attempting to convince others of something. This again raises suspicions about the child's identity. The narrator links the failure to convince to the girl's hair, which is of indeterminate length and colour, but which appears almost grey, thereby hinting at a characteristic of an older, adult woman.

The girl is referred to throughout as 'das Mädchen' [the girl]. Even after she is taken to the children's home, the narrator never refers to her with a proper name. In Kaschnitz's text the child's lack of a proper name prevents the realization of identity; in Erpenbeck's text, the lack of a name emphasizes the girl's lack of identity. She is also referred to throughout by the neuter pronoun 'es', even though the other girls warrant the pronoun 'sie'. This refusal of gender has the effect of emphasizing her status as a child rather than a woman. As well as referring to the girl without a proper name or gender, the narrator also frequently refers to her as a thing or mere body: as a 'Holzkloben' (p. 8) [block of wood, p. 11] 'verkommene Masse' (p. 31) [ruinous mass, p. 51], 'Ochse' (35) [ox, p. 55], 'Klumpen' (p. 45) [blackened lump, p. 73], 'Knochensack' (p. 63) [bag of bones, p. 103], and even as a 'riesiger atmender Kadaver' (p. 62) [massive, breathing cadaver, p. 101]. All of these nouns have negative associations, and imply that the girl is an insensible, unpleasant physical body rather than a person. The adjective 'verkommen' [ruinous] insinuates that something is wrong with the girl, as is also implied when the narrator speaks of 'seinen vertrackten Körper' (p. 32) [this difficult body of hers (p. 50)]. The sense of there being something wrong, as conveyed by the repeated use of the prefix 'ver-', is linked to the idea of lack and abnormality. In referring to her 'vertrackten Körper', the narrator claims that the child lacks resistance, or is completely passive. As with Kaschnitz's story, we might consider whether Erpenbeck is drawing on (and perhaps critiquing) a cultural association between bodily fatness and apathetic behaviour.

As in 'Das dicke Kind', the child is positioned as an object of disgust, apparent both in the narrator's choice of language and in the way the other children view the girl. In particular, the girl arouses the children's disgust through her immoderate and indiscriminate eating habits, which include eating the other children's leftovers. Katie Jones reads this behaviour as a 'ritual of purification' signalling the girl's longing for physical integration into the collective.[40] The girl enjoys being in the closed, institutional children's home, which might be read as an allegory of the GDR. However, although the children consider the girl disgusting, the narrator describes their disgust as normal:

> So erregt das Mädchen zwar den Unwillen und Ekel derer, vor denen Blicken es so unmäßig viel ißt, hat aber auch teil an der allgemeinen Geselligkeit, und der Unwillen und Ekel sind ganz gewöhnlicher Unwillen und Ekel, ganz alltäglich. (p. 34)
>
> [Thus while the girl arouses the displeasure and disgust of those before whose eyes she is eating so immoderately, she is nonetheless partaking in the general conviviality, and this displeasure and disgust are quite ordinary displeasure and disgust, they are perfectly quotidian. (p. 54)]

The narrator stresses that the children's feelings remain within normal bounds: they are 'gewöhnlich' [ordinary] and 'alltäglich' [quotidian]. Though the other children are repulsed by her, crucially the girl is accepted into the group as she hoped: the children find her unpleasant, but this is a 'ganz normale Grausamkeit' (p. 34) [perfectly normal cruelty (p. 54)], and not a sign of anything deeper. By emphasizing the normality of the children's feelings, the narrator simultaneously raises the possibility that there might be something more insidious at stake to account for their repulsion.

Throughout the text, the narrator insinuates that the other children are missing crucial information. For example, in a later passage, the girl's voracious and indiscriminate manner of eating is correlated with her habit of forgetting. The girl's room-mates are able to tell her their secrets, because they know that she will not divulge them, but they do not make the connection between her inclination to forget and her inclination to eat:

> Ein wenig erinnert das Verhalten des Mädchens an die Art und Weise, mit welcher es immer das viele Essen in sich hineinfrißt, auch hier zeigt sich diese stille Gefräßigkeit, die alles in sich aufnimmt, um es niemals wieder herauszurücken, *aber dieser Zusammenhang fällt den anderen nicht auf.* (p. 47, my italics)
>
> [The girl's behaviour might remind one a little of the way she stuffs herself with large quantities of food, for here, too, one can behold a silent gluttony which

takes in everything, never to release it again, *but this similarity does not occur to the others.* (p. 76, my italics)]

By adverting us to connections that are being missed, the narrator suggests that there is a riddle to be solved. Close observation of the girl's behaviour, psychological disposition, and appearance may help to solve the riddle. In the passage above, the narrator's link between eating and forgetting stresses the child's tendency to take in, without giving out, suggesting that a process of repression may be at work. Through this association, the girl's fat body becomes a correlative of her mental state, which is one of passive absorption.

The passage above has also been read as a reference to Ludwig Tieck's uncanny Romantic *Märchen* 'Der blonde Eckbert' [Blond Eckbert] (1797). Nancy Nobile parallels Erpenbeck's scene of secret sharing with the episode in Tieck's story when Eckbert decides to share a secret with his friend Walther, but afterwards fears that his secret will be divulged. Eckbert's fear is well founded, for the unveiling of secret pasts and hidden identities is at the heart of Tieck's tale. Eckbert continually re-encounters his past, despite trying to escape it: having killed his friend Walther, he discovers that his new friend Hugo is Walther, and is also the old woman with whom his wife had lived as a child. At the end, even Eckbert's wife Bertha is revealed as having an unknown identity — she is Eckbert's sister. An intertextual parallel offers itself not only through the final revelation of identity, but also through the way in which all identities appear to fall together as one, as the past continually returns. Nobile highlights Tieck's use of 'Niemand' to suggest that Walther may not even exist, and may represent a 'failure of selfhood', in the same way that Erpenbeck's girl is surrounded by an aura of 'nichts'.[41]

In Erpenbeck's scene, as the girl listens to Nicole, 'der Blonden' (which Nobile reads as an allusion to blond Eckbert), the girl's nose runs and with it her memory also seems to run out of her:

> es scheint ihm so, als hätte es mit der Erinnerung an das, was war, auch die Erinnerung an das was sein soll, verloren. Es kommt sich vor wie jemand, der zusammengeschnurrt ist, wie jemand, der in der Zeit zusammengeschnurrt ist wie in einem Feuer, und jetzt ein Klumpen ist in einem Kinderheim. (p. 45)
>
> [it seems to her as if she has lost, along with her memory of what used to be, her memory of what is supposed to be some day. She appears to herself like someone who has been charred into a little ball, someone who has been charred in time as in a fire and is now nothing more than a blackened lump that has been deposited at a home for children. (pp. 72–73)]

Losing memory has the effect of confining the girl within a continuous present. The cumbrous paratactic style and use of repetition reflects the emphasis on the present. Not only has the girl forgotten the past, but she has come to a point of stasis, as expressed through the curious phrase: 'in der Zeit zusammengeschnurrt [. . .] wie in einem Feuer' [charred in time as in a fire].

The simile is significant because it prefigures a later episode in the text, when the school holds a commemoration day to recall the bombing of the city (pp. 52–53). Although it is never made clear when and where the novella is set, the description of the bombing suggests the allied air raids on cities such as Dresden in 1945, in which tens of thousands of civilians died: an event commemorated in the GDR. In Erpenbeck's novella, the children are told a horrific account of people jumping into a boiling river to escape the fire. During the recounting of this narrative, several children make joking comments, whereas the girl loses her appetite and has to leave the room. Her intense affect separates her from the other children, as she struggles to understand the connection between the horrific events and the cake that has been laid out for the occasion, asking: 'Warum wird eine Geburtstagsfeier veranstaltet, wenn die Menschen gekocht worden sind?' (p. 53) [Why is there a birthday party when the people were boiled alive? (p. 86)]. The girl's response suggests that she is unable to regard the events with the distanced perspective of the other children, and is in this respect similar to the cook, who answers the girl's question with: 'Man muss es feiern, wenn man es nicht vergessen kann' (p. 53) [You have to celebrate what you cannot forget (p. 87)].

The image of being trapped in the fire of a burning city is echoed in the writer W. G. Sebald's *Luftkrieg und Literatur* (1999), in which Sebald criticizes literature for failing to deal properly with the air raids of the Second World War. He also gives a graphic account of events, including burned bodies, which he describes as 'zusammengeschnurrt auf ein Drittel ihrer natürlichen Größe' [charred down to a third of their normal size].[42] While Sebald's book, which was based on his lectures a couple of years previously, was only published in 1999 — the same year as Erpenbeck's novella — the issues were already in the public eye when Erpenbeck was writing. Sebald claimed that German writers failed to inscribe such events into collective memory because they were tied up with Nazi guilt. By referencing the bombing in her text, Erpenbeck highlights the experience of the bombing as a lasting trauma in the consciousness of the older generation like the cook, but also shows how access to it is blocked, both through the way in which the older generation hope to forget it, and the younger generation's inability to comprehend it.

The unusual and horrible expression of being 'zusammengeschnurrt' in a fire is also found in a tale by the brothers Grimm, called 'Das junggeglühte Männlein' [The old man made young] (1857 edition), which, like Erpenbeck's tale, is about temporal reversal. In the Grimms' tale, an old woman witnesses a beggar being made young again ('junggeglüht') by being thrown into a blacksmith's fire by a saint. The next day, the woman decides to copy this by throwing herself into the fire. However, it causes her to scream horribly and come out 'ganz zusammen geschnurrt' [completely charred].[43] In the Grimms' story, the fire is a means for becoming young again when under saintly enchantment, but without the saint's influence it is the source of horrific pain. If we read Erpenbeck's novella alongside 'Das junggeglühte Männlein', we might ask whether the girl's temporal confinement ('zusammengeschnurrt in der Zeit') will be an experience of enchanted youthfulness like the beggar, or rather a traumatic experience, an attempt at reversing time that will fail horribly. Read through the potential, and thematically very apt intertext provided by the Grimm's tale of attempting to return to youth, Erpenbeck's reference to the girl being 'in der Zeit zusammengeschnurrt [. . .] wie in einem Feuer' gains ominous undercurrents, suggesting that the girl's attempt at reversing time is misguided and will end badly, like that of the old woman.

The Art of Forgetting

Not only does the girl appear at the start of the story without a past, but she continues to relinquish her past while in the orphanage, practising the 'Kunst des Vergessens' (p. 35) [art of forgetting (p. 56)]. For example, she does not attempt to remember what she learns in class, nor does she care about progressing to the next year: unlike her classmates she hopes to remain in the school forever. The narrator explains that the girl knows what true freedom is: 'sich nicht selber schubsen zu müssen' (p.14) [not having to shove anyone yourself (p. 20)], which means being able to relinquish agency, a freedom, the narrator claims, that exists only in the institution.

The other children learn to take advantage of the girl's forgetful behaviour. This begins with incidents such as them telling the girl to clap, which she immediately does, while they take her plate of food away. They repeat this the next day with the same results: the child claps readily, despite having been upset by having her food taken away the day before (p. 35). As she is forgetful and obedient, the children find that they can make use of the girl. She is used to carry stolen items (which she forgets having been given), to stand watch outside doors and knock when a teacher approaches, to tell secrets to without fear that she will divulge those secrets.

The girl is obedient to the point of blindness. Because she wants to relinquish agency she gives herself over to whatever is asked of her. She even stays in the playground all night when, during a game, the other children forget to call her. The narrator explains this by claiming: 'Das Mädchen weiß, daß sein Körper eine Schuld ist, es will dieser Schuld gern abtragen, daher befolgt es die Gebote seiner Kameraden aufs peinlichste' (p. 26) [The girl knows that her body is a transgression, she would like to atone for it, and so she obeys the decrees issued by her classmates to the letter (p. 41)]. The narrator's explanation of the girl's compliant behaviour remains enigmatic, since we do not know why the girl believes her body to be a transgression or debt. It seems, however, that the girl's willingness to submit to others and to disregard her body is connected to her past: it is a way of paying off a previous debt or guilt. Since the post-war period *Schuld* has often been used in just this dual sense, as both physical affect (guilt) and in economic terms, as debt, an account that needs to be balanced. As Sigrid Weigel claims: 'Seit Ende des "Dritten Reiches" wird über die *Schuld* der Deutschen im Diskurs von *Schulden*, Bilanz oder Bilanzen gesprochen' [Since the end of the Third Reich, German *Schuld* (guilt) has been spoken about in discourse on *Schulden* (debts), budgetary balance or balances].[44] However, it is unclear why the girl feels that her body is the source of *Schuld*. Is it because of some action or experience that lies in the past? Or is her body itself something to be guilty about, a body that ought not to be the way it is? Both readings are possible, but the text provides no definitive answer. However, we might read the girl's childlike body as a way of absolving herself of *Schuld* if we consider that through her identity as a child she positions herself within a state of *Unschuld* [innocence]. By attempting to exist as a child, she attempts to reach a state of innocence, free of any guilt that may have attached to her in the past.

For the girl, maintaining a state of innocence means rejecting any memories of a past prior to her life in the children's home, and rejecting anything that suggests growing up. For example, she is intensely repelled by all matters involving sexuality, showing extreme responses that break through her otherwise passive exterior. Once when she sees a couple kissing she suddenly becomes unable to see:

> es schaut hin, aber es kann nichts mehr sehen, nicht nur das Paar nicht, sondern auch sonst nichts, nicht das Treppenhaus, nicht die hölzernen Stufen, nichts vor sich, nichts hinter sich, nichts. Es reißt die Augen auf, aber es sieht nichts. (p. 16)

> [she looks but sees nothing, it is not only the couple she cannot see, she sees nothing at all, not the stairwell, not the wooden steps, nothing in front of her and nothing behind, nothing. She opens her eyes as wide as she can, but she sees nothing. (p. 24)]

The extreme repetition is characteristic of Erpenbeck's text as a whole: stylistically the text reflects the girl's ponderous thought process and gives a sense of being locked into a repetitive present. In the passage above the emphasis is on the word 'nichts', on the way in which the girl blocks out everything so that nothing remains. The fact that she has nothing in front or behind her might be read as a comment on her situation as a whole: blind to the past and future, she falls into a state of blankness. By violently rejecting anything but a non-sexual, innocent, childish identity, the girl ends up blocking out everything around her. Yet where she differs from an ordinary child is in her determined lack of curiosity, as her internal life becomes as blank and empty as possible. For example, she lacks opinions of her own: 'Das Mädchen hat an der Stelle wo bei den anderen eine solche Meinung sitzt eine Leere' (p. 19) [In the girl's head, at the spot which in all the others is occupied by an opinion of this sort, there is only emptiness (p. 29)]. 'Leer' [empty] is an adjective applied to the girl a number of times in the novella, emphasizing her lack of subjectivity as well as her lack of past and future.

There are no direct descriptions of, or reflections on, the girl's past prior to arriving at the school. However, there are traces, moments of affective intensity which provide clues to the girl's attitudes, past relationships, and history, just as psychoanalysis reads affects as links to a buried past. For example, there are the notes the girl writes on scraps of paper, which she buries in an animal graveyard. These are all addressed from the girl's mother, and contain violent messages such as 'SEI NETT SONST WIRST DU ERSCHLAGEN. VIELE GRÜßE, DEINE MAMA' (58) [BE NICE, OR ELSE YOU'LL BE STRUCK DEAD. BEST WISHES — YOUR MAMA (p. 94)]. The messages seem to indicate a violent and traumatic past. According to Freud, the experience of trauma is one that is strong enough to shatter the protective shield of the self.[45] If trauma creates a rupture in personal identity, the traumatic experience could lead to a rejection of an entire past identity, and an attempt to distance oneself from an experience that resurfaces involuntarily, like the 'Wiederholungszwang' [repetition compulsion] of traumatic experience.[46]

Although the girl's notes hint at a past trauma, it is impossible to get any objective perspective on her past, since the notes intertwine with more recent events. For example there is the command: 'STECK DEINEN KOPF NICHT SO WEIT AUS DEM FENSTER, ER KÖNNTE SONST ABBRECHEN.' (p. 58) [DON'T STICK

YOUR HEAD SO FAR OUT OF THE WINDOW, OR ELSE IT MIGHT FALL OFF (p. 95)]. This recalls the words of a school caretaker earlier in the narrative, when he warned the girl about a window falling on her neck. Whatever the notes may suggest about the girl's past, they remain as forgotten, unexamined, ephemeral traces: 'niemand findet die Briefe, niemand faltet sie auseinander, und niemand macht die Mühe, sie zu lesen' (p. 58) [no one finds these letters, no one unfolds them, and no one makes the effort to read them (p. 94)].

The notes also denounce the child's body. One shows a very fat person who has been crossed out and the words 'HUNGER UND DURST' [HUNGER AND THIRST] written underneath (p. 58). In this way, the girl suggests that her fat body is an object of rejection, although it is unclear how to read the note. It could be read as a reference to a point in history in which there was hunger and thirst, for example during the war years. The note points to a disjunction between the girl's present fatness and the experience of hunger and thirst, which, read alongside the other notes, may be part of a traumatic past. The girl's fatness may even be seen as a response to wartime experience, as a bodily manifestation of the hoarding behaviour common in the post-war period, in which a release from rationing and the spectre of potential hardship spurred a desire to accumulate.[47] A psychological explanation of the girl's fatness is one that the text continually encourages, through linking the girl's bodily state to her obscure past with its lingering traces of traumatic experience.

In his study of the cultural history of obesity, Sander Gilman claims that over the twentieth century, and particularly during the post-war period, obesity became increasingly pathologized, rather than being viewed as primarily a matter of physiology.[48] In particular, obesity was often ascribed to family pathologies, influenced to a considerable extent by the work of psychologist Hilde Bruch, who explained childhood obesity as arising from an absence of love in the mother. In her influential study *Eating Disorders* of 1973, Bruch considers the case of a girl who was accidentally conceived during the war and who was initially rejected by her mother. Bruch reads the mother's later overfeeding of the girl as an attempt to expiate her guilt over her initial rejection.[49] A similar pathologization of obesity can be read in *Geschichte vom alten Kind*, in which the girl's physical compulsion to eat is linked to her psychological compulsion to forget. Her eating is also strategic, for it allows her to remain in a bodily form that provides the identity she desires. Bruch's model of obesity being caused by a mother's guilt may also inform a reading of Erpenbeck's text, since the notes that the girl writes, as though from her mother, suggest a disturbed mother–daughter relationship and a pathological condition of the mother as well as the daughter. According to Bruch's model, becoming fat is a way of attempting to negate the guilt of the past, and an attempt to make up for a previous lack of affection. In this way, the fat body becomes an embodiment of guilt and a past lack of love. In suggesting that the girl's body is a 'Schuld', and in linking the girl's fatness to a traumatic past, and particularly to a disturbing relationship with her mother, Erpenbeck draws upon a model of obesity as a pathological state.

Metamorphosis: Body as Costume

As in Kaschnitz's story, the final metamorphosis is a turning-point in the narrative, and can be read as a crisis of subjectivity and bodily existence. In Erpenbeck's text, the metamorphosis comes after the girl starts to realize the impossibility of living without individual agency. Previously she had mimicked the opinions and behaviour of the other children, but after she starts to notice the others as individuals with different personalities, this no longer becomes possible. She realizes that there is an individual will or intention that lies behind people's actions:

> Kaum hat man etwas getan, steht schon der Wille ganz nackt dahinter, und das ist dem Mädchen so außerordentlich Peinliches, das Mädchen will ja gerade nichts, es will das, was alle wollen, aber das gibt es nicht. Und in dem Moment, da ihm das klar wird, wird ihm auch klar, daß seine Kräfte es verlassen. (p. 57)
>
> [The moment you do anything at all, your volition can be seen standing naked behind it, and this the girl finds so utterly embarrassing that she chooses to want nothing. She wants what all the others want, but there is no such thing. And the moment she realizes this, she realizes also that her strength is waning. (p. 92)]

Once she realizes that her actions are grounded in individual will, and that collective will is impossible, she loses her ability to act altogether. Nancy Nobile has suggested that this passage may be a commentary on Erpenbeck's father's manuscript on free will, in which he discusses a form of pseudo-will, a will to submit to authority and evade responsibility, which culminates in a 'Zerstörungstrieb' [drive towards self-destruction].[50] This is the situation in which the girl finds herself when she realizes that she can act only as an individual or not at all.

Soon after this, the girl finds that she is unable to get out of bed (p. 59). She is taken to the school infirmary, where she has already spent much time, after being subject to an unusually large number of colds ('Verkühlungen', p. 32). The lexical choice 'Verkühlung' (rather than the more standard 'Erkältung'), also used in Kafka's *Verwandlung*, when Gregor interprets his transformation as a result of a 'Verkühlung', poses more scope for figurative meaning. The word opens up the possibility of emotional coldness and disengagement, which leads to a mental and physical process of shutting down. The girl resists completely shutting down by attempting to remain mentally in the school routine: 'So empfindet es am Montag von acht Uhr bis neun Uhr fünfunddreißig Englisch, mit einer kleinen Pause dazwischen' (p. 60) [And so on Monday from eight o'clock until nine thirty-five she feels English, with a little break in the middle (p. 98)]. However, eventually, she loses track: 'wie eine Blinde ist es an die Zeit gestoßen, da muß es weinen' (p. 61) [She has bumped up against time like a blind person, at this she has to weep (p. 100)]. The girl's attempt to remain temporally in the school environment fails. Eventually, she is taken out of the school and brought to a hospital.

In the hospital she remains in bed, in a state that has been described throughout using the lexis of death. The girl's body is 'irgendwie tot' (p. 31) [somehow dead, p. 50], is a 'riesiger atmenden Kadaver' (p. 62) [massive breathing cadaver, p. 101], and is referred to by the doctors as a 'Knochensack' (p. 63) [bag of bones, p. 102]. It is in this de-subjectified, immobile, deathlike state, that the girl begins to transform bodily. She has been placed on a strict diet, and as she loses weight, her skin begins to reveal a different identity: 'An seinem Körper beginnt die überflüssig gewordene Haut Falten zu schlagen, das Gesicht nimmt in ungeheuerer Weise Form an: Es wird ein erwachsenes Gesicht' (p. 63) [her now superfluous skin begins to droop in folds, and her face takes shape in a monstrous way: It is becoming the face of an adult (p. 104)].

As in Kaschnitz's story, the metamorphosis comes as a result of the girl being overweight. In 'Das dicke Kind', the girl's weight breaks the ice, which leads to the crisis that necessitates her metamorphosis and the revelation of her identity. In Erpenbeck's text, the forcible loss of weight leads to a bodily metamorphosis and a revelation of identity. However, the metamorphosis is not, as in Kaschnitz, a positive transformation, but a grotesque process. It is described through a lexis of horror and repulsion, as the word 'ungeheuer' [monstrous] suggests, a potential allusion to the 'ungeheueres Ungeziefer' in Kafka. There is also an emphasis on the unnatural nature of the transformation, described as an 'unnatürlich anmutender Alterungsprozeß' (p. 64) [unnatural [. . .] aging process, (p. 105)]. The narrator stresses the abnormality of her aging process through a comparison with rapid ageing disorders:

> Das Mädchen aber vergreist nicht vorzeitig und kontinuierlich, wie man es bei den altgeborenen kennt, deren Krankheit bekannt und beschrieben ist, sondern verharrt in seinem Älterwerden nach ungefähr zwei Wochen, als es das aussehen einer etwa dreißigjährige Frau erreicht hat. (p. 64)

> [the girl does not continue to age and turn grey prematurely as happens with those children who are born old, whose illness is well-known and has been studied, rather she ceases to age after approximately two weeks, when she has come to resemble a woman of thirty (p. 105)]

The girl's aging process is described using the negative verb 'vergreisen', which suggests extreme old age rather than the age of thirty. By contrasting the girl's ageing process to those with a 'known illness', the narrator insinuates that there is something abnormal taking place that does not fit known medical categories. The narrator also highlights a temporal difference in the two cases: the girl's unusually rapid ageing does not continue to progress indefinitely, but ends in a point of stasis. This point is described using 'verharren', a repetition of the 'ver-' prefix, with its negative connotations of something diverging from normality. As Nancy Nobile points out, the age the girl reaches is roughly the same as the Berlin Wall at its falling.[51] Nobile's parallel supports readings of the girl's experience as an allegory of the GDR. On this account, the girl's attempt at relinquishing herself to the collective, separating herself from the outside world, and even from the past, ultimately fails, just as the new and seemingly timeless socialist state gave way to the *Wende*. The age can also be read biographically as Erpenbeck's age when she wrote the novella after having conducted research by returning to school aged twenty-seven and passing herself off as a seventeen-year-old. In this way, we may read the metamorphosis both as personal experience, and as an index of the key historical rupture of late twentieth-century Germany, supported by the allegorical narrative style, for example in the girl's lack of a proper name.

The narrator's negative attitude towards the metamorphosis is particularly striking. The discourse of 'unnaturalness' culminates in outright condemnation:

> [w]as bisher als wirkliche Existenz wahrgenommen wird, [wird] nun als gezielte Täuschung erkennbar, als Maskerade, und weiter nichts. Das Mädchen, das nun kein Mädchen mehr ist, hat sein Kostüm abgelegt, die eigene Haut, und den Mummenschanz vor aller Augen beendet, so als sei seine Kindheit nichts als ein Scherz gewesen, in der Zeit herumzuspazieren wie in einem Garten, und in dieser Haltung liegt, bei aller Bescheidenheit, die das Mädchen an den Tag legt, und die es auch jetzt unverändert an den Tag legt, etwas Anstößiges, etwas Hochmütiges, den Lauf der Dinge Verachtendes, ja Gott Versuchendes. (p. 65)
>
> [what was previously perceived as a genuine existence now is seen to have been a calculated deception, a masquerade and nothing more. The girl, who is no longer a girl, has laid aside her costume, her own skin, and before everyone's eyes has put an end to this carnival performance, as if her childhood were nothing but a joke, as if it had been given to her to stroll up and down in time as in a garden, and in this attitude, despite all the modesty the girl displayed as a child and now continues to display unchanged, there is something offensive, something arrogant, a certain contempt for the natural course of things, even a challenge to God. (p. 106)]

The narrator stresses the radical change between the existence as a girl and the new identity through the temporal contrast of 'bisher' [previously] and 'nun' [now], as well as the contrast between perceived real identity and false identity. The narrator's claim that the girl's previous identity was a form of deception is stressed repeatedly ('gezielte Täuschung', 'Maskerade', 'Kostüm', 'Mummenschanz', 'Scherz'). These accusations suggest that the girl has set out to deceive, to subvert norms, to perform a false identity. In particular, the narrator is revolted by the girl's attempt to subvert time, to 'to stroll up and down in time as in a garden'. This is what leads to the final string of grandiose incriminations, culminating in 'Gott Versuchendes' [challenge to God]. The girl's subversion of time is interpreted as going against nature. This view is presented not just as the narrator's own, but as the general consensus of a 'weißbekitteltes Publikum' (p. 65) [lab-coated audience (p. 106)]. These representatives of science are gratified to see that the girl, now referred to as a 'Patientin', is now often crying, and that her 'Versuch, die Zeit anzuhalten ist fehlgeschlagen' (p. 65) [her attempt to stop time in its tracks has failed (p. 107)]. This statement might be read as a triumph of scientific inevitability, that time cannot be halted or reversed. Alternatively, if we read the text as a parable of the GDR, we might read this passage as West German gratification over the fall of communism. Most striking, however, is the narrator's treatment of the girl as object of condemnation.

The impact of the metamorphosis on the former girl is left open, and is not developed beyond what we learn in the final paragraph. In the final paragraph, a 'greise Dame' [grey-haired old lady] arrives, who is presented as the mother. Only two things are mentioned about her: that she is exhausted, and that her face is filled with shame. The mother's shame appears to reiterate the view of the hospital staff that the girl's ageing is an instance of 'Schamlosigkeit' (p. 64) [shamelessness], but beyond this her feelings and character remain enigmatic. When the former girl is introduced to the old woman, she responds with emotional disinterest: 'Ach du bist meine Mutter, sagt die, welche das Mädchen gewesen war, und öffnet sehr langsam die Augen, ich kann mich gar nicht mehr an dich erinnern' (p. 65) [Oh, are you my mother? Says the woman who used to be the girl, and very slowly she opens her eyes. I don't remember you at all (p. 107)]. With the final word 'erinnern' [remember] suggesting the breaking-off of memory, the girl's project of forgetting appears ultimately to have been successful. The conspicuous alteration of reference from 'das Mädchen' [the girl] to the cumbersome 'die, welche das Mädchen gewesen war' [woman who used to be the girl] emphasizes the radical nature of the change. The girl's words cited above come in the final line of the novella, and are one of the longest examples of reported speech from the girl. However, they do not represent a movement towards understanding, individual subjectivity, and recognition of one's past, as in Kaschnitz's story. Rather, they suggest that the past has been completely blocked, that the painful memories of the mother, of whom traces appeared earlier, have now been completely erased. By ending the novella at this point, the text suggests a blockage both of the past and of the future. Like the girl herself, the narrative remains locked in the present, resisting access to the past, resisting moving on.

Whereas in both texts, by Kaschnitz and Erpenbeck, the turning point is a metamorphosis that works as a final revelation of identity, the narrative trajectory is very different. In Kaschnitz's text, the metamorphosis signals a movement towards individual agency, self-understanding and recollection of the past, while in Erpenbeck's text the metamorphosis does not bring with it a change in the girl's behaviour, in our understanding of her behaviour and her past, and in the narrative attitude towards her. As readers, our access to her past is foreclosed, hinted at only through enigmatic, affective fragments, and a final sense of resolution and understanding is withheld.

Comparative Analysis

Both texts deal with key moments of life transition, using metamorphosis to starkly convey extreme physical or psychological change. The child becomes the site of metamorphosis, while the transformation happens through a process of re-encountering a repressed aspect of the self. In this sense, the metamorphosis acts as temporal subversion, challenging not only the unbroken continuation of the self through time, but also raising potential links to the breaks in socio-political continuity that have marked the authors' own experiences. In what follows, the core issues of the texts are set into a wider context to allow for a broader investigation of the relationship between literary metamorphosis and life transition, the challenge posed to personal continuity by difficult pasts, and the relationship between narratives of personal transformation and socio-political upheaval.

Sites of Transition: Metamorphic Bodies and Narratives

Both texts involve child figures apparently around the age of puberty who finally undergo a metamorphosis. In this way, metamorphosis is indexed to the major life transition from childhood to adulthood. Rather than explore this process as gradual development or maturation, as would be characteristic of a *Bildungsroman*, the process is represented as metamorphosis — as rapid change, but also as a turning point within the narrative and a moment of revelation. In Kaschnitz's story there is a psychological transformation at work, a change in attitude and understanding that is brought into conjunction with the physical motif of butterfly metamorphosis. In Erpenbeck, the metamorphosis is an extreme bodily transformation.

The short form of both texts lends itself well to the topic of metamorphosis. As a form, the short story often emphasizes moments of transition. Leonie Marx highlights the use of the short story in post-war Germany as a way of exploring processes of transition:

> zeitliche Übergänge bei Altersstufen (Kindheit, Jugend, Alter); räumliche Übergänge: Fahrt mit dem Schiff, Zug oder Flugzeug, Schauplätze am Rande der Stadt; psychische Übergänge: Mögliches und Unmögliches werden verschränkt, die Grenzen zwischen Traum und rational erfasster Wirklichkeit verwischen sich.[52]
>
> [temporal transitions at particular life stages (childhood, youth, old age); spatial transitions: travel by ship, train or plane, scenes at the edge of the city; psychological transitions: the possible and impossible become entangled, the boundaries between dream and rationally grasped reality become blurred.]

Marx's characterization is particularly apt in connection with 'Das dicke Kind', which involves not only the temporal transition of puberty, but also a spatial transition as the narrator follows the child out to a lake surrounded by woods. The lake is not only geographically removed from the earlier scene inside the narrator's house, but also temporally, for it is a location that existed in the narrator's childhood, but according to a neighbour, no longer exists. The personal transformation in Kaschnitz can thus be linked to a wider emphasis on transition. As is characteristic of post-war short stories, 'Das dicke Kind' remains open-ended, with the consequences of the metamorphosis yet to be played out.

As a novella, Erpenbeck's narrative centres on a single, strange incident — that of the protagonist passing herself off as a child. The girl's true identity is heavily hinted at throughout, but is only revealed in the metamorphosis at the end. The *Dingsymbol* of the novella can also be found in the form of the empty bucket suggesting the girl's empty past.

When metamorphosis is used to express life transition, it may be mapped onto moments of coming into or out of being. In both texts, the metamorphosis is described using the lexis of death, a central theme of the post-war short story.[53] In 'Das dicke Kind', the metamorphosis takes place during a struggle between life and death. The motif of the caterpillar becoming a butterfly can also be read, following classical mythology, as a symbol of the soul leaving the body upon death. As in the poetry of Nelly Sachs, metamorphosis is thus used as a move towards the unknown. At the same time, metamorphosis is also conceptualized as a birth, a breaking from a shell as well as a cocoon (p. 34). In this respect, the story differs from Erpenbeck's, in which the transformation is described as a form of death, but not as birth or rebirth with its hopeful, positive connotations. In *Geschichte vom alten Kind* the transformation does not bring new life, or the resurfacing of forgotten memories, but stasis and total repression.

Both metamorphoses follow a childlike state in which the child is configured as fat and inexpressive, her physical body marking a psychological process of repression. While Erpenbeck does not explicitly use a caterpillar motif, the metamorphosis in her text comes after a cocoon-like state of immobility. The fact that both texts continually refer to the girl with the neuter pronoun 'es' emphasizes the girl's childlike status, prior to the acquisition of adult identity, hence prefiguring the later metamorphosis. The metamorphosis is thus not only a transition into adulthood, but a move into womanhood after an ungendered child's identity and a state of pupa-like dormancy. Metamorphosis has frequently been configured as the beginning of gendered existence, and particularly, the beginning of female identity: for Nabokov, for example, 'the caterpillar is a *he*, the pupa an *it*, and the butterfly a *she*'.[54] However, in neither text is there a clear affirmation of the new, female, identity. Rather, the emphasis of the narrative is on the conditions that lead towards the metamorphosis, which results from a change in the child's fat, apathetic state.

Memory and the Construction of Identity

Strikingly, neither child is an idealized figure of innocence, but is an object of extreme narrative abjection, and is configured as lacking in independent subjectivity. Both accept their consignment to the lowest place in the hierarchy of family and school. Both figures reproduce a cultural stereotype in which fatness is linked to apathetic behaviour, and even to a propensity to repress undesirable past experiences, a process signalled visually through excess bodily fat.

The girls speak very little, giving out only the information required of them. Their muteness can be interpreted in varying ways. Anna Richards argues that silence and reticence in female literary characters has been variously characterized as a sign of patriarchal oppression and, conversely, as a more authentic, physical means of expression.[55] Both of these interpretations might be brought to bear on the texts. In Kaschnitz's story, the child's silence can be read as a sign of oppression, although an oppression stemming from her own sense of inadequacy in comparison to her sister. Her silence and reticence may also be read as a protective device to mask her unhappiness. Similarly, in Erpenbeck's story, the girl's silence and reticence might be read as a mask to hide her thoughts and feelings, but here, reticence is employed strategically to conceal the girl's real identity as an adult. While reticent behaviour may have its roots in structures of oppression, it also protects the figures from having their real feelings and identities uncovered.

Although the two children are depicted as passive and disengaged, their unemotional demeanour is broken by brief flashes of intense affect. In 'Das dicke Kind', the narrator only notices the girl's intense affect when recalling the encounter later on: 'ich glaube mich jetzt zu erinnern, das sein Gesicht sich in diesem Augenblick schmerzlich verzog. Aber ich achtete nicht darauf' (p. 28) [I think I now remember that her face crumpled up at this point. But I paid no attention to it]. Although the child claims that she does not care about being called

'Dicke', her face reveals a different story. By contrast, Erpenbeck's narrator does not reflect upon the girl's feelings. Nevertheless, the narrative reveals the girl's intense affects that surface when she observes sexual behaviour, and when she is taken out of school. Her physical expressions of affect, shown by being sick, dizzy, or crying, suggest that she is invested in her identity as a child, and is strongly repelled by any threat to that identity.

Intense flashes of affect reveal hidden aspects of the girls' identity. In *Geschichte vom alten Kind*, traces of the girl's past are suggested through the violent messages that the girl writes and throws away. Like the photograph in Kaschnitz's tale, the notes act as material links to a buried past, affective ties between the present and the intense, difficult feelings of the past. In Kaschnitz's text, it is not the child's affect, but the narrator's intense affect that points to an unwanted, repressed past that resurfaces through the figure of the child and is revealed through the metamorphosis.

The intensely negative attitude of the narrator is a source of narrative tension in both texts. The discrepancy between the child's neutral behaviour and the seemingly disproportionate and inappropriate narrative hatred make both texts particularly intriguing as they build up towards the final metamorphosis. The ending of 'Das dicke Kind' retrospectively explains the narrator's hatred of the child as intense self-criticism based on feelings of inadequacy rooted in the past. However, Erpenbeck leaves the identity of her narrator obscure, making it impossible to situate and explain the narrator's judgemental viewpoint. Crucially, the narrator's negative perspective of the girl's behaviour is presented as objective fact, without alternative or constructive interpretations, thus forcing the reader to work at understanding the girl's behaviour if they choose not to side with the narrator's condemnation. The narrative perspective in Erpenbeck's text contributes to the sense of enigma and blocked access to narrative understanding that Erpenbeck claims to have aimed for.

Forgetting one's past is one way of causing a break in personal identity, understood as the spatio-temporal continuity of a person. Both texts fashion the later metamorphosis as a result of an earlier rift in identity, with characters attempting to distance themselves from their pasts. When realization of the past identity resurfaces in 'Das dicke Kind', the scene of metamorphosis functions like a return of the repressed. By contrast, Erpenbeck's scene of bodily metamorphosis only serves to contrast with the lack of psychological change, as the girl progresses further with her project of forgetting to a point where the past appears completely repressed. The rift in personal identity that comes from forgetting negative experiences might be related to trauma as an extreme example of self-threatening experience. According to Freud (in his *Jenseits des Lustprinzips* [Beyond the Pleasure Principle]), the experience of trauma is one that shatters the protective shield of the self and leaves the self as fragments, unable to register or to integrate the traumatic event as part of history and identity.[56] The inability to integrate a past identity into a present identity is radically apparent in Erpenbeck's figure. The girl's behaviour may be the result of a traumatic experience, as hinted at through the fragmentary traces of a troubled past, but no clear traumatic source is ever revealed.

The ability to survive trauma is often related to the ability to incorporate the traumatic experience into one's life, to remember and to encompass it in a narrative that spans from one's past to one's present identity.[57] However, Erpenbeck's protagonist does not do this. In Kaschnitz's text, the narrator is able to recognize her past self and move towards greater understanding. In Erpenbeck's text, however, the girl does not recognize her past, as is made clear at the end, when she claims not to remember her mother. Whereas in Kaschnitz's text the metamorphosis brings with it a return of the repressed and a psychological transformation, in Erpenbeck's text the metamorphosis is only a bodily one, and the girl's past remains repressed.

The different narrative trajectories of the texts are striking: in 'Das dicke Kind' the metamorphosis brings with it a move towards understanding; in *Geschichte vom alten Kind*, the metamorphosis involves a move towards forgetting. In attempting to view this difference in a wider context, one might consider relating it to the changing ways of approaching the past that scholars have identified in German literature over the latter half of the twentieth century. Reiko Tachibana argues that autobiographical narratives are common in the immediate post-war period, whereas later writers dealing with the wartime past tend to use multi-layered narratives to emphasize even further the difficulties in grasping an objective vision of history. At the same time, there also tends to be an expansion of time and place in later narratives.[58] Certainly, Erpenbeck's story does not use an autobiographical narrator like Kaschnitz, but emphasizes to an extreme degree the lack of access to the girl's past. Erpenbeck's intention to create a narrative block might be related to the changing attitudes towards memory in the 1990s, particularly the memory debates around that time, in which the term 'Vergangenheitsbewältigung' came under pressure. According to Anne Fuchs and Mary Cosgrove, a need arose for the new term 'memory contests', which does not assume that there is a single, objective past that can be mastered but which 'embraces the idea that individuals and groups advance and edit competing stories about themselves that forge their changing sense of identity'.[59] An understanding of identities changing through the ways in which we integrate past behaviour and experience into present identities, or repress aspects of ourselves, allows for a new form of metamorphosis in late twentieth-century narratives: the metamorphic self as a heightened expression of the ruptures in identity caused by difficult pasts. While Erpenbeck's text is more sceptical than Kaschnitz's of the possibility of understanding and integrating the past into present identity, both texts suggest that historicity is an important part of identity, that having an identity requires recognizing one's past.

The Crisis of Metamorphosis: Personal and Public Upheavals

In both texts, metamorphosis comes as a final crisis in which the girl's identity is revealed. Unlike Kafka's *Die Verwandlung*, which begins with a metamorphosis, in Kaschnitz's and Erpenbeck's texts the consequences of the metamorphosis are left open, and the focus is instead on the lead-up to the metamorphosis. The metamorphosis thus acts as the resolution to an unsustainable situation, a situation in which knowledge of the child's true identity is suppressed, but must eventually come to the surface.

Like Kafka's metamorphosis, however, the metamorphosis is not freely chosen, but is forced upon the protagonists. The metamorphosis is a physical consequence of a physical state: the fatness that causes the ice to crack or the girl to be put on a diet. The metamorphosis is also a crisis in subjectivity, marking the point at which the child's apathetic behaviour becomes untenable. However, whereas Kaschnitz's child discovers a strong individual will in the attempt to escape from the ice, Erpenbeck's novella ends with the girl losing individual will completely. The differing trajectories, into and from self-awareness, are also apparent in the texts' use of mirrors, symbols of self-recognition: Erpenbeck's girl is happy to learn that there are no mirrors in the school, whereas Kaschnitz's narrator recognizes the child as herself when she sees her mirror image in the lake.

In metamorphosis the temporal process is one of crisis rather than gradual evolution. The use of metamorphosis in both texts opens up a model of history that is not one of progress, but one of crisis. History might be envisioned as Walter Benjamin described in 1940, in *Über den Begriff der Geschichte* [On the Concept of History], in which he discusses Paul Klee's painting *Angelus Novus*. Benjamin imagines Klee's painting as depicting the angel of history, his face towards the past, seeing not a chain of interlinked events, but a single catastrophe piling wreckage at his feet. Although the angel would like to put right the damage, he is propelled violently towards the future.[60] In both texts, the past creates wreckage that has not been put right, but which leaves a legacy of negative affect. The catastrophe that comes at the end of the texts is a result of suppressed knowledge of an unwanted, unresolved past being suddenly forced into the present day, either to be understood and overcome, as Kaschnitz optimistically suggests, or to be repressed once more.

If we see history not as an unbroken continuum but as a pile of wreckage then we have a model of history as something that cannot be grasped in its entirety. The engagement with a buried past in both texts reflects such a model of history as fragmentary. As a writer, Erpenbeck is particularly concerned with the impossibility of complete memory. For example, she comments in an interview: 'Was man im Moment erlebt, bleibt nur in Bruchstücken übrig, und die ganze Komplexität verschwindet in nichts' [What you experience in one moment remains only in fragments, and the whole complexity disappears into nothingness].[61] The idea of memory as broken fragments is apparent in the notes thrown away by the child in *Geschichte vom alten Kind*. In restricting access even to the fragments of the past, Erpenbeck's novella is more radically sceptical than Kaschnitz's story about the possibility of grasping an awareness and understanding of the past.

The metamorphoses of these texts are not straightforward allegories of historical rupture, but they may reflect an understanding of history that has been shaped by experience and awareness of the socio-political upheavals of twentieth-century Germany. As well as being a moment of personal crisis, the metamorphosis in both texts is also a temporal crisis, a moment in which the past erupts into the present, either to be understood or to be erased. For Erpenbeck, engagement with history means understanding the key moments of transition within individual lives. In an interview she comments:

> Mich interessiert Geschichte wahrscheinlich als Individualgeschichte, weil ich

glaube, dass Geschichte anders nicht wirklich von Menschen wahrzunehmen ist. Sowohl im Leben also auch in der Theorie interessiert es mich, wie Geschichte konkret wird, wo die Umbrüche wirklich zu sehen sind.[62]

[I am probably interested in history as individual history because I think that history cannot be understood by people in any other way. Both in life and in theory I'm interested in how history becomes concrete, where change can really be seen.]

The metamorphosis of *Geschichte vom alten Kind* is a particularly striking way of engaging with radical change. Erpenbeck's interest in the upheavals within individual lives can be related to her own socio-historical position, as she has pointed out:

Eines der Motive, die in jedem meiner Bücher auftauchen, ist die Frage, wie man mit verschwundener Vergangenheit umgeht. Wie ist das, wenn die Verbindung von der Kindheit zum Erwachsensein gekappt wird? In gewisser Weise bin ich froh, dass ich etwas so Wichtiges verloren habe [wie die DDR], es schärft den Blick für die Endlichkeit des menschlichen Lebens.[63]

[One of the motifs that turns up in all of my books is the question of how one deals with a past that has been lost. What does it mean for the link between childhood and adulthood to be cut off? In a way, I'm happy that I've lost something so important [as the GDR], it sharpens my awareness of the finite nature of human life]

Erpenbeck's interest in lost histories is particularly apparent in *Geschichte vom alten Kind*, which might be seen as an experiment in temporal rupture, cutting off not only the past, but foreclosing the future for a person who has completely relinquished her past identity. The extent to which we might read the story as a comment on the resistance to a future beyond the institutional environment of the GDR remains open. However, reading the refusal to grow up as a resistance to broader socio-political conditions has its literary precedents. For example, Günter Grass's *Die Blechtrommel* (1959) [The Tin Drum], in which the child protagonist stops growing aged three, has been interpreted as resistance to a threatening adult world troubled by war.[64] In Erpenbeck's novella it remains uncertain why the girl so strongly resists adulthood, thus inviting interpretations based on socio-political allegory as well as psychological speculation. But what is clear is that the girl's eventual metamorphosis is a consequence of her resistance to the past, and her refusal to grow up, which is eventually forced upon her physically. The two texts reveal differing attitudes towards the buried past that resurface through the metamorphosis: the focus upon the erasure of the past in Erpenbeck, and in Kaschnitz the prospect of self-understanding through the confrontation with one's past identity.

Conclusion

While my previous chapters dealt with human–animal transformation, in these texts metamorphosis takes the form of radical physical or psychological change indexed to the transition between childhood and adulthood. For Kaschnitz, the motif of butterfly metamorphosis helps to convey the profound nature of the change, configured as a form of rebirth that occurs during a life-or-death struggle. The process of metamorphosis in 'Das dicke Kind' can be read as an emergence of self-consciousness and individual will. This contrasts markedly with *Geschichte vom alten Kind*, in which the physical metamorphosis does not bring with it psychological change, but is accompanied by a continued process of forgetting and relinquishing subjectivity.

As they deal with the process leading up to metamorphosis, it is striking that both texts represent the child figure as fat, apathetic, and the object of narrative abjection. The texts draw on a cultural association between physical fatness and psychological repression, suggesting not only the buried affects of the children, but raising the enigma of the narrator's intense hatred of the child. If we read abjection as involved in the process of self-formation, then we can read the child figures as representing undesired aspects of the self.

Although the texts on the one hand use metamorphosis to mark a profound personal change and moment of anagnorisis, or recognition of identity, metamorphosis also serves as a temporal juncture in which a repressed past is forced to the surface. The past can be further repressed, as in Erpenbeck's text, but both texts suggest that acceptance of the undesirable aspects of past or present identity is necessary for self-understanding and the full subjecthood and agency without which individuals remain passive and lacking in will.

In dealing with unwanted pasts, the texts reflect the authors' concerns with the legacy of both personal experiences and the radical socio-political changes that they have lived through. For Kaschnitz, writing shortly after the Second World War, there is hope of accepting an unwanted past and reaffirming one's identity. For Erpenbeck, writing after the fall of the wall, there will always be blocks in our understanding of the past, and perhaps a desire to repress the past and to resist change that persists despite being subjected to metamorphosis.

Notes to Chapter 3

1. Darko Suvin and Carla Dente, 'Some Thoughts on Metamorphosis: An Interview with Darko Suvin', in *Proteus: The Language of Metamorphosis*, ed. by Carla Dente and others (Aldershot: Ashgate, 2005), pp. 13–22 (p. 18).
2. Cited in Marie Luise Kaschnitz, *Das dicke Kind und andere Erzählungen*, Text und Commentar, ed. by Asta-Maria Bachmann and Uwe Schweikert (Frankfurt a.M: Suhrkamp BasisBibliothek, 2002), p. 200.
3. Jenny Erpenbeck's father John Erpenbeck as well as two grandparents, Fritz Erpenbeck and Hedda Zinner, were novelists. Her mother, Doris Kilias, worked as a translator.
4. Both texts have been published in school editions: The edition of *Das dicke Kind* already cited is in the series 'Arbeitstexte für Schule und Studium'. The cited edition of *Geschichte vom alten Kind* is published by Büchners's 'Schulbibliothek der Moderne'.
5. Julia Kristeva, *Powers of Horror: An Essay on Abjection*, trans. by Leon S. Roudiez (New York: Columbia University Press, 1982).
6. Cited in Kaschnitz, *Das dicke Kind*, p. 227.
7. Elsbeth Pulver, *Marie Luise Kaschnitz* (Munich: C. H. Beck, 1984), p. 49.
8. Leonie Marx, *Die deutsche Kurzgeschichte* (Stuttgart: J. B. Metzler, 2005), p. 113.
9. Cited in Marx, *Die deutsche Kurzgeschichte*, p. 131.
10. Klaus Doderer, *Die Kurzgeschichte in Deutschland: Ihre Form und ihre Entwicklung* (Darmstadt: Wissenschaftliche Buchgesellschaft, 1977), p. 44.

11. Pulver, p. 50.
12. Sigmund Freud, *Gesammelte Werke*, ed. by Anna Freud, 18 vols (Frankfurt a.M.: Fischer, 1948–99), XII, 259.
13. William Ian Miller, *The Anatomy of Disgust* (Cambridge, MA: Harvard University Press, 1997), p. x.
14. Kristeva, p. 2.
15. Sander Gilman, *Obesity: The Biography* (Oxford: Oxford University Press, 2010), p. 5.
16. Ibid., p. 16.
17. Nikola Roßbach, ' "Gepeinigt von Phantasie": Autobiographische Kindheitsentwürfe bei Marie Luise Kaschnitz', in *'Für eine aufmerksamere und nachdenklichere Welt': Beiträge zu Marie Luise Kaschnitz*, ed. by Dirk Göttsche (Stuttgart and Weimar: Metzler, 2001), pp. 49–64 (p. 55).
18. Debbie Pinfold, *The Child's View of the Third Reich in German Literature: The Eye among the Blind* (Oxford: Oxford University Press, 2001), p. 15.
19. Roßbach, pp. 55–56.
20. Ibid., p. 53.
21. In a 1961 discussion with Horst Bieneck, Kaschnitz stated: 'Ja, das Kind bin ich selbst. Die Schwester ist meine Schwester Lonja, der See ist der Jungfernsee in Potsdam.' She also claimed: 'Ich halte die Geschichte "Das dicke Kind" für meine stärkste Erzählung, weil sie am kühnsten und grausamsten ist. So grausam zu sein konnte mir nur gelingen weil das Objekt dieser Grausamkeit ich selber war'. Cited in Kaschnitz, *Das dicke Kind*, p. 227.
22. Martin von Koppenfels, *Immune Erzähler: Flaubert und die Affektpoetik des modernen Romans* (Munich: Wilhelm Fink Verlag, 2007), pp. 10–13.
23. Ibid., pp. 37–102.
24. Tyler cites Elizabeth Abel's 'Reflections on the Female Double' (paper presented at the meeting of the Modern Language Association, 1980) in her chapter 'Revisionary Revelations: Women and Self-Worth in Two West-German Short Stories', in *The German Mosaic: Cultural and Linguistic Diversity in Society*, ed. by Carol Aisha Blackshire-Belay (Westport: Greenwood, 1994), pp. 63–71 (p. 66).
25. Cited in Pulver, p. 39.
26. Ibid., p. 38.
27. Deleuze, cited in Göttsche, ed., *'Für eine aufmerksamere und nachdenklichere Welt'*, p. 40.
28. Georg Wilhelm Friedrich Hegel, *Phänomenologie des Geistes*, in *Werke*, III, ed. by Eva Moldenhauer and Karl Markus Michel (Frankfurt a.M.: Suhrkamp, 1986), pp. 137–55 (esp. p. 145).
29. Jacques Lacan, 'Some Reflections on the Ego', *International Journal of Psychoanalysis*, 34 (1951), 11–17.
30. Tyler, p. 66.
31. E.g. Hans Werner Richter claimed in 1956 'daß die Vergangenheit vergessen und vergeben werden soll'. Cited in Stuart Parkes and John J. White, eds, *German Monitor: Gruppe 47 Fifty Years On* (Amsterdam: Rodopi, 1999), p. xv.
32. Marina Warner, *Fantastic Metamorphoses, Other Worlds: Ways of Telling the Self* (Oxford and New York: Oxford University Press, 2002), p. 19.
33. Pulver, p. 50.
34. Tobias Dennehy, 'Weise Einfältigkeit vom unteren Ende der Hierarchieleiter: Jenny Erpenbecks nüchterne und anstrengende "Geschichte vom alten Kind"', *Literaturkritik*, 2 (2000) <http://www.literaturkritik.de/public/rezension.php?rez_id=835> [accessed 4 December 2015].
35. Ibid.
36. Nancy Nobile, ' "So morgen wie heut": Time and Context in Jenny Erpenbeck's *Geschichte vom alten Kind*', *Gegenwartsliteratur*, II, ed. by Paul Michael Lützeler and Stephan K. Schneider (Tübingen: Stauffenburg, 2003), pp. 283–84.
37. Ibid., p. 285.
38. Jenny Erpenbeck, *The Old Child and The Book of Words*, trans. by Susan Bernofsky (London: Portabello, 2008), p. 5. All subsequent translations of *Die Geschichte vom alten Kind* are taken from this edition.
39. Isabel Wirtz, 'Jenny Erpenbeck: Geschichte vom alten Kind', *Bayrischer Rundfunk Online*, 28 December 2000.

40. Katie Jones, 'Ganz gewöhnlicher Ekel? Disgust and Body Motifs in Jenny Erpenbeck's *Geschichte vom alten Kind*. *Pushing at Boundaries: Approaches to Contemporary German Women Writers from Karen Duve to Jenny Erpenbeck*, ed. by Heike Bartel and Elizabeth Boa, German Monitor, 64 (Amsterdam and New York: Rodopi, 2006), pp. 119–34 (p. 127).
41. Nobile, p. 296.
42. W. G. Sebald, *Luftkrieg und Literatur: Mit einem Essay zu Alfred Andersch* (Munich: Hanser, 1999), p. 35.
43. Jakob Grimm and Wilhelm Grimm, *Kinder und Hausmärchen: Ausgabe letzter Hand*, ed. by Heinz Rölleke (Stuttgart: Reclam, 2009), p. 640.
44. Sigrid Weigel, 'Shylocks Wiederkehr: Die Verwandlung von Schuld in Schulden', in *Fünfzig Jahre danach: Zur Nachgeschichte des Nationalsozialismus*, ed. by Sigrid Weigel and Birgit R. Erdle (Zurich: VDF, 1996), pp. 165–92 (p. 170).
45. Freud, XIII, 29.
46. Ibid., 17.
47. Franz Severin Berger and Christiane Holler, *Trümmerfrauen: Alltag zwischen Hamstern und Hoffen* (Vienna: Ueberreuter, 1994).
48. Gilman, *Obesity*, p. 96.
49. Bruch, pp. 96–104.
50. Nobile, p. 303.
51. Ibid., p. 304.
52. Marx, *Die deutsche Kurzgeschichte*, p. 142.
53. Ibid.
54. Vladimir Nabokov, 'Nabokov's Butterflies, On Transformation', *The Atlantic Monthly*, 2854 (2000), 51–56 (p. 54).
55. Anna Richards, 'Suffering, Silence and the Female Voice in German Fiction around 1800', *Women in German Yearbook*, 18 (2002), 89–100 (p. 89).
56. Freud, XII, 29.
57. Susan Brison, *Aftermath: Violence and the Remaking of a Self* (Princeton, NJ: Princeton University Press, 2002), p. 68.
58. Reiko Tachibana, *Narrative as Counter-Memory* (New York: State University of New York Press, 1998), pp. 7–8.
59. Mary Cosgrove and Anne Fuchs, 'Introduction', in *Memory Contests: The Quest for Identity in Literature, Film and Discourse since 1990*, ed. by Anne Fuchs (Rochester, NY: Camden House, 2007), pp. 1–24 (p. 2).
60. Walter Benjamin, 'Über den Begriff der Geschichte', in *Gesammelte Schriften*, ed. by Rolf Tiedemann and Hermann Schweppenhäuser, I.2: *Abhandlungen 2* (Frankfurt a.M.: Suhrkamp, 1980), pp. 691–700 (pp. 697–98).
61. Jenny Erpenbeck, 'Erinnerung ist nur ein Blick zurück', derStandard.at, interview with Adalbert Reif, 6 Nov. 2009 (Printed edition 8 Nov.2009) <http://derstandard.at/1256744249081/Album-Interview-Erinnerung-ist-nur-ein-Blick-zurueck> [accessed 7 May 2015].
62. Jenny Erpenbeck, 'Man kann sich sein Verhältnis zur Vergangenheit nicht aussuchen', *Planet Interview*, interview with Maren Schuster and Martin Paul, 1 September 2008 <http://www.planet-interview.de/interviews/jenny-erpenbeck/34662/> [accessed 7 May 2015].
63. Erpenbeck, 'Erinnerung ist nur ein Blick zurück'.
64. E.g. Elizabeth Boa, 'Günter Grass and the German Gremlin', *German Life and Letters*, 23.2 (1970), pp. 144–51.

CHAPTER 4

❖

Metamorphoses under the Influence: Transformation Politics, Poetics, and Affects in Yoko Tawada

Movement and Metamorphosis

In what further ways may metamorphosis be configured in late twentieth- and early twenty-first-century literature? While the previous chapter was concerned with the temporality of metamorphosis, this chapter turns to the spatial dimensions of metamorphosis. In a context of increasing global mobility, both physical and virtual, the idea of identities 'on the move' becomes a familiar concept. Under such conditions, radical bodily transformations can become part of the process of exploring the shifts in identity that often accompany geographical movement and intercultural interaction. In German literature of this period, increased emphasis is placed on processes of movement and identity change. This is apparent in works such as Ilija Trojanow's bestselling novel *Der Weltensammler* [The Collector of Worlds] (2006), in which the main protagonist adopts a new identity in every place he lives. By raising questions about identity under conditions of cross-cultural movement, Trojanow's novel touches on concerns that have been central in narratives of metamorphosis.

Trojanow is also one of a growing number of authors of non-German background writing in German. Yoko Tawada might also be placed in this category, although unlike Trojanow as well as many German-Turkish writers, Tawada came to Germany not out of necessity but out of choice as a young adult. Born in Tokyo in 1960, Tawada first visited Germany in 1979 and moved to Hamburg in 1982, where she studied German literature. Her first literary publication, in 1987, was a collection of poetry and prose written in Japanese and translated into German by Peter Pörtner. Since then she has published a large number of literary works, written in both Japanese and German, including poetry, prose, stories, novels, plays, poetry accompanied by pianist Aki Takase, and an experimental film. She also completed a doctoral thesis under the supervision of Sigrid Weigel, which was published in 2000 under the title *Spielzeug und Sprachmagie in der europäischen Literatur: Eine ethnologische Poetologie* [Toys and Language Magic in European Literature: An Ethnological Poetology].[1] Many of Tawada's works have now been translated, but to a considerable extent she is still known in Germany and Japan on the basis of a separate, substantial oeuvre. Her works have been awarded literary prizes such as the Akutagawa Prize (1993), Japan's foremost prize for emerging writers; the Adelbert von Chamisso Prize (1996), awarded to authors of non-German-speaking background writing in German; and the Goethe Medal (2005), awarded to foreign personalities performing outstanding service to German intercultural relations. During the past couple of decades Tawada has become increasingly prominent in both German and Japanese studies, as well as in studies of transcultural literature.

Tawada's background is important for understanding the particular prominence she places on metamorphosis, and the specific forms that transformations take in her work. While Tawada writes in German as a non-native language (a mode of writing which has been termed exophonic[2]), her writing does not attempt assimilation, but becomes productive by playfully reflecting upon words, often opening up alternative meanings and associations, and thereby enacting transformations at a linguistic level. Transformation thus becomes part of the literary process, and not necessarily the unwelcome, forcibly enacted process explored in previous chapters. Moving across boundaries, both bodily boundaries as well as geographical and linguistic boundaries, opens up potential for new ways of thinking and acting.

This chapter investigates the new ways of thinking about metamorphosis offered by Tawada's work, and considers the understanding of changing identity and subjectivity that emerges. The increasingly global and multicultural conditions of the late twentieth century are important factors in understanding the changing forms of subjectivity in this period. For example, in her analysis of Tawada's texts, Leslie Adelson has drawn attention to Doris Bachmann-Medick's suggestion that scholars need to pay more refined critical attention to specific 'forms of movement' in order to understand cultural transformations in subjectivity in this period. Bachmann-Medick characterizes a paradigmatic shift in European cultures of subjectivity around the year 2000, as social life is transformed by diverse new technologies of 'spatial appropriation'.[3] This chapter aims to investigate the relationship between changing forms of subjectivity and movement, though not with exclusive focus on geographical movement (which has been the subject of several studies of Tawada[4]), but rather on movement of the body, as corporeal transformation, and of the affects, as emotional 'movement'. I also investigate the link between bodily transformation and the transformation of literary and theoretical texts, which is important within Tawada's literary production. In particular, I return to Hoffmann and Kafka, whose work Tawada discusses in *Spielzeug und Sprachmagie*, and draws upon intertextually in her literary work. Tawada's engagement with, and even transformation of, some of the metamorphosis texts will be explored with attention to new forms of subjectivity and affective practices in the late twentieth century.[5]

Although many of Tawada's works deal with transformation, including extraordinary corporeal transformations, this chapter focuses primarily on *Opium für Ovid: Ein Kopfkissenbuch von 22 Frauen* [Opium for Ovid: A Pillow Book of 22 Women], published in 2000. Written first in German, and afterwards translated by Tawada into Japanese (*Henshin no tame no opiumu*, 2001), *Opium für Ovid* is a collection of twenty-two intertwined stories that foreground bodily transformation. Ovid's *Metamorphoses* turn up in new guises, with the twenty-two chapters named after women from Ovid's tales, though these women live in a present-day city not unlike Hamburg. Their narratives link loosely to the women's mythological namesakes, implicating them in bodily transformations that range from the mythical and surreal to everyday changes such as ageing or illness. Many of the transformations are made possible through the use of material substances, such as the opium of the title.

I also draw on some of Tawada's other works, written around the end of the twentieth century, including her three poetics lectures *Verwandlungen* [Transformations] given in Tübingen in 1997–98. In these she explores what it is to speak a foreign language ('Stimme eines Vogels oder das Problem der Fremdheit' [Voice of a Bird or the Problem of the Foreign]), translation ('Schrift einer Schildkröte oder das Problem der Übersetzung' [Writing of a Tortoise or the Problem of Translation]), and transformation ('Gesicht eines Fisches oder das Problem der Verwandlung' [Face of a Fish or the Problem of Transformation]). I also draw upon *Spielzeug und Sprachmagie* (2000) to explore Tawada's interest in metamorphosis.

Transformation Politics

Social and Political Transformations of Bodies in 'Opium für Ovid'

Given the central role of metamorphosis and other forms of transformation (such as textual or linguistic transformations) in Tawada's texts,[6] it is unsurprising that scholarship on Tawada's work often focuses on Tawada's destabilizing of subject positions.[7] In summarizing the main approaches to Tawada's work, Susan Anderson includes examinations of heterogeneous identities and new subject positions as one major area of focus along with other approaches that foreground the creative exploration of language, culture, and (mis-)communication, being foreign, the strangeness of language, exophony, and criticisms of dualistic thinking about cultural difference.[8] Leslie Adelson also provides an overview of Tawada scholarship, in which she identifies three major trajectories: studies that relate Tawada's work to contemporary contexts of cultural globalization, studies drawing upon the historical traditions of surrealist aesthetics, and recent work on the social labour of literary translation.[9]

This chapter builds upon existing scholarship by situating Tawada's use of metamorphosis in connection to existing literary traditions of metamorphosis. While studies of Tawada often link the destabilizing of identities and subject positions to contemporary contexts of postmodernism or cultural globalization, the literary trope of metamorphosis has, at least since as far back as the Romantic texts I begin with, been used to explore unstable identities. However, the literary engagement with metamorphic bodies and identities may take specific new forms in the late twentieth century. In particular, the playful treatment of metamorphosis in Tawada's texts marks out a territory that differs from some of the previous metamorphosis texts I examined, in which the metamorphosis is a forcibly enacted, unwelcome transition. In Tawada's *Opium für Ovid*, transformations happen on multiple levels, both as bodily processes (ageing, injury, surreal and mythological transformations) as well as literary ones (rewriting texts, linguistic creativity).

The twenty-two chapters of *Opium für Ovid* foreground experiences of bodily change in twenty-two women protagonists. The first chapter begins with Leda, whose arms are paralysed and who refuses to show her naked body to anyone. The narrator reflects upon attitudes towards bodily change, asking: 'Je älter desto schöner empfindet man eine Teekanne, ein Buch und ein Haus. Warum soll das bei Menschen anders sein' (p. 9) [The older a teapot, a book and a house become, the more beautiful one finds them. Why should that be different with people]. As well as ordinary temporal change, bodies are also altered as a result of social and political changes. These include changes brought about through tax reforms, changes in health insurance policies or city council regulations. The impact such social and political changes have on bodily experience is a major issue in *Opium für Ovid*, though critical studies have said little about the social and political shaping of identities and bodies, instead foregrounding Tawada's use of myth,[10] or her destabilizing of identity with reference to language and style.[11] For example, in the first chapter, a controversial new law is described:

> Die Krankenkasse müsse nicht mehr die Kosten für medizinische Behandlungen des Unterleibs übernehmen. Ein Spezialist für soziale Wandlungen sagte im Radio, in Zukunft würden öfter Transplantationen vorkommen, bei denen Unterleibsorgane auf den Oberleib übertragen würden. (p. 9)
>
> [The health insurance company no longer needs to cover the costs of medical treatments of the lower body. A specialist for social change said in the radio that in the future, transplants of organs from the lower to the upper body would become more common.]

Tawada explores social change in an absurd surrealist scenario that leads to bizarre bodily transformation. The surrealist style that Tawada employs here provokes questions about what 'normal' social and bodily change would be. Surrealist literature has much in common with the fantastic, the genre of many tales of metamorphosis. However, whereas the protagonist of a fantastic text characteristically hesitates over the reality of a situation, the protagonist in a surrealist text accepts the extraordinary happenings with bland indifference.[12] Whereas the fantastic calls into question the nature of reality, the surrealist technique that Tawada employs provokes questions about normality, revealing the absurd and arbitrary basis of some social norms and practices.[13]

A further example in *Opium für Ovid* is the introduction of a tax on hair, after a club of hamster lovers complains about paying the same mammal tax as for a German shepherd dog. To avoid discrimination against fat people, the finance office introduces a tax, not on body surface, but on *haired* body surface. This leads to a fashion for hairy furniture, watches, and credit cards for those who can afford it (made possible through genetic technology), while impoverished students shave themselves completely (pp. 38–40). This episode playfully raises issues of transformation through new bio-technological possibilities that were in the public eye at the time. In her discussion of a text in which Tawada writes about a typewriter as a 'Sprachmutter' ['language mother', a play on 'mother tongue'],[14] Yasemin Yıldız links Tawada's 'crossing of technology and organic body' to Donna Haraway's feminist approach to technoscience, stressing Haraway's emphasis on 'rethinking relation as neither purely organic, nor purely mechanical'.[15] The hair tax episode also suggests ways in which bodies and technologies intertwine, as bodies, objects, behaviours, and fashions are affected and reconfigured not only through biotechnology, but as a result of political and social changes. The transformations that happen in Tawada's text are not caused by mysterious or unknown forces, as is often the case in tales of metamorphosis, but are anchored in the social world, amongst the constant social changes that affect bodily attitudes and result in bodily transformations.

In *Opium für Ovid* bodily transformations happen through organic processes (such as ageing), through medical, technological, and social processes, and, in particular, through material substances such as hormones and drugs. The use of opium as a central motif in the book serves to emphasize the physical and material means by which transformations of bodies and feelings are brought about. Opium not only acts upon the body, causing a state of intoxication or 'Rausch', in which transformations occur, but it is also implicated in political power relationships in the context of the opium wars, which are referenced in the book. In one passage, a student tells Limnaea about the Opium Wars, saying that England was once dependent on China for tea, but managed to emancipate itself through forcing India to produce tea. However, he claims, England was not content with escaping dependence, but also wanted to dominate China:

> England hatte wieder eine geniale Idee: Wer unter Tee gelitten hat, kann die Teekultur überspitzen und damit zurückschlagen. Das ist beinahe eine postkolonialistische Strategie. Und was wäre die Überspitzung der Teekultur? Die Opiumpolitik! England zwang Indien, Opium zu produzieren und verkaufte es für viel Geld an China. Opium war verdammt teuer und unwiderstehlich. (p. 130)

> [England had another ingenious idea: Whoever has suffered from tea can go one better than tea culture and so strike back. That's almost a postcolonial strategy. And what would be one better than tea culture? Opium politics! England forced India to produce opium and sold it to China for a lot of money. Opium was bloody expensive and irresistible.]

In this description of opium politics, dependence at a political level is linked to dependence at an individual, bodily level on substances such as tea or opium. England not only resists dependence, but also reverses the direction of dependence. Thus, the material substances that affect and transform bodies are used in political power struggles to create relations of dependence. The postcolonial gestures that have been identified in Tawada's work[16] belong to Tawada's broader interest in the political power relationships that lead to transformations at a social and individual level.

Narrative Contingency: The Metamorphic Text

Given that the characters in *Opium für Ovid* are continually subject to transformation, there is no coherent, developing plot, but rather a series of loosely related episodes. The structure of the narrative gives rise to some interpretative difficulties in situating the figures and understanding their relation to one another. In particular, the narrator is difficult to locate. Sometimes she situates herself as author of the characters, for example, in discussing Iuno she asserts 'Ich bin ihre Autorin' (p. 201) [I am her author]. She also positions the characters as products of her imagination, for example: 'In meiner Puppenstube arbeitet die Puppe Leda als Apothekerin' (p. 21) [In my puppet theatre, the puppet Leda works as a chemist]. Leda is described as a 'Puppe', which can mean both a 'puppet', the narrator's toy, or a 'pupa', a creature that will undergo metamorphosis. As well as claiming to be the author of the characters, however, the narrator also interacts with them. For example, she tells Coronis that she admires her literature (p. 89).

The slippage between the roles of creator and subject, as well as the narrator's close ties with the metamorphic characters, is a common feature of narratives of metamorphosis. Often the writer is both observer of transformation and part of the transformation. As Nabokov put it, the writer is both the entomologist and the butterfly.[17] Tawada makes a similar claim in her *Verwandlungen* lectures when she says that whoever speaks a foreign language is an ornithologist and a bird in the same person (p. 22). Observing processes of transformation, whether physical or linguistic, happens alongside feeling and experiencing such processes. Close experiential narration is a central feature of texts such as Kafka's *Die Verwandlung*, and can be seen as part of the broader project of transformation, which the narrator also undergoes while becoming involved in the story. In *Opium für Ovid*, the narrator transforms into a character within the book, while the book is also characterized as a work of fiction, of which she is the author.

The positioning of the characters as the narrator's imagined play-figures gives the narrative a sense of contingency. The changeability of the narrative is underscored through the narrator's metatextual reflections, such as the remark: 'Auf einmal fiel mir ein, das sich Latona und Scylla nie kennengelernt hatten. Die hier beschriebene Szene muß also aus dem Text gestrichen werden' (p. 36) [Suddenly I realized that Latona and Scylla had never met. The scene described here will have to be crossed out of the text]. In this way, the text itself becomes subject to change and transformation. Moreover, it is not only the narrator who comments on and alters the narrative, but also the characters themselves. For example, in a scene where Salamacis is talking to her mother, Salamacis suddenly realizes that her mother no longer exists (p. 67). This means that the scene cannot have happened in reality, but only in the imagination of the character Salamacis. Even the characters do not live within a stable reality but within a contingent narrative.

The uncertain narrative positioning has led to some interpretative attempts to understand the status of the narrator and characters. In particular, it has been suggested that the characters might be considered not only as figments of the narrator's imagination but as fragments of a single persona.[18] This view is partly supported by the narrator being injured in a traffic accident in the second chapter, which causes pain followed by a sensation that the narrator can only describe 'mit dem ganz unpassenden Wort Glück' (p. 19) [With the quite inappropriate word 'happiness']. Theodore Ziolkowski has suggested that the narrator's drug-like state akin to happiness is central to understanding the status of the characters, since it raises the possibility that the characters are products of the narrator's hallucinations following the accident (p. 217). The text does not confirm this interpretation, but there are suggestions that the narratives might be considered as the narrator's dreams. For example, the narrator claims that she sends her messenger 'Prinz Taschenlampe' [prince torch] to a different woman every night (p. 148). The idea of sending a messenger to the characters, whose names are all to be found in Ovid's *Metamorphoses*, suggests that the characters are not the narrator's conscious creations, but figures encountered in a dream-like state. If the narratives of the twenty-two women are dreams, this raises the question of where the narrator is situated. Is she to be understood as belonging to an external real world, or is she, as she speculates at one point 'in einer Schlafblase eines Menschen, den ich noch nicht kenne?'(p. 71) [in a sleep bubble of a person I don't yet know]. It is not clear that there is an external reality outside of the contingent, changeable dream-like realm of the text; therefore there is no basis with which to distinguish between dream and reality.

From arguing that the characters are dreamed-up constructs of the narrator, a number of commentators take the further step to say that the characters are all aspects of the author-narrator's personality. For example, Ziolkowski writes that 'all the persons in these scenes, despite their Ovidean names and traits, are inventions of the nameless author, who uses them to explore and project aspects of her own personality'.[19] The image of the broken vessel, a reference to Walter Benjamin's 'Die Aufgabe des Übersetzers' [The Task of the Translator], has also been used as a way of understanding the relationship between narrator and characters.[20] On such an account, the characters are to be thought of as shards of a single persona, that of the narrator.

Kari van Dijk's argument that the twenty-two characters are fragments of a single persona also draws on the significance of the number twenty-two as a number suggesting transformation. Van Dijk points out that Tawada writes of the number two in *Spielzeug und Sprachmagie* as revealing 'eine unübersehbare Spur der Verwandlung' [an unmistakable trace of transformation].[21] However, if we look at Tawada's sentence more closely, Tawada is actually writing of the two apprentices in Kafka's story 'Blumfeld, ein ältere Junggeselle' [Blumfeld, an old Bachelor] revealing, because of the fact that there are two of them, a trace of having been transformed from balls: 'Die Zahl zwei bildet eine unübersehbare Spur der Verwandlung der zwei Bälle in den zwei Praktikanten' (p. 146) [The number two forms an unmistakable trace of the transformation of the two balls into the two apprentices]. In this sentence Tawada is not making a generic claim about the significance of the number two, but only about its significance in this textual passage. However, elsewhere in her dissertation, as van Dijk also points out, Tawada cites a passage from Daniela Hodrová's *Città Dolente*, in which Tawada claims that the number two contains 'das Prinzip der Teilung, der Vielzahl und

Unterscheidung, der Stofflichkeit und der Verwandlung' [the principle of division, multiplicity, difference, materiality, and transformation].[22] If we can relate Tawada's symbolism of the number two to the choice to include twenty-two characters, then the number of women becomes associated with the idea of transformation. The twenty-two women might also be brought into connection with Kafka's text 'Elf Söhne' [Eleven Sons], which alludes to the eleven tales in the collection. As in 'Elf Söhne', the individual chapters of Tawada's book are also the twenty-two characters, though Tawada does not configure these as sons or even as daughters, but as women, thereby resisting the notion of family relationship.

However, the number twenty-two carries slightly different connotations from the number two. While two suggests binaries, and would be applicable to a model of metamorphosis based on the idea of one thing becoming another thing (as is commonly the case in Kafka), the number twenty-two suggests multiplicity. Moreover, as van Dijk fails to mention, Tawada also writes specifically about the number twenty-two in *Spielzeug und Sprachmagie*. When discussing the golem, a figure from the Jewish literary tradition that is created from inanimate matter, Tawada references the twelfth-century Hebrew commentary on 'Safer Ezra' [Book of Creation], in which it is explained that the soul is created through the combination of the twenty-two letters in the alphabet.[23] The idea of the soul being created from twenty-two letters supports the idea that the twenty-two women are all parts of a single soul.[24] To follow this analogy, the twenty-two women in the narrative give rise to a soul, but on their own they have no individual souls. Like the golem, the Ovidean characters are brought to life through being placed together in Tawada's narrative. Moreover, by likening the soul to an alphabet, the idea arises that the soul is constituted through language. The importance of language as a means of creating the self is suggested in other passages in the book, such as: 'Das Ich, das eine Melodie hört, das Ich, das sie nachspielt, das Ich, das von einem Musikerleben träumt, das Ich, das von diesem Traum erzählt. Das Ich vermehrt sich täglich, in jedem Satz mindestens eine neue Geburt' (p. 14) [The I that hears a melody, the I that plays it back, the I that dreams of being a musician, the I that tells of this dream. The I increases daily, in every sentence at least one new birth]. It is only in the act of speaking that the 'Ich' emerges. However, the 'Ich' is not like an unchanging soul, but is constantly occupying new subject positions depending on what activities the person is engaged in.

To return to the interpretation that the characters are projections of a single persona (Ziolkowski), fragments of a whole (van Dijk), or manifestations of a single 'Ich' (Cho-Sobotka), it will, however, be necessary to take issue with the idea of there existing a single persona, single whole, single 'Ich', or single soul in this text. Not only does Tawada undercut the notion of the single 'Ich' and the idea of the narrator as occupying a stable position, but she also undercuts the idea of the text as finished or whole. Neither the text nor the narrator is a singular entity but they each carry metamorphic qualities.

Another problem with the argument that the characters are manifestations of a single persona is that this claim elides the physical and material distinctions between the characters. In *Opium für Ovid*, the characters are distinct individuals, with specific names, ages, jobs, bodily forms, interests, family circumstances, experiences, opinions, and personalities. To say that they are all manifestations of the same persona is to accept this persona as multiple at a very material level. We might ask, therefore, in what sense the characters can be fragments of a single persona. Physically, the characters are clearly different from one another. However, they could be seen as part of the narrator to the extent that they are all products of her imagination. Yet I would argue that it is a mistake to attempt to trace the characters back to a single identity, such as that of the narrator or author, for in *Opium für Ovid* it is not possible to find a single, clearly situated identity. If the characters are all part of a single soul, as the number twenty-two suggests, then the soul must be understood as a heterogeneous entity, just as an alphabet is made up of different letters.

Rather than attempting to trace the characters back to a single identity, it would be worth considering other models of relatedness. For example, the narrator and characters could be said to link together in the manner of a rhizome, an important image in the philosophy of Deleuze, who used it to conceptualize relationships that are multidirectional, rather than a root that goes straight down. Such a concept fits well with the way in which *Opium für Ovid* challenges structures of political dependence and dependence on material substances, as discussed earlier. Rhizomes are even referenced briefly in *Opium für Ovid* when Pomona is seduced through scents that are 'durch Rhizome miteinander verbunden, wie zusammengewachsene Männerbeine' (p. 165) [connected by rhizomes, like men's legs that have grown together]. The idea of individual scents being linked via rhizomes could be read as a nod towards the rhizomatic structure of the narrative more broadly. Instead of a linear, chronological narrative and plot, the disjointed scenes and reflections within the chapters are tied together by interlinking themes and motifs. The multi-directional and multi-relational structure at work in the narrative as a whole is also central to understanding Tawada's model of metamorphosis, which differs from binary models that trace the transformation of one single thing to another single thing. Rhizomes can also be used to conceptualize models of identity that pose challenges to ideas of rootedness, instead offering what Édouard Glissant, taking up Deleuze's image of the rhizome, calls a 'poetics of relation', in which identities are extended through multiple relationships.[25] In *Opium für Ovid* it is not only the narrative structure and the interpersonal relationships that are rhizomatic, but the model of identity and metamorphosis, including the metamorphic process of writing.

Textual Transformations: Ovid, Hoffmann, Kafka

Tawada's work draws on a rich source of literary and theoretical material, including some of the metamorphosis texts encountered in my previous chapters. Through dialogue with other tales of metamorphosis, Tawada is able to articulate her own understanding of what it means to transform. *Opium für Ovid* has as its most obvious intertext Ovid's *Metamorphoses*, a link that has been often discussed.[26] Tawada engages with Ovid's work and characters in a way that allows for critique and transformation of the classical material.

Each of the twenty-two chapters is named after a woman who features in Ovid's *Metamorphoses*, but who is now situated in a contemporary context. The metamorphoses in Ovid's stories are frequently alluded to, but have often been altered. For example, the first chapter, 'Leda', recalls Ovid's story of Zeus becoming a swan to seduce Leda. Allusions to Ovid's story can be found in lexical choices such 'es ist *federleicht*, pünktlich aus dem Haus zu gehen' [it's *easy/light as a feather* to leave the house on time] or 'Als Leda zwanzig war, *schwamm* sie durch die Menschenmenge' [When Leda was twenty, she *swam* through the crowds] (p. 10, my emphases). In Tawada's text, however, it is Leda who appears as the swan, thereby reversing the mythic power dynamic, and making Leda the subject undergoing transformation, as is the case with all the twenty-two women in Tawada's text.

The suggestion of Leda as a swan is reinforced when the narrator envisions Leda, whose arms are paralysed, in the bathtub: 'Vielleicht saß sie im Wasser mit ausgebreiteten Flügeln, die kraftlos an den Rändern der Badewanne lagen. Mit den Schnabel reinigte sie die wasserdichten cremeweißen Federn' (p. 9) [Perhaps she lay in the bathtub with wings spread out. With her beak she cleaned her watertight creamy white feathers]. Here a physical characteristic (Leda's paralysis) gives rise to the comparison, which takes place through references to the bodily features of a swan. The adverb 'vielleicht' [perhaps] makes the characterization as a swan hypothetical, a construct of the narrator, who is not able to observe the scene directly, since it is earlier claimed that Leda refuses to show her naked body to anyone. Leda is thus envisioned as a swan, but whether we should read the description of Leda as a swan as metaphorical or literal is itself called into question through metatextual reflections. For example, in the following chapter Daphne discusses a 'spannendes Buch' [an exciting book], referring to the book by Marx, which has unexpectedly replaced the book of poetry she had put into her bag. Without specifying which author she is referring to, Daphne claims: 'Ein Autor, der viel von der Materialität der Welt hält, kann keine Metaphern benutzen. Wenn er schreiben würde, seine Frau sei ein Schwan, dann hieße es, daß sie wirklich ein Schwan ist' (p. 30) [An author who places a lot of importance on the materiality of the world cannot use metaphors. If he should write that his wife is swan, that means that she really is a swan]. Daphne's statement could be applied to the author Tawada, whose book *Opium für Ovid* emphasizes materiality, though it could also be applied to a hybrid Marx–Ovid, or to Kafka, another writer who was famously sceptical of metaphor.

The problem of how to read metamorphosis — as metaphor or as literal — is a problem raised not only by Kafka's *Verwandlung*, as discussed in chapter 2, but by metamorphosis in literature more generally. In Tawada's text, the transformations are not offered as metaphors, but neither are they to be taken literally, for there is always some distancing technique preventing this, such as the adjective 'vielleicht' in the passage above. Rather than depicting transformations that we might read as literal, transformation is alluded to suggestively through allusions to Ovid's *Metamorphoses*, or through the women's characteristics and behaviour. For example, Daphne does not play tennis but 'spielt die Rolle einer Birke, die an der Ecke eines Tennisplatzes steht' (p. 33) [plays the role of a birch tree that stands on the edge of the tennis court]. Daphne also imagines her skin as a protective rind (p. 33) and would rather be an 'Eiche' [oak] than an 'Eichhörnchen' [squirrel] (p. 32). Daphne imagines herself in terms that lexically allude to Ovid's story, but not always faithfully, for whereas Ovid has Daphne transform into a laurel tree, Tawada's Daphne is imagined as various different trees.

Ovid's *Metamorphoses* contrast starkly with Kafka's *Die Verwandlung* in that they tell of numerous transformations rather than a one-off exceptional event. Tawada's book follows the Ovidean model, with characters whose behaviour not only recalls the transformations of their mythic namesakes, but who also transform through ageing, drug-use, dressing-up and acting, or as a result of social and political changes. As in Ovid, transformability is a property of all things, an aspect that Tawada emphasizes in her third *Verwandlungen* lecture:

> In Ovids 'Metamorphosen' wird im ersten Kapitel auf eine Weise von der Entstehung der Welt erzählt, die gleichzeitig eine Erklärung für die Verwandelbarkeit der einzelne Wesen ist. Die Vorstellung, daß ein Wesen sich überhaupt in ein anderes verwandeln kann, stammt aus der Erinnerung an die Zeit in der die Gestalten der Lebewesen und der Dinge noch nicht bestimmt waren. (p. 54)

> [In Ovid's *Metamorphoses*, the first chapter tells of the formation of the world in a way that is also an explanation of the transformability of individual beings. The whole idea that a being can transform into another comes from the memory of a time in which the forms of living beings and things were not yet determined.]

According to Tawada, the concept of metamorphosis originates in the animistic idea of living beings and objects as categories that are not fully separate and that contain the possibility of moving from one to the other. The idea of animistic transformation is central within Tawada's poetics, and something that she highlights in discussing the work of E. T. A. Hoffmann. As well as focusing on Hoffmann's puppets and animate toys in *Spielzeug und Sprachmagie*, she discusses Hoffmann's story 'Das fremde Kind' [The Strange Child] in her first *Verwandlungen* lecture (entitled 'Stimme eines Vogels, oder das Problem der Fremdheit'). In 'Das Fremde Kind' birds compete with the music of an automated puppet, and their song brings things to life. Tawada compares the voice of birds in this story with the linguistic capacity to bring things to life. Through regarding the boundaries between living things, objects and words as permeable, transformation becomes possible. Like Hoffmann, Tawada's literary imagination often works through destabilizing boundaries between things, allowing objects and figures to be brought to life or transformed.

Tawada also explores objects coming to life in Kafka's tales. In *Spielzeug und Sprachmagie* she discusses Kafka's 'Blumfeld, ein älterer Junggeselle', in which Blumfeld unexpectedly finds two balls bouncing independently around his room. Tawada considers what could account for the balls' appearance in the story, and argues that two processes are at work. First, when Blumfeld is walking upstairs to his room he is thinking about a dog and its 'Bellen' [barking], which raises an acoustic association with 'Bällen' [balls]. Secondly, Tawada claims, a metonymic process is at work based on dogs liking to play with balls (p. 140). In this way, Kafka's narrative comes about through linguistic associations, a process that is also at work in *Die Verwandlung*, as the rich connotations of the word 'Ungeziefer' raise the possibility of Gregor actually becoming an 'Ungeziefer'. In highlighting the linguistic inspiration behind Kafka's literary work, Tawada draws attention to the second major topic of her dissertation, 'Sprachmagie' [language magic]. Like the texts she examines, Tawada's own literary work enacts a form of language magic, using language to provoke new associations that direct the narrative and that generate transformation.

In works by both Hoffmann and Kafka, transformation also involves animals taking on human qualities, particularly the capacity for linguistic communication. In Hoffmann's *Lebens-Ansichten des Katers Murr* or Kafka's 'Forschungen eines Hundes' animals narrate their own biographies, and describe their contact with humans. In her *Verwandlungen* lectures Tawada discusses Kafka's ape figure 'Rotpeter', and claims that Kafka likes to invert the relationship between researcher and object of research (p. 59). Instead of being the object of research, animals become ethnographers of their surroundings, providing an alternative perspective with which to view human life. In *Opium für Ovid*, the only specific reference to Kafka's texts is when Semele's son sees dead silkworm larvae on the ground, which are described as being like 'winzige Gregor Samsas' [tiny Gregor Samsas]. Here Tawada inverts the standard direction of analogy, by comparing insects to a particular human. As in Kafka, the insects are objects of disgust, which make Semele's son sick. In the passage cited, the insects are being eaten by a dog. To understand the significance of the dog eating the Gregor Samsas we might turn to Tawada's *Spielzeug und Sprachmagie*, written shortly before *Opium für Ovid*, in which she refers to Benjamin's essay on Kafka, in which Benjamin describes Kafka's animals as receptacles of the forgotten (Tawada, p. 148). Benjamin makes particular reference to dogs, and goes on to speak of the dog 'Strohmian' in Tieck's 'Der blonde Eckbert'.[27] Following Benjamin, via Tawada, we might read the dog eating the Gregor Samsas as a nod to that otherwise unmentioned transformation story, Kafka's *Die Verwandlung*, and indeed perhaps also to 'Der Blonde Eckbert'.

The reversal of relationship that Tawada notes in Kafka's work is central in Tawada's own poetic project, which she terms 'ethnologische Poetologie' [ethnological poetology] (the subtitle of *Spielzeug und Sprachmagie*). Tawada's adoption of the perspective of an outsider has frequently been commented on.[28] Yet the reversal of relationship used to present an alternative perspective is also part of her textual practice as a whole, informing the way in which Tawada engages with literary material in her own work.

Transformation Poetics

Intertextual Relations: Giving Opium to Ovid

As argued above, Ovid's *Metamorphoses* is a central intertext in *Opium für Ovid*, but Tawada does not straightforwardly appropriate Ovid's text. Instead, she alludes to it playfully, often altering key features in the process. This section examines more closely the literary process at work in Tawada's transformations of Ovid's stories, and the relationship between Tawada's text and her intertexts.

Theodore Ziolkowski, writing on the use of Ovidean material in modern literature, links Tawada's intertextual approach to a statement by Tawada's character Coronis, a writer, who asserts that she does not want any predecessors or successors.[29] Ziolkowski argues: 'Ovid, too, belongs among these rejected predecessors. [Tawada's] figures are precisely not postfigurations of the mythological women whose names they bear. Her metamorphoses are not adaptations but contemporary analogues' (p. 217). Whereas an adaptation might be thought of in similar terms to family relationships, an analogue, Ziolkowski suggests, cannot. An analogue might play with the same plot and characters, but it does not bear responsibility towards the source text as an adaptation might, nor is there a strong connection between source material and text. Coronis's literary style further illustrates resistance towards family-style relationships: Coronis 'findet es verdächtig, wenn Menschen von ihren Vorfahren oder von ihren Kindern erzählen. Deshalb schreibt sie auch keinen Roman, denn dort sind die Menschen nur durch Blut oder durch Liebschaften verbunden' (p. 85) [finds it suspicious when people speak of their ancestors or their children. That's why she also doesn't write novels, for in novels people are connected only through blood or love affairs]. *Opium für Ovid* is also such a text, since the twenty-two characters are not related to one another as family members or lovers, but only by fleeting acquaintance. *Opium für Ovid* resists structures that involve dependence, both in terms of character relationships, in terms of narrative structure, by using chapters that are independent from the previous and following chapters, and also through her use of intertexts, which are alluded to in a playful and transformative manner.

Issues of dependence and relationship structures are also central in debates surrounding translation. Tawada's engagement with Walter Benjamin's essay 'Die Aufgabe des Übersetzers' has been particularly commented upon. Christine Ivanović, for example, has analysed the ways in which Tawada follows Benjamin, but also departs from him by rejecting Benjamin's dichotomy of original and translation.[30] Benjamin argues for a model of translation that does not try to reproduce the meaning of the original but that participates in its ongoing life ('Fortleben'). Tawada's engagement with Ovid's work in *Opium für Ovid* could be seen as working on a similar principle, in that she does not aim to capture or reproduce the content and meaning of Ovid's tales, but to use them in ways that are creatively productive, and that thereby allow for their continued life. The translations that Benjamin particularly admires (such as Hölderlin's translation of Sophocles) touch on the meaning of the original only lightly, Benjamin argues, akin to the wind on an Aeolian harp. Such a casual, tangential relationship also marks Tawada's allusions to Ovid.

Opium für Ovid not only alludes creatively to Ovid's tales, but also lays claim to a particular power structure in the relationship between Ovid's *Metamorphoses* and Tawada's book. Ovid is only mentioned a couple of times in *Opium für Ovid*, notably in the chapter 'Pomona', about a character who is addicted to painkillers. In this chapter the narrator claims that, unlike Pomona, she refuses to be dependent on substances:

> Bei mir begann es genau umgekehrt. Alles ablehnen, was wasserlöslich ist, alles, was pulverartig ist. Keine Schmerzen wegnehmen lassen, alle Krankheiten

bei mir behalten, geizig bis an die Grenze. Ich hatte Angst vor chemischen Angriffen. Sie wollen mich beeinflussen und langsam beherrschen. Nein, ich will meine Schmerzen selbst komponieren, keine Abhängigkeit von einer Kolonialmacht. Wird die Tablette meine Haut in Baumrinde verwandeln, werde ich sie durch einen Rausch wieder einweichen. Ein Opium gegen Ovid, mein Opiumkrieg ist noch nicht zu Ende. (p. 172)

[With me it happened the other way around. Rejecting anything that was water-soluble, anything powder-like. Let no pains be taken away, keep all illness with me, stingy to the very limit. I was afraid of chemical assaults. They wanted to influence me and gradually rule me. No, I want to compose my own pain, not be dependent on a colonial power. If the tablet transforms my skin into tree bark I will soften it again through a *Rausch*. An opium against Ovid, my opium war is not yet at an end.]

In this passage, the narrator moves from refusing dependence on chemical substances in the form of tablets, powders, and liquids, to refusing dependence at the level of colonial power politics, finally ending by asserting a rejection of Ovid. Through these transitions, dependence at the level of the individual body becomes implicated in the lexis of colonialism with its political structures of dependence. Linking individual relationships with social or political relationships, as well as with textual relationships, is a technique employed throughout the book, particularly in the allusions to the Opium Wars. In the passage above, the narrator operates as England did, by reversing the direction of dependence. By selling opium to China via India, England makes China becomes dependent on her. Similarly, the narrator resists the transformative influence of substances by producing her own substance to send back in reverse. The 'Rausch' which the narrator uses to transform back and soften her skin is her own imagination or writing, for at other points in the text she speaks of getting up early to produce 'Rauschmittel' (p. 68) [*Rausch* substances], or of how objects appear in the state of 'Rausch' (p. 78), or of how Coronis's writing reminds her of a particular 'Rauschmittel' (p. 89). In the passage above, the narrator's writing becomes a kind of opium to use against Ovid as a way of reversing the kind of power dynamics at work in colonial politics.

The title *Opium für Ovid* might now be understood as signalling a reversal of the power relationship between the literary source material and the new text. Tawada's text allows for a 'Fortleben' of Ovid's stories but only after significantly transforming them through her own writing, which functions as a kind of opium, a material substance that causes transformations of thoughts and feelings. My interpretation of the title differs in this sense from that of some other commentators. For example, Monika Schmitz-Emans suggests that the title could imply either that the narrator herself is Ovid or that opium takes the place of Ovid.[31] However, in the passage cited above the narrator positions herself in opposition to Ovid rather than suggesting that she is Ovid. Schmitz-Emans's second suggestion is that Ovid is no longer necessary because the narrator can produce her own opium. Yet in the passage above, the narrator is speaking not so much of replacing Ovid, as of providing Ovid with opium as a means of transformation. The Japanese version of the book, published one year later, also indicates the sense in which we might understand the title: 'Henshin no tame no opiumu' has the sense of 'opium for transformations', which places emphasis on opium as a material agent of transformation, including the transformation of Ovid's material.

It is also significant that the German title (though not the Japanese) makes two potential intertexts apparent. The full title *Opium für Ovid: Ein Kopfkissenbuch von 22 Frauen* suggests a link to Sei Shōnagon's *Pillow Book* as well as to Ovid's *Metamorphoses*. Commentators on the German book often make reference to this subtitle, and in particular, tend to read it as an indication of Tawada's situatedness between Western and Eastern (or Japanese) literary traditions.[32] Because Shōnagon was writing in late tenth to early eleventh century Japan, at a time when writing literary prose in Japanese was an activity generally carried out by women, the reference to her *Pillow Book* could be read as a counterpoint to a male-dominated Western literary tradition, represented by Ovid. Cho-Sobotka, for example, writes: 'Führt die Wiederbelebung einiger weiblicher Figuren Ovids auf eine westliche literarische Tradition zurück, so ist die Bezeichnung Kopfkissenbuch als eine Würdigung der weiblichen Schreibenden aus der Kultur der Autorin zu verstehen' (p. 174) [If the revival of some of Ovid's female characters can be traced back to a Western literary tradition, so too can the term Pillow Book be understood as an appraisal of the female writers from the author's culture]. Yet although the title appears to invite such a reading, it is inherently problematic to situate Tawada in the context of two singular literary traditions and cultures, particularly as characterized through a West–East binary.[33] We might also consider whether the allusion to the *Pillow Book* is a specific choice on Tawada's behalf, or a publishing decision (especially since the allusion does not appear in the Japanese version). In any case, Tawada often undermines the adherence to a concept of East and West, for example, in her essay 'Eigentlich darf man es niemandem sagen, aber Europa gibt es nicht' [You're not supposed to tell anyone this, but Europe doesn't exist].[34] Or in the answer Tawada gives to a Kurdish writer who asks her whether the theme of the literary festival they are attending ('The Orient') is discriminatory or stereotypical. Tawada responds: 'isn't it appropriate in that it points to the imaginary place that exists in the European mind'.[35]

Shōnagon's *Pillow Book* invites comparison with Tawada's text, however, since, like Tawada's text, it is not a chronological narrative but a collection of fragmentary episodes and reflections.[36] Shōnagon's text is made up of reminiscences, accounts of court life, poems, opinions, character sketches, imaginative scenes, and lists of 'Amusing Things', 'Disappointing Things', and the like. While the book makes for an interesting comparison, the *Pillow Book* should not be regarded as representative of a singular literary tradition. If we compare it, for example, with *The Tale of Genji*, a now canonical work by Shōnagon's contemporary Murasaki Shikibu, it will be apparent how different in style the two works are. In particular, *The Tale of Genji* operates on a more or less chronological structure, following the life of Genji and related characters. Indeed, in the only known text in which Murasaki Shikibu comments on Shōnagon's writing, she comments scathingly upon it, remarking that it is extraordinarily self-satisfied, full of imperfect, presumptuous scatterings of Chinese texts, and claims that Shōnagon makes too much effort to be different from others, ending with: 'if one has to sample each interesting thing that comes along, people are bound to regard one as frivolous. And how can things turn out well for such a woman?'[37] Yet if we apply Shikibu's question to Tawada, there longer seems to be a problem, in the postmodern age, in jumping from one episode to another in a text that alludes to its intertexts only imperfectly.

Opium für Ovid engages with the *Metamorphoses* in a way that allows for the continued life of Ovid's stories, but that also transforms them significantly and thereby resists dependence upon them. In this respect, Tawada's model of transformation involves a reversal of power structures that can be paralleled with the reversal of the political structures of colonialism. For Tawada, transforming literary material means resisting dependence. Therefore, the idea of posing Shōnagon as a counterpoint to Ovid is not enough. Transformation means liberation from all forms of political and personal dependence, linear chronology, and concepts of singular tradition or culture.

Metamorphosis as Literary Practice: Tawada's Model of Authorship

Tawada's model of the textual process of transformation can be related to her understanding of authorship and subjectivity. Tawada's idea of writing as a process of transforming existing material involves taking stories, ideas, or words, following the associations they provoke, integrating them into a new narrative, and often reversing or challenging their original usage. This idea of transformation as a particular kind of literary practice involves a different model of authorship from the kind associated with Ovid's text. While the *Metamorphoses* begin with the creation of the world, positing transformation as a result of divine, purposeful creation, the transformations in Tawada's texts are more aleatory and not authoritatively directed by an omnipotent agent.

Tawada discussed her idea of authorship in her lecture 'Tawada Yoko Does Not Exist' (2004), in which she claimed: 'The God of a monotheistic religion is a man who creates sons without a wife, and it seems that the "creator" of literary works shares some of these qualities, at least in the West'.[38] The idea of creation as stemming from a single (male) progenitor is a model that Tawada resists in her work. Tawada also comments in her lecture on the English word 'author', which is associated with 'authority' and sounds very grand. In Japanese, Tawada is able to choose from a number of words, of which her favourite, she claims, is 'monogaki' ('writer of things'). She also notes that 'kaku' is used both for writing and for scratching trenches. She continues:

> Then we remember that the 'thing' of monogaki, the 'writer of things', is semantically connected to mononoke, a 'changeling'. Which means that this 'writer of things' also describes a person in the clutches of changelings and shapeshifters, a person under the spell of things. The writer takes what the things have said, and carves them into shapes by scratching out lines, making the wounds and scars on paper that we call texts. But when these writers begin writing they have no clear idea what sort of tale it will turn into because even as they write, the 'ling' underlying these changes takes charge and decides how the tale will progress.[39]

According to this model of writing, the author is not so much a god-like original creator, but rather a person who is responding to the things already existing in the world. By suggesting the idea of the writer as a person 'under the spell of things' Tawada reverses the direction of power. For rather than the author being the original creator of the text, it is instead the things that create the text through the medium of the writer. The idea of the writer as 'under the spell' further suggests a connection to *Opium für Ovid*, in which writing happens while in a state of 'Rausch', a state in which a person relinquishes full control and becomes moved and affected through the influence of drug-like substances.

The writer's spellbound state leads to a text with magical and aleatory qualities, as Tawada suggests by saying that the author has no idea how the text will progress. This assertion recalls in particular Kafka's writing practice, especially since Kafka is known for having written numerous openings, but no completed novels. It has been argued that Kafka's narratives often unfold in dream-like sequence from an initial striking idea, which then determines the plot.[40] In her *Verwandlungen* lectures Tawada also remarks that before the work is finished it can be transformed, but afterwards the possibility of transformation is ruled out (p. 58). However Tawada's *Opium für Ovid* undoes the apparent fixity of the finished text by suggesting alternative ways in which the characters or text could be written. In this way, Tawada maintains a trace of the process of transformation in her finished work.

The idea of writing as scratching or scraping suggests the idea of an author as a craftsperson, but by linking the scratching process to 'wounds and scars on paper' Tawada brings in a lexis of bodily pain and disfigurement. However, in Tawada's work wounds frequently function, not as one might expect, as purely markers of past trauma, but as sites of boundary-crossing, which contain transformative potential. By offering an alternative image of the wound, a frequent motif in literatures of migration and exile, Tawada is rejecting the idea of boundary-crossing as a form of violence. In the 'Semele' chapter, for example, the narrator ends by noticing a wound on Semele's neck: 'Im Dunkelrot der Wunde werde ich eingezogen' (p. 154) [I'm drawn into the dark red of the wound]. Cho-Sobotka highlights what she calls an 'Akzeptanz des Mangels' [acceptance of blemishes] in *Opium für Ovid* (p. 195). For example, the narrator buys a table made from 'Schwellenholz' [railway sleeper wood, also literally 'boundary wood'] that was once a railway sleeper and has a dark burn mark on the side (p. 55). Because of the burn mark, the narrator says that she starts to accept the whole table and can now sleep better. These marks, scars, and wounds are not negative attributes to be accepted reluctantly, but rather, wounds are reconceived as traces of contact that lead into other, interesting spaces, and allow for immersion, self-abandonment, or sleep as states of potential transformation.

As the passage above suggests, writing and metamorphosis are intimately linked. By Tawada's account, writing is not creation *ex nihilo* but scratching, shaping, and transforming things. In the context of transformation as a creative process, the motif of insect metamorphosis is sometimes used as a metaphor for writing. As Cho-Sobotka has suggested in relation to a passage in *Opium für Ovid*, the image of silkworms creating their cocoons could be read as a reflection on literary production, since the writer also takes threads and weaves them into a coherent whole (p. 218). In Tawada's passage, the finished cocoon is described as a 'Wohnraum ohne Ausgänge, abgeschlossen und zum Einschlafen gemacht, die Verwandlung passiert in einem erfüllten Schlaf' (p. 147) [living room without exits, enclosed and designed for sleeping, transformation happens in fulfilled sleep]. Cho-Sobotka interprets the emphasis on the inside of the cocoon as recalling a characteristic of Japanese poetry, namely the foregrounding of secret or indefinable aspects of the psyche (p. 218). If we are to read the cocoon as the literary text, then the idea of being enclosed inside the text while undergoing metamorphosis suggests a particular quality of the text, though not one of secrecy, as Cho-Sobotka claims. Rather, it suggests the process of transformation. The text does not by itself cause transformation in its writer or readers, but by being immersed and wrapped up in the text, transformation is made possible. In many tales, metamorphosis happens during the self-abandonment of sleep, but unlike in Kafka's *Die Verwandlung*, in which the metamorphosis happens during 'unruhigen Träumen' (p. 115) [uneasy dreams], Tawada's passage suggests that metamorphosis can be a fulfilling process.

In order to transform material into texts, literary writers must be able to let themselves be immersed into and transformed by their material. As I argued in my chapter on Kafka, transformation as a literary process also means being able to transform oneself into the characters. In her third *Verwandlungen* lecture, Tawada speaks of the writer's propensity to transform into other beings as part of an artistic impulse: 'Die Verwandlung ist der Traum vieler Künstler' (p. 57) [transformation is the dream of many artists]. Tawada discusses a tale by eighteenth-century Japanese writer Ueda Akinari, about a monk who has painted hundreds of fish and becomes transformed into a fish. While the monk is ill in bed, his soul separates from him and becomes a carp, which is caught and brought to the monk's house. Just before the carp is about to be killed, the monk wakes up and asks for the fish to be released, thereby saving himself from dying (p. 58). By becoming so absorbed in his paintings, the painter becomes the object of his art. In this way, transformation disrupts the boundary between artist and artwork or between literary writer and text. The disruption of boundaries is apparent in *Opium für Ovid* in the slippage between the narrator as author and as character.

As a literary practice, metamorphosis requires giving up authoritative control and letting transformation take over. This means becoming immersed in what Tawada calls the 'language of things', and abandoning oneself to the world of the text in a process that resembles falling asleep. In the next section, I consider what a non-authoritative, dreamlike, and transformable text might look like.

Narrative Material: Textual Wrapping and Folding

If writing and reading involves transforming and being transformed by texts, then the metaphor of the text as a material fabric, an idea played upon in *Opium für Ovid*, can be further used to portray texts as transformable and transformative.

The etymological link between the word 'text' and textiles or fabrics has often been commented upon, including by literary theorists such as Roland Barthes, whose work Tawada has closely engaged with. *Opium für Ovid* stresses this etymological link through the use of fabrics and clothing as recurrent motifs, often in ways that allow for reflection upon the nature of literary texts. For example, Scylla wraps herself up completely in white gauze like a cocoon:

> Wickeln, das ist ihr neues Konzept. Eine instinktive Kunst wäre nichts für sie. Man muß ein Konzept haben. Sie will sich nicht mehr von dem großväterlichen Fluß ihrer Erzählkunst treiben lassen, sondern ein Konzept haben, und das neueste Konzept lautet einfach: Wickeln. (p. 64)
>
> [Wrapping, that's her new concept. An instinctive art is meaningless for her. One needs a concept. She doesn't want to let her narrative art be swept along by the grandfatherly flood, but to have a concept, and the latest concept is basically: wrapping.]

In this passage, the idea of wrapping is used to refer to a form of artistic practice. Scylla wants a concept to define her art, rather than to follow tradition. The adjective 'großväterlich' [grandfatherly] recalls the resistance demonstrated in *Opium für Ovid* towards copying one's predecessors and following existing currents of literary practice. If, as argued earlier, Tawada transforms, rather than appropriates, literary material, then her literary practice could be compared to the process of wrapping and thereby creating a cocoon in which metamorphosis occurs. The practice of wrapping is particularly prominent in Japanese culture, as anthropologist Joy Hendry claims in *Wrapping Culture: Politeness, Presentation, and Power in Japan and Other Societies*. As well as discussing gift-wrapping, Hendry considers honorific language (keigo) as a form of 'linguistic wrapping', clothing as 'bodily wrapping', 'spatial wrapping' in architectural design, and 'temporal wrapping' in the organization of significant events.[41] When applied to literary production, wrapping highlights a process of textual layering, which differs from a model of literary transformation that posits a linear transit from original to final text. In contrast to a linear model, Tawada's text involves multiple layers of literary material rather than being based around a single original.

A particularly important fabric in connection with metamorphosis is silk, given that it is produced from silkworm cocoons. Silk plays an important role in *Opium für Ovid*, both at an individual and at a socio-political level. Like opium and tea, silk is implicated in political power struggles and relations of dependency. As a major Chinese export for hundreds of years, the dependence on China for silk is paralleled by the dependence of humans on the silkworms for their fabric. The fact that the silkworms have to die in order for the silk to be produced raises a relationship of exploitation, expressed in the text by Semele's son being sick when Semele explains to him that the silkworms die (pp. 147–48).

In *Opium für Ovid*, silk evokes diverse, strong emotions ranging from disgust to longing. Semele, a fashion designer, loves fabrics, especially silk, in which she encloses or cocoons herself at night as she sleeps. She speaks of the 'Zauber der Stoffe' [magic of fabrics] and exclaims: 'Die Stoffe, sie werfen duftende Falten! Mir wird schwindelig, das ist es ja, das ist es' (p. 147) [Fabrics, they cast scented folds! I'm becoming dizzy, that's it, that's it]. Semele's entrancement is connected to the movement of the surface of the fabric. As the fabric moves, folds appear and disappear, giving the surface the impression of continual transformation: 'Plötzlich fließt Licht in die schattigen Gräben der Falten, und schon verändert sich das Muster auf dem Stoff' (p. 147) [Suddenly light floods into the shadowy trenches of the folds, and already the pattern on the fabric changes]. The 'schattigen Gräben' [shadowy trenches] recall Tawada's description of writing a text as a process of scraping trenches. These shadowy trenches make fabrics and texts appear to transform. Transformability is a quality of the fabric or text (particularly those that are pliant enough to form folds), but the transformation happens through the reading of the surface, through observing the play of light and shadow.

Several scholars have drawn attention to Tawada's use of the fold motif. Gabrielle Brandstetter, writing on the motif of the fold in Rilke, Warburg, and Tawada, argues that Tawada's 'Semele' chapter touches upon all possibilities of folding and draping.[42] Brandstetter highlights the way in which the body itself becomes material whose topography can be read, for example when Semele claims that silk is her skin.[43] In German, 'Falten' can mean both folds and wrinkles. Tawada plays upon the dual meaning when Semele applies make-up to cover her wrinkles, which, however, reappear over the course of the day, betraying what Brandstetter calls 'der Zwiefalt von Sein und Schein' [the duality of being and appearance].[44] The folds on the surface of Semele's skin reveal a further type of transformation, that of age.

Another of Tawada's texts that uses the fold motif is the story 'Sumidagawa no shiwaotoko' (1994) [The Fold Man of the Sumida River]. In her discussion of this text, Yumiko Washinosu links Tawada's statement that literature without scars, seams, rips, incoherence, and disharmony is uninteresting, with the figure of the fold man. Washinosu writes:

> Solche Unebenheiten im literarischen Text verkörpert der Faltenmann. Er ist in diesem Zusammenhang Personifikation eines offenen Textes mit Narben, Gräbern und Rissen. Zugleich bilden die Heterogenität der Referenztexte wie die Disharmonie verschiedener Episoden Falten im Text und stellen dessen Linearität und Geschlossenheit in Frage.[45]

> [The fold man embodies such unevenness in the literary text. In this context he is the personification of an open text with scars, trenches, and rips. At the same time, the heterogeneity of the reference texts and the disharmony of different episodes create folds in the text and call into question the text's linearity and enclosedness.]

Washinosu suggests that the fold motif can be linked to Tawada's style of writing, particularly Tawada's use of diverse intertexts and her non-linear style, which give her texts an uneven surface. Tawada's uneven textual style is particularly apparent in *Opium für Ovid* with its constant shifting from one brief episode, scene, or idea to another, which creates textual gaps that might be thought of as folds, as unfilled spaces that point towards unknown possibilities and that give the impression of transformability.

In her discussion of *Opium für Ovid*, Cho-Sobotka brings Tawada's work into contact with Barthes's writings about texts. For example, in his essay on Japan, *L'Empire des Signes* [Empire of Signs] (1970) Barthes writes of the haiku as: 'a faint plication by which is creased, with a rapid touch, the page of life, the silk of language'.[46] For Barthes, the faint plication or fold is an intensity of life and language, an idea that may find its way into Tawada's use of the fold motif. As well as engaging with Barthes, Tawada has often drawn upon the work of Walter Benjamin, who also writes about folds. Washinosu brings Tawada's fold motif into contact with Benjamin's claim that the language of a translation wraps the content only loosely, 'wie ein Königsmantel in weiten Falten. Denn sie [die Übersetzung] bedeutet eine höhere Sprache als sie ist und bleibt dadurch ihrem eigenen Gehalt gegenüber unangemessen, gewaltig und fremd' [like a king's robe in wide folds. For it [the translation] signifies a higher language than its own and thus remains unsuited to its content, tremendous and alien].[47] Unlike the original text, whose language and content form a unity, for Benjamin, the language of a translation wraps the content in opulent folds. Benjamin admires translations that are not natural sounding, but that sound foreign because every word is translated individually, making no attempt to fit in with conventional language use. By translating in this way, the authors of these translations raise the possibility of a higher form of language, which Benjamin refers to as 'reine Sprache' [pure language].

In Benjamin's poetic image of language as a cloak, the wide folds suggest the looseness between language and content. As in *Opium für Ovid*, folds signal points of departure in which language can detach from content. Although *Opium für Ovid* is not a translation of an original in Benjamin's sense, Tawada employs the technique of detaching language from its meaning, allowing it to enter into new associations and rendering it 'fremd' [alien] in Benjamin's sense. For example at the end of the 'Semele' chapter, Semele pulls on a trailing thread on the narrator's trousers ('Hose'), which unravel like a cyclone ('Windhose'). Brandstetter comments on Tawada's linguistic usage here, claiming that Tawada writes texts 'als *Faltsachen*' [as folded things].[48] Tawada's linguistic and textual leaps create a textual surface with folds, though these folds do not point towards Benjamin's 'pure language', free of all content, but towards continually new associations and possibilities.

Although scholars have related Tawada's use of the fold motif to the work of Barthes and Benjamin, both writers whom Tawada has engaged with, to understand how productive the concept of the fold is in Tawada's work, we might also turn to Deleuze. In *The Fold: Leibniz and the Baroque* Deleuze identifies as 'baroque' a certain trait, which is to produce endless folds.[49] Using the concept of the fold, Deleuze develops an account of matter and subjectivity in which the multiple can be thought of not only as that which has many parts, but as that which is folded in many ways.[50] Applied to Tawada's text, Deleuze's concept of the multiple as a series of folds might be useful in thinking about the individual chapters and episodes not as disparate pieces, but as part of a continuum in which themes and motifs continually resurface in altered fashion. Moreover, as Deleuze points out, folding means diminishing or withdrawing into the recesses, whereas unfolding means increasing or growing.[51] Following Deleuze, we might characterize the folded points in the text as those places where things are left unsaid, and which thereby point beyond themselves, allowing the possibility for unfolding. Deleuze also characterizes metamorphosis as a process of unfolding: 'every animal is double — but as a heterogeneous or heteromorphic creature, just as the butterfly is folded into the caterpillar that will soon unfold'.[52] The idea that the potential for metamorphosis is contained within the subject like a fold resonates with certain passages of Tawada's text. For example,

Clymene's hands have all of her past hands within them, traceable through the wrinkles or folds ('Falten') that mark the transformation that has occurred.[53]

Deleuze's writing on the fold is also useful for thinking about subjectivity. Using the concept of the fold, Deleuze proposes a model of subjectivity that is not split into simple interior and exterior (or depth and surface), but rather the inside is no more than a fold of the outside. The concept of the fold undermines the distinction between inner self, as stable entity and source of agency, and subjective surface, as something constantly being worked upon and shaped by the environment. Using Deleuze's model, we might return to Tawada's concept of authorship as being directed by the 'language of things'. According to Tawada, literary creation rests neither on the 'inner' authority of a single, omnipotent creator, nor solely on 'exterior' material, but on the combination of both: the things work upon the subject to produce the text and the subject works upon the things. The idea of folds can thus be used to conceptualize literary creativity in a way that does not involve an 'inner' self acting upon 'external' material. It can also be used to arrive at a model of subjectivity in which the 'inner self' is no more than an inflection of the 'outer self'. *Opium für Ovid* raises the possibility of such a model through its constant undermining of distinctions between inner and outer, with the narrator being both external to the narrative and internal to it.

Not only is there no true interiority, on Deleuze's account, but there is also no single substance, but rather an endlessly differentiating process, always folding, unfolding, and refolding.[54] Deleuze's emphasis on process rather than being might be linked to the importance of transformation in Tawada's work. In Tawada's texts, transformations are constantly taking place and subjects continually change. Tawada's model of subjectivity might indeed be understood, following Deleuze, as a series of folds, each of which has the potential to unfold and transform. *Opium für Ovid* explores what it means to inhabit such a folded space, and to unfold and transform.

The Affects of Transformation

Empty Points in the Text: Spaces of 'Rausch'

In Tawada's work, the transformative text is one with an uneven folded surface, for it is in the folds and gaps that transformation becomes possible. In his discussion of Tawada and Kafka, Hansjörg Bay considers the letter 'O' as a way of exploring the holes, openings, and transformations in both authors' texts, while considering the letter 'A' in connection with the idea of entrapment ('Verhaftung'). Bay argues that Kafka's 'O' never manages to get free of 'A', or in other words, transformation is a flight *from* a cultural order, but never *to* another culture.[55] In contrast, Tawada's 'O' provides the escape from entrapment that Kafka's transformation stories never completely achieved. In *Opium für Ovid* it is in the empty spaces that the possibility of transformation arises. In her *Verwandlungen* lectures Tawada speaks of Gregor Samsa's transformation as involving an empty mid-point, for in contrast to Ovid's *Metamorphoses*, in Kafka's *Die Verwandlung* it is never made apparent what transgression has led to Gregor's transformation: 'Im Text wird nicht einmal das

Gesetz benannt, das er übertreten haben soll. Das ungenannte Gesetz bildet den leeren Mittelpunkt im Text' (p. 56) [In the text, we don't even know which law he is supposed to have violated. The unnamed law forms the empty mid-point of the text.] The empty point at the centre of Kafka's text is not knowing why the transformation has taken place.

Tawada has discussed the idea of an empty mid-point in *Spielzeug und Sprachmagie*, in which she considers the cabalistic model of soul transmigration in Daniela Hodrová's *Città Dolente*. The process of transmigration is made possible through spinning, which creates an empty mid-point: 'Die Drehbewegung macht die Mitte leer, in der sonst das Bewußtsein des Menschen sitzt, und schleudert seine Seele nach außen' (p. 209) [Spinning empties the centre, in which a person's consciousness would normally sit, and catapults the soul to the outside]. Through spinning, a person is voided of consciousness or soul, which migrates towards the outside. A similar idea is at work in *Opium für Ovid*. For example, Leda loses hold of herself as she spins along with the record player: 'Zu dem Nullpunkt zurückkehren' (p. 17) [return to the zero point]. Leda's spinning movement is a way of reaching an empty or zero point, and is associated with the intoxicated state of *Rausch*, which Leda has achieved through taking tablets and listening to music, but which other characters achieve through writing, alcohol, dancing, acting, or other means. The state of *Rausch* is central within *Opium für Ovid*, because it is the state in which all the transformations happen: 'Im Rauschzustand öffnen sich überall kleine Löcher, zwischen den Lauten, zwischen dem Ein- und Ausatmen, beim Blinzeln. Sie stellen die Kontinuität in Frage' (p. 97) [In a state of *Rausch* small holes open up everywhere, between sounds, between breathing in and out, when blinking. They call continuity into question]. These holes break linear progression, and form spaces of uncertainty and potential transformation.

Rausch can refer to the experience of ecstasy or enrapture, though it can also mean intoxication, suggesting the operation of a material substance. The term *Rausch* has a long history of being associated with literary production and aesthetic experience. For example, it is a central term in Hölderlin and in Nietzsche, signifying a highly affective state of immersion or self-abandonment in which creative work can be produced. In *Opium für Ovid*, the narrator produces 'Rausch' through writing, opening up the possibility of a zero point:

> Pausenlos sollte der Rausch neu hergestellt werden, denn er vergeht immer schneller [. . .] Es reicht nicht, wenn man gleichmäßig schneller wird. Der Punkt Null ruft mich, eine Sehnsucht nach der Zahl ohne Menge. Die Zahl Hundert kann man leicht erreichen, indem man langsam und pausenlos fortschreitet. Aber den Punkt Null kann man nur dann erreichen, wenn man sich selbst in der Geschwindigkeit verliert. Es gibt einen seltsamen Sprung zwischen schnell sein und schneller werden. Ein Sprung, in dem man seine eigene Abwesenheit erreicht. (p. 153)

> [*Rausch* must be constantly produced anew, for it disappears ever quicker [. . .] it is not enough to accelerate evenly. The zero point beckons to me, a longing for the number without quantity. The number one hundred can be reached easily, by advancing slowly and continually. But the zero point can only be reached when one loses oneself in speed. There is a strange leap between being fast and

becoming faster. A leap in which one reaches one's own absence.]

The narrator longs for the zero point, a point in which the subject disappears. As with Leda, the zero point is not reached through gradual linear movement. Rather, the zero point is reached through speed. In her article on Tawada's *Das Nackte Auge* [The Naked Eye], Leslie Adelson argues that the novel's configuration of lateral movement, parallel to the railway tracks, rather than movement across or in-between two lines, allows for new ways of thinking about translation, movement, and transformation.[56] In *Opium für Ovid*, movement into the zero point can only be achieved indirectly, unlike models of translational movement that posit a linear progression from original to translation, or models of transformation in which an original form is completely replaced by a new form. The zero point cannot be reached directly because it does not exist independently, but is only created through the process of rapid movement.

The striving towards the zero point recalls Barthes's notion of 'writing at the zero degree'. In Barthes's *Writing Degree Zero* (1953), the zero degree characterizes a certain type of literary writing that is free from stylistic embellishment and from conformance to conventional language use. Barthes finds this kind of writing in Albert Camus's 1942 novel *L'Étranger* [*The Stranger*]. Camus's style of writing is one without personal involvement, in which the subject appears to be absent, and which Barthes describes as non-emotive:

> Proportionately speaking, writing at the zero degree is basically in the indicative mood, or if you like amodal; it would be accurate to say that it is a journalist's writing, if it were not precisely the case that journalism develops, in general, optative or imperative (that is, emotive) forms. The new neutral writing takes place in the midst of all those ejaculations and judgments, without becoming involved in any of them; it consists precisely in their absence.[57]

Barthes's description could even be applied to Tawada's writing, which not only engages with the motif of the zero point, but which can stylistically be seen as 'zero degree' writing, in which distance is created between emotional content and narrative observation.

The affective dimension of Tawada's work has been little commented on, perhaps for the very reason that her work is not overtly emotional. However, if affective style can provide insight into models of subjectivity, then analysis of Tawada's use of affect can inform an understanding of Tawada's approach to subjectivity and personal identity. In particular, Tawada's work characteristically adopts the tone of interested observer rather than that of impassioned actor. Tawada's protagonists often seek to interpret an unfamiliar environment, and do not understand or show the expected emotional response. For example:

> Im Licht der Küchenlampe glänzten schwach weiße Kaffeetassen. Ich erinnerte mich, daß in jenem Roman einmal eine Szene wie diese beschrieben worden war, um ein bestimmtes Gefühl einer Person auszudrücken. Ich haßte diese Textstelle. Ich konnte mich aber zum Glück nicht mehr daran erinnern, welches Gefühl dort beschrieben werden sollte.[58]

[In the light of the kitchen lamp white coffee cups gleamed faintly. I remembered that in that novel a scene like this was described in order to express a person's particular feeling. I hated this passage. Luckily I couldn't remember any more which feeling was supposed to be described.]

What the narrator dislikes is not the expression of emotion, but the oblique transferring of feelings onto things, the creation of emotional atmosphere. Tawada's work itself is free from the overt creation of atmosphere, and is more concerned with calling standard emotional responses into question. Her work does this through the unexpected attitudes and behaviours of her childlike narrators. For example, in one story, the narrator is not angry at being called an 'Arschloch', but reflects upon how the arsehole is an important part of the body.[59]

While Tawada's style is not overtly emotional, affect does play a central role, especially in moments of transformation. In *Opium für Ovid*, transformation often happens in the intensely affective state of *Rausch*, but also under everyday circumstances, which nevertheless are affectively charged. Seemingly insignificant transformations arouse strong feelings, for example, when Semele cries at finding that her bread has gone mouldy overnight. Semele's friend Ariadne tells her with a touch of Schadenfreude: 'Das kommt alles vom Alter' (p. 152) [that's all because of ageing]. Tawada links the transformation of the bread with Semele's experience of becoming older, which involves heightened emotion: 'Alt zu werden fühlt sich genauso an, wie verliebt zu sein, denkt Semele. Das Bauchweh, die Unruhe, die Schlaflosigkeit und die Tränen: Älter zu werden heißt, pausenlos verliebt zu sein' (p. 152) [Ageing feels exactly like being in love, thinks Semele. The stomach ache, the unease, the sleeplessness and the tears: ageing means being constantly in love]. Becoming older evokes mixed feelings, which is characteristic of bodily transformation in general, as something both desirable and abject. For van Dijk, the fragments that make up *Opium for Ovid* are all characterized by a sense of desire ('Begehren') (p. 76). Tawada's texts may not be overtly emotional, but longing for transformation is a frequent topos.

In her third *Verwandlungen* lecture Tawada claims: 'Poetische Verwandlungen bilden einen Raum zwischen der Sehnsucht nach einer tödlichen Verwandlung in ein Tier und dem Entsetzen über die Verwandlung in einen Menschen' (p. 60) [Poetic transformations form a space between the longing for a fatal transformation into an animal, and the horror over the transformation into a human]. Tawada is partly referring back to her discussion of Kafka's *Die Verwandlung* and 'Ein Bericht für eine Akademie', but the statement can also apply to her own work. In *Opium für Ovid* transformation and boundary-crossing evoke both desire and horror. While Leda desires to lose herself in the 'Rausch' of music, she also has fears about bodily intrusion:

> Wegen der unsichtbaren Stacheln ißt sie kein Obst. Sie ißt kein Getreide, weil es im Magen gärt und Giftgas erzeugt. Salat nimmt ihr die Körperwärme weg, Suppe verdünnt ihre Kraft, Zucker macht sie nervös, Essig sticht ihr Gefühl feindlich und Milch ekelt sie. (p. 12)

> [Because of the invisible thorns she eats no fruit. She eats no grains, because they ferment in her stomach and produce poison gas. Salad takes away her

bodily warmth, soup weakens her strength, sugar makes her nervous, vinegar adversely pierces her feelings, and milk disgusts her.]

Almost anything Leda encounters has a negative effect on her body and feelings. She is also intensely disturbed by the noises of the electrical appliances of the house. Daphne also has fears about boundaries being transgressed, for example, she is disgusted by fabric suitcases because of the possibility of liquids seeping through: rainwater, engine oil, sweat or even blood on the hands of the baggage handlers (p. 34). In *Opium für Ovid*, intense desires and fears of transgression are part of the central exploration of transformation as a profoundly affective change.

Feelings as Transformative Substances

In *Opium für Ovid* transformation often happens in the highly affective state of *Rausch*, which can be induced by various material means. Emphasis is put on exploring the material ways in which bodies and feelings can be affected and transformed. Indeed, the narrator frequently reflects upon the processes at work in producing feeling. A key passage comes after the narrator has been injured in a traffic accident and feels a sensation that she tentatively calls 'Glück' [happiness], even though the word seems inappropriate. Later, she wants to know how this feeling came about, and asks the nurse:

> Kann es sein, daß ich eine Art Drogenfabrik bin? Wenn mir etwas Schlimmes zustößt, wird sofort ein Mittel in meinem Körper hergestellt, so daß es mir danach gar nicht schlecht geht. Im Gegenteil. Ich bin danach high. Sind das Drogen? Wenn Sie wissen, wie diese Substanz heißt, sagen Sie es mir bitte. Kann ich diese Substanz vielleicht bewusst produzieren? (p. 25)
>
> [Could it be the case that I'm a kind of drug factory? When something bad happens to me, a substance is suddenly produced in my body making me no longer feel at all bad. On the contrary. I feel high. Is that drugs? If you know what this substance is called, please tell me. Can I possibly produce this substance knowingly?]

The narrator experiences her feeling as a kind of drug that has been produced by her body. The idea of feelings as unknown agents affecting the body is not a new one. Indeed, in my chapter on Hoffmann, I highlighted a model of being subjected to emotions as though to external agents. However, ideas of emotions as external agents may develop in new directions in light of late twentieth-century advances in biotechnology. In particular, the possibility of hormone manipulation (which plays a role in some of the transformations in *Opium für Ovid*) raises questions about the extent to which our feelings are personal responses or chemical changes within us. A number of literary works of this period have engaged with the effects of biotechnology upon the individual.[60] Botho Strauß provides an interesting example in his 2003 novel *Die Nacht mit Alice als Julia ums Haus schlich* [The night with Alice, as Julia crept around the house], when the narrator considers the possibility that in the future we might be able to use hormone injections to provide us with whatever feelings we want to have.[61] In the passage above, Tawada's narrator similarly views feelings as drug-induced states. The idea that her own body can produce a drug that makes her feel good leads to the question of whether she can produce the substance consciously. A key gesture in the book is that of resisting dependence on substances. In the passage above, the narrator wants to take control of the drug-like operations of her body in order to be in charge of her own bodily transformations.

Since the word 'Glück' seems inappropriate in the context of a traffic injury, the narrator begins the following chapter by explaining her decision to replace the word 'Glück' by the word 'Opium':

> Daß ich mich von dem Wort 'Glück' verabschieden und mich für das Wort 'Opium' entscheiden konnte, verdanke ich Karl Marx. Eines Tages blätterte ich in seinen Schriften, ohne sie wirklich zu lesen [. . .] In dem Moment flog mir ein Satz ins Auge: 'Religion ist Opium für das Volk.' Warum war ich nicht schon früher darauf gekommen, auch diese Substanz als Materie zu verstehen? Marx schreibt: Eisen, Weizen, Kaffee, Getreide, Baumwolle, Edelmetalle, Gold. Er schreibt: Opium. (p. 27)

> [Being able to depart from the word 'happiness' and to decide upon the word 'opium' is thanks to Karl Marx. One day I was leafing through his writings without really reading them [. . .] At that moment, a sentence flew into my eye: 'Religion is opium for the people.' Why didn't I think of this earlier, to understand this substance as material too? Marx writes: iron, wheat, coffee, grain, cotton, precious metals, gold. He writes: opium.]

By replacing an intangible feeling with the substance opium, the focus shifts from feelings as inner states to feelings as material substances. It is not happiness as a feeling state that brings about transformation, but as a material substance that moves around the body and causes change. By casting feeling as a substance, the emphasis turns to on what feelings do and how they circulate within bodies and societies. This emphasis correlates with an approach to understanding affect that has been influential across the humanities and social sciences over the past couple of decades, and which involves regarding emotions not simply as psychological states, but instead examining the ways in which emotions are at work in the politics of social life, and in particular, in its relations of power (e.g. Abu-Lughod and Lutz). For example, Tawada's idea of emotions circulating between bodies like material substances, recalls approaches taken in studies such as Sara Ahmed's *The Cultural Politics of Emotion* (2004).[62] In the passage above, the feeling 'Glück' is transformed into the substance 'Opium' as the narrator comes into contact with the works of Marx. The sentence 'Religion ist Opium für das Volk' is not a correct quotation from Marx, who wrote that 'Religion [. . .] ist das Opium *des* Volkes' [religion is the opiate *of* the people] (my emphasis),[63] but a transformation into Lenin's later variant, that religion is opium *for* the people.[64] The alteration is characteristic of *Opium für Ovid*, and is marked in the text by the fact that the narrator is not reading the book carefully and mosquitoes are flying around obscuring the letters. Once 'Glück' has become opium, it becomes implicated in issues of addiction and dependence, both at an individual level and at a political level. The drug-like state of happiness or *Rausch* is not simply to be understood as a static psychological state, but as a material operator upon and between bodies. The feeling is thus bound up with the social politics of circulation and is configured as constantly moving and being moved.

Tawada's emphasis on emotions as substances that affect and are affected reflects the emphasis of the 'affective turn' in the 1990s, whose most enduring contribution, according to Patricia Clough, was the way in which it allowed for thinking about the dynamism of bodily matter.[65]

The social, political, cultural, and linguistic shaping of feeling is reflected upon throughout *Opium für Ovid*. For example, linguist Clymene notes that people first get annoyed about someone, then they calm down, and later they experience affection. They experience feelings one after the other rather than simultaneously, which Clymene claims is a result of language: 'Weil ihre Münder nicht gleichzeitig Abneigung und Zuneigung aussprechen können. In Wirklichkeit empfinden sie beide Gefühle im selben Moment' (p. 106) [Because their mouths cannot express disaffection and affection at once. In reality they experience both feelings at the same moment]. For Clymene, language encourages a linear experience of feelings, but she challenges this model, similarly to the way in which the narrative structure of *Opium für Ovid* challenges linearity.

Our experience and articulation of feelings is not only shaped by language, but by historically changing social conditions. In her chapter 'Echo', Tawada brings in the figure of Thomas de Quincey, author of *Confessions of an English Opium-Eater* (1821). De Quincey narrates his experience to journalist Echo in strongly emotive terms, emphasizing the 'Hass, Mitleid und Angst' [Hatred, Pity and Fear] that he felt towards the millions of other opium-eaters (p. 175). He also reflects upon his affective style as historically contingent:

> Zu meiner Zeit war das Bekenntnis eine Technik, mit der man die Lust verdoppelte, verstärkte [. . .] Das funktioniert nicht mehr, die Zeiten verändern sich. Bei Ihnen hätte ich mein Bekenntnis ausarbeiten und verkaufen müssen. Dazu war ich zu faul. (p. 180)

> [In my day, confession was a technique by which to double desire, to increase it [. . .] That no longer works, times change. For you I'd have had to flesh out the confession and sell it. I was too lazy for that.]

De Quincey's reflections reinforce the portrayal of feelings as subject to socio-historical transformation, rather than as static, ahistorical inner states. Today, de Quincey suggests, it is not enough to confess to and re-arouse strong feelings, but feelings must also be reflected upon, as they are in Tawada's text.

Rather than creating emotional atmosphere, Tawada's texts engage with feeling through playful reflection, for example, the narrator of *Überseezungen* considers the word 'Gefühl':

> Ein Gefühl haben, unterdrücken oder zeigen: Das Gefühl ist heute verdinglicht worden und deshalb kann man es verletzen. Ein Gefühl stelle ich mir wie ein Stück Fleisch vor, rosa, feucht und lauwarm. Wenn eine Lüge ins Gefühl kommen würde, könnte ein Geflügel entstehen. (p. 152)

> [To have, suppress, or show a feeling: feeling is considered a thing nowadays, and so it is possible to hurt it. I imagine a feeling like a piece of meat, pink, damp, and lukewarm. If a lie [Lüge] came into a feeling [Gefühl], a bird of poultry [Geflügel] could arise.]

The narrator reflects on the idea of feelings as things, objects external to the self rather than direct expressions of it. The narrator situates the idea in language; for her, the idea of feelings as things is rooted in a linguistic tradition that allows feelings to be expressed as nouns rather than as verbs and adjectives. The narrator plays with this idea by imagining a feeling as a concrete object, and enacting a linguistic transformation of 'Gefühl'. By inserting the word 'Lüge' into the word 'Gefühl', the feeling comically becomes a 'Geflügel'. This surprising linguistic transformation serves to provoke reflection upon the ways in which we conceptualize feeling. Since the feeling becomes a bird that could fly away or be eaten, the focus turns to the things that can happen to feelings, and the ways they can be transformed.

In *Opium für Ovid*, feelings are also reflected upon as things or objects outside the self. In particular, after the narrator is injured in the traffic accident she experiences her pain as if it were outside her body: 'auf einmal stand der Schmerz wie ein Totempfahl neben mir' [suddenly pain stood beside me like a totem pole] (p. 18). The phenomenon of pain is also investigated by Clymene, who is interested in what she calls 'die Grammatik der Schmerzen' [the grammar of pain]. Clymene notices that pains seem to make a foreign materiality apparent, such as the appearance of a screwdriver or a hammer in the body (p. 101). Clymene manages to locate the source of the pain, but finds that it lies outside her skin: 'Anscheiend gab es einen sphärischen Körper, der viel größer ist als der Fleischkörper' [Apparently there was a spherical body that is much bigger than that of the flesh body] (p. 101). The sphere that Clymene refers to brings the boundary of the self into question, for the experiential self-boundary is no longer the surface of the body. The uncertain boundary of the self makes it easy to view feelings as external agents.

The model of affect at work here — feelings as objects of reflection in an otherwise unemotional narrative — has been the focus of important debates within affect scholarship. Initial impetus came from Fredric Jameson's claim that affect is 'waning' in postmodern culture.[66] Jameson's argument is not that feelings disappear entirely, but that 'there is no longer a self present to do the feeling'.[67] Jameson argues that, in postmodernism, feelings (though he notes that it may be better to term feelings 'intensities', following Lyotard) 'are now free-floating and impersonal and tend to be dominated by a peculiar kind of euphoria'.[68] *Opium für Ovid* seems initially to support Jameson's claim, particularly with its emphasis on a peculiar kind of euphoria named *Rausch*. The euphoric state of *Rausch* is connected to the possibility of transformation, of changing bodies and identities and indeed losing the idea of an inner self, a key postmodern move, according to Jameson.

However, Jameson's thesis has been criticized for suggesting that feelings and emotions are only possible if there is a subject, that is, a unitary, autonomous person, to have the emotions. Rei Terada argues that even after the 'death of the subject' emotions are possible. Indeed, according to Terada, emotions are not only possible without a subject, but they are essentially non-subjective. In her conclusion to *Feeling in Theory: Emotion after the 'Death of the Subject'* Terada calls for a reversal of views such as Jameson's, claiming that if we were really subjects we would have no emotions at all.[69] Although we might think of the 'dead subject' as zombie-like, Terada argues that the idea of a subject is more like that of a zombie, a being that is pure intentionality, its needs directed towards one thing at a time. The non-subject or 'dead subject' (meaning the death of the traditional notion of subject) that Terada upholds is a self-differential living system, something that wavers in different directions and crucially, that feels (p. 156). To return to *Opium für Ovid*, we can see how a text without stable subject positions can still involve feelings, which do not have to be 'free floating' and 'impersonal' as Jameson claims. While the feelings in Tawada's text are often positioned as external things, it would be strange to call them 'impersonal', for they are often deeply personal, in the sense that they genuinely affect the person concerned. However, Jameson does pick up on an aspect of postmodern literature that is useful for understanding Tawada's text, which is the positioning of feelings as things to be reflected upon rather than to be evoked in the narrative. Feelings are not indications of an inner self, but are things that are produced and shaped in social interaction, and which, while they can be deeply moving, can also be subject to scrutiny.

Feelings circulate between and through bodies, transforming them in the process. In the chapter 'Ariadne' feelings even play a role in spatial orientation:

> Die Wegbeschreibung zu dem Haus der Geliebten könnte zum Beispiel so aussehen: minus-plus-minus-plus-plus. So wird eine Wegbeschreibung im Gefühl eines Menschen aufbewahrt und nirgendwo anders. (p. 205)
>
> [The directions towards a lover's house could, for example, look like this: minus-plus-minus-plus-plus. In this way, directions could be stored in the feeling of a person and nowhere else.]

Since the streets in the city have no names, as is common in Japan, the inhabitants orientate themselves through feelings, which make the environment meaningful. As the inhabitants read the varied surface geography of the city, feelings emerge.

Reading Faces: Surface, Affect, Identity

I have argued against the possibility raised by Jameson that Tawada's work exhibits a waning of feeling. Instead I would like to propose a different geography of affect and subjectivity, which is less concerned with interiority, and more with surface. Tawada's emphasis on surfaces has been remarked upon by critics. In particular, Susan Anderson has drawn attention to Tawada's technique of 'surface translation', which involves translating from the surface of language (for example, at the level of sound rather than meaning). I build on this by considering bodily transformation as surface change, rather than as replacement of one inner self by another.

The idea of transformation as surface change is apparent in Tawada's third *Verwandlungen* lecture, entitled 'Gesicht eines Fisches, oder das Problem der Verwandlung' [Face of a Fish or the Problem of Transformation]. In her discussion of bodily transformation, Tawada does not speak of changing subjects, selves, or identities, but begins with the surface of the body, by discussing the face. Tawada's emphasis on the material and the bodily, rather than on abstract concepts, is a feature of her work as a whole. For example, Tawada explores language through the motif of the tongue (e.g. in *Überseezungen*), vision and perception through the motif of the eye (e.g. in *Das Nackte Auge*), cultural identity through the motif of heels (in her early tale 'Missing Heels',[70] a Japanese metaphor for those who live, uprooted, in foreign lands), as well as personality, identity, or emotional expression through the motif of the face. Tawada's bodily literalism is brought out in Hiltrud Arens's claim that Tawada 'goes beyond the body of language (*Sprachkörper*) to incorporate the language of the body (*Körpersprache*)'.[71] The turn towards the body as locus for experience and as central in the construction of identity might also be connected to the bodily turn of the 1990s, with feminist theorists such as Elizabeth Grosz in the early 1990s claiming that the body still remains a conceptual blindspot in both mainstream Western philosophical thought and contemporary feminist theory.[72] Sharalyn Orbaugh, however, argues that Japanese women's fiction of this period constantly returns 'to the female body as source of metaphor'.[73] In Tawada's work, the body is not just a metaphor for something else, but part of a process of corporeal thinking.

Tawada begins her lecture by wondering where the face of a fish begins or ends, thereby calling into question the idea of the face as a clearly defined body part. Instead, Tawada considers the possibility of a face as something that appears in the process of reading (p. 46). Tawada finds support for her concept of face in a passage by Walter Benjamin on the 'physiognomy of things'. In the passage Tawada cites, Benjamin writes of a passion for collecting as showing its true face in the figure of the collector. Tawada points out that it is not the collector's face that shows the passion, but the other way round: passion shows its face in the collector. Rather than understanding a face as the outward manifestation of a self, Tawada, drawing on Benjamin, considers the idea of a face as that which becomes visible in the process of reading (p. 47). In this way, faces are not just parts of the body, but rather, things, cities, and objects can also reveal faces (p. 46). Faces are surfaces that can be read in different ways, and which constantly change through these different readings.

The variability of reading faces becomes particularly apparent when dealing with foreignness:

> Man kann das Thema des Gesichtes kaum umgehen, wenn man sich mit der Fremdheit beschäftigt. Reisende bekommen von den Einheimischen deshalb so viele Masken aufs Gesicht gedrückt, weil sie sonst unsichtbar bleiben. (pp. 52–53)
>
> [You can hardly avoid the topic of the face if you are concerned with foreignness. Travellers have so many masks placed upon their faces by the locals since they would otherwise remain invisible.]

Reading a face can be like placing a mask on it, which means interpreting the face through preconceptions or stereotypes, although it is only through such means that unfamiliar faces can become visible or interpretable. Tawada gives an example of such a reading process from her early short novel *Das Bad* [The Bath] (1989). The narrator returns to Japan after being in Europe for a long time, and her mother asks her why she has acquired such an Asian face, like that of Japanese people in American films. The narrator's face has taken on the stereotypical mask of what a Japanese face is supposed to look like according to American culture. Tawada comments: 'Die Erwartungen der Betrachter erzeugen Masken, und die wachsen ins Fleisch der Fremden hinein' [The expectations of the onlooker create masks, and these grow into the flesh of the foreigner] (p. 53). On Tawada's account, there is no 'true identity' behind the mask, since the mask (the way in which someone is interpreted) becomes part of the face. The idea that there is no 'naked self' behind the mask, but just another mask is also a common one in discourse surrounding classical Japanese Noh theatre.[74] In Tawada's example from *Das Bad*, faces are not externalizations of an inner self, but changeable surfaces that appear to take on particular forms through the effects of social and cultural ideologies.

Facial expression and affect display is also shaped by social and cultural practices under particular political conditions. In *Opium für Ovid*, Coronis, a writer who has emigrated from an Eastern European country with a dictatorship, reflects upon different forms of affect display:

> Coronis verachtet die einheimischen Mädchen. In der Demokratie hat sich scheinbar ein inzestuöses Verhältnis zwischen den Beamten und den Mädchen entwickelt. Wenn die Mädchen beim Schwarzfahren erwischt werden, beginnen sie, die Kontrolleure laut anzuschreien, mit ihnen zu schimpfen und manchmal noch zu schluchzen, als wären die Kontrolleure ihre Eltern. Coronis kann den Anblick nicht ertragen, sie versteht nicht, warum diese jungen Menschen ihre Gefühle auf den Teller legen und ihrem Feind anbieten. Eine emotionale Reaktion verbindet Menschen miteinander. Von Coronis bekommt ein Bote der staatlichen Macht keine einzige Reaktion, keine Spucke, keine Tränen, keine zitternde Stimme, kein Schimpfwort. Coronis bleibt unfaßbar und ungreifbar wie eine Abgemeldete. (p. 81)

> [Coronis despises the local girls. Under democracy an incestuous relationship between the officials and the girls seems to have developed. When the girls are caught fare-dodging they start crying out at the ticket inspectors, ranting and sometimes even sobbing, as if the ticket inspectors were their parents. Coronis can't stand the sight; she doesn't understand why these young people lay their feelings on a plate and offer them to their enemy. An emotional reaction connects people together. From Coronis, a messenger of the state power receives not a single reaction, no spit, no tears, no trembling voice, no swear word. Coronis remains as unreachable and untouchable as a deregistered person.]

Coronis does not lack feeling, as it might appear, but refuses to display it. In the passage above, feelings are things or foodstuffs (suggested by their 'lying on a plate') that can be used as commodities in social relationships. However, by remaining emotionally distant, Coronis refuses to enter into a close relationship with the state. Coronis's affective style is shaped by her social background and attitude, which makes it hard for those from a different social background to read her face. The difficulty of reading foreigners' faces is also noted in Tawada's *Talisman*, when the narrator comments that people become uneasy if they cannot read her face like a book (p. 40).

Klaus-Peter Köpping discusses the problem of reading faces as emotionless in an article dealing with the stereotype (also widespread in Japan) of Japanese people appearing to foreigners as lacking feeling. Köpping argues that a face that appears emotionless or emotionally controlled could be read in Japan as a sign of a rich inner life.[75] He refers to the phenomenon of emotional non-display as the 'Performanz des Gesichts' [performance of the face],[76] but also contrasts this with a different form of bodily performance carried out at festivals when people engage in uncontrolled behaviour and dancing learnt 'through the belly' (which Köpping refers to as 'Bauchverhalten').[77] Köpping's contrast between surface performance and 'belly behaviour' might be useful in thinking about the moments of *Rausch* in this text as moments in which self-control is given over to intuitive behaviour, moments that Köpping describes as 'Grenzzeit' [transitional time], which lie outside apportioned time, and in which social norms and hierarchies do not apply.[78] If the text is otherwise a smooth, controlled surface, such moments form the folds that alter the surfaces, and make gaps possible.

The idea of the gap or empty space is also discussed in Tawada's 'Eine leere Flasche' [An Empty Bottle] (2002). The narrator of this text imagines the German pronoun 'Ich' as an empty bottle and claims that it constitutes a freedom from the Japanese system, which marks personal pronouns in terms of gender and social position. However, the narrator's claim is ironic, because, as Tawada explains in an interview, people in Europe do not enjoy the freedom of empty identity. Tawada says:

> Für viele Leute bedeutet 'nicht zu sein' etwas Schreckliches und sie suchen danach, diese Leere zu füllen. Sie empfinden sie nicht als Freiheit oder Gefäß für viele Möglichkeiten, sondern als 'ich bin niemand'. So wollen sie eine Arbeitsstelle haben, Familie haben, Erfolg haben oder einen Partner haben, der immer sagt, wie sie sind. Denn in Anbetracht des Rätsels dieser Leere weiß man ja nicht, ob man ohne die Identitätszuschreibungen klar kommt.
>
> [For many people, 'not being' means something terrifying and they want to fill this emptiness. They don't experience it as freedom, or as a vessel for many possibilities, but as 'I am nothing'. So they want to have a job, family, success, or a partner, who always tells them what they are. For faced with the puzzle of this emptiness they don't know whether it's possible to cope without these ascriptions of identity.][79]

John Namjun Kim also highlights the irony in 'Eine leere Flasche' by pointing out that the German text is forced to convey pronominal gender information (for example, in 'das Mädchen'). He thus claims that: 'The text is not allied to its narrator, making her words do what she does not want to say'.[80] The idea of empty identity is not one that can actually be found in European language, even if Tawada imagines the possibility of 'Ich' as container for multiple possibilities.

In her third *Verwandlungen* lecture, Tawada claims that having multiple faces is regarded negatively in Germany, whereas Buddhist art often has statues with many faces (pp. 51–52). Tawada says of the Buddhist figure Senju-Kannon, that the existence of many faces 'zeigt die großartige Verwandlungskunst' [shows the great art of transformation] (p. 52). For Tawada, having many faces is to enact multiple transformations. The constantly transforming surface is what makes people and texts interesting. Whether there is any depth or 'inner self' behind the surface, or whether there are just more surfaces folded inside another, is not as important as how the surfaces fold and constantly transform. Tawada concludes her lecture with the claim: 'Das Modewort "Identitätsverlust" hat den Begriff der Verwandlung in die Ecke verdrängt. Die Verwandlung ist aber seit der Antike — sei es der griechischen oder der chinesischen — eines der wichtigsten Motive der Literatur' (p. 60) [The fashionable phrase "loss of identity" has pushed the concept of metamorphosis aside. Yet since antiquity — whether Greek or Chinese — metamorphosis has been one of the most important motifs of literature]. Transformation, as Tawada points out, is not about losing identity, but about the continual changes that can be traced on faces and on textual surfaces. For Tawada, transformation is the exciting process of surface change.

Conclusion

To understand what is unique about Tawada's model of metamorphosis it is worth recalling alternative models. In a short essay on Goethe's poem 'Heidenröslein' [Rose on the Heath], Tawada writes of being disappointed to find that Goethe ignores the contradictions inherent in the idea of metamorphosis as progressive development.[81] Tawada argues that even though Goethe's botanical account of metamorphosis makes use of such concepts as regressive metamorphosis, or reversal of growth, his poetic account serves only to confirm an idealized concept of love, with metamorphosis as the striving towards a final, perfect identity ('die Vollkommenheit einer Identität', p. 55).[82]

In contrast, Tawada's own poetics of transformation do not look towards a unified identity, but emphasize the ways in which identities are constantly transforming under changing social and political conditions. Unlike the progressive development characteristic of a *Bildungsroman*, Tawada's *Opium für Ovid* involves multiple transformations that neither end in nor originate from a single identity. The lack of any stable subject position is underscored by the contingent, metamorphic form of the text itself, with its rhizomatic structures of relationship, and the multiple possibilities that are constantly being unfolded. From the first lines of the book ('Es ist federleicht, pünktlich aus dem Haus zu gehen. Man kommt dennoch immer später an als geplant' [It's easy as a feather to leave the house on time. Yet one always arrives later than intended]) it is apparent that this is a narrative with diversions and unexpected turns, perhaps easy to write but not possible to predict.[83]

As a literary process, transformation in Tawada's sense means beginning with the things, bodies, ideas, stories, and words already in the world, and allowing these to enter into new associations and relationships. The process of transformation does not depend upon an omnipotent creator, but takes shape organically once released from the ideology of the fully determining author-subject. In *Opium für Ovid* transformation happens above all when the subject disappears, when the subject is absorbed into the empty space of possibility that is opened up in a state of *Rausch*. This highly affective state of transformability is reached through accelerated circular movement, through textual leaps and loops, through returning to texts of the past and moving through them into the present.

Under such conditions, a form of subjectivity emerges that is free of inner depth, but that is constantly on the move, whose folded, uneven surface gives rise to a proliferation of new possibilities. The surfaces of subject and text are constantly being affected and transformed as they are read and interpreted in different ways. This process of transforming and being transformed by the text as you enter into it can be a joyful one, as Diana discovers at the end of *Opium für Ovid*, when she wants to read and read, during nights that become longer and longer and never end. By opening up such endless possibilities of transformation, Tawada offers her metamorphoses as part of a creative process into which the reader can also enter.

Notes to Chapter 4

1. Yoko Tawada, *Spielzeug und Sprachmagie in der europäischen Literatur: Eine ethnologische Poetologie* (Tübingen: Konkursbuchverlag, 2000).
2. Marjorie Perloff, 'Foreword', in *Yōko Tawada: Voices from Everywhere*, ed. by Doug Slaymaker (Lanham: Lexington Books, 2007), pp. vii–ix (p. vii).
3. Leslie Adelson, 'The Future of Futurity: Alexander Kluge and Yoko Tawada', *The Germanic Review*, 86.3 (2011) 153–84 (pp. 159–60).
4. In particular Christine Kraenzle explores travel as a spatial metaphor for the travelling subject (esp. 'Mobility, Space and Subjectivity: Yoko Tawada and German-Language Transnational Literature' (Diss. University of Toronto, 2004)).
5. On new forms of subjectivity and affective practices see, for example, Margaret Wetherell, ed., *Identity in the 21st Century: New Trends in Changing Times* (Basingstoke: Palgrave Macmillan, 2011); Lisa Blackman, *Immaterial Bodies: Affect, Embodiment, Mediation* (London: Sage, 2012).
6. For example, the title of a particularly comprehensive recent volume devoted to Tawada's work is *Yoko Tawada. Poetik der Transformation: Beiträge zum Gesamtwerk*, ed. by Christine Ivanović (Tübingen: Stauffenburg, 2010).
7. For example: Myung-Hwa Cho-Sobotka, *Auf der Suche nach dem weiblichen Subjekt: Studien zu Ingeborg Bachmanns 'Malina', Elfriede Jelineks 'Die Klavierspielerin' und Yoko Tawadas 'Opium für Ovid'* (Heidelberg: Universitätsverlag Winter, 2007); Linda Koiran, *Schreiben in fremder Sprache: Yoko Tawada und Galsan Tschinag* (Munich: Iudicium, 2009); Kraenzle, 'Mobility, Space and Subjectivity' and 'Travelling without Moving: Physical and Linguistic Mobility, Translation, and Identity in Yoko Tawada's *Überseezungen*', *Transit*, 2.1 (2006), 1–15; Doug Slaymaker, ed., *Yōko Tawada: Voices from Everywhere* (Lanham: Lexington Books, 2007).
8. Susan C. Anderson, 'Surface Translations: Meaning and Difference in Yoko Tawada's German Prose', *Seminar: A Journal of Germanic Studies*, 46.1 (2010), 50–70.
9. Adelson, 'The Future of Futurity', p. 158.
10. Monika Schmitz-Emans, *Poetiken der Verwandlung* (Innsbruck: Studienverlag, 2008); Theodore Ziolkowski, *Ovid and the Moderns* (Ithaca, NY: Cornell University Press, 2005).
11. Cho-Sobotka, *Auf der Suche nach dem weiblichen Subjekt*; Koiran, *Schreiben in fremder Sprache*.
12. Rosemary Jackson, *Fantasy: The Literature of Subversion* (London and New York: Routledge, 1981), p. 21.
13. For an account of Tawada's use of surrealism see Bettina Brandt, 'The Unknown Character: Traces of the Surreal in Yoko Tawada's Writings', in *Yōko Tawada: Voices from Everywhere*, ed. by Doug Slaymaker (Lanham: Lexington Books, 2007), pp. 111–24.
14. Yoko Tawada, 'Von der Muttersprache zur Sprachmutter', in Yoko Tawada, *Talisman* (Tübingen: Konkursbuchverlag, 1996), pp. 9–15.
15. Yasemin Yıldız, *Beyond the Mother Tongue: The Postmonolingual Condition* (New York: Fordham University Press, 2012), p. 129.
16. Claudia Breger, 'Mimikry als Grenzverwirrung. Parodistische Posen bei Yoko Tawada', in *Über Grenzen: Limitation und Transgression in Literatur und Ästhetik*, ed. by Claudia Benthien and Irmela Krüger-Fürhoff (Stuttgart: Metzler, 1999), pp. 176–206.
17. Vladimir Nabokov, 'Metamorphosen', *Masken, Metamorphosen*, Literaturmagazin, 45 (2000), 45–46 (p. 45).
18. E.g. Monika Schmitz-Emans suggests that the characters may be partial manifestations of a self: 'Metamorphose und Metempsychose: Zwei konkurrierende Modelle von Verwandlungen im Spiegel der Gegenwartsliteratur', *Arcadia*, 40 (2005), 390–413 (p. 410); Kari van Dijk describes the narrator as a 'fragmented ich', and the characters as shards of a container, with reference to the fact that Tawada, following Walter Benjamin, often references broken vessels in her work: '"Starting out with fragments": Zur androgynen Poetologie Yoko Tawadas unter besonderer

Berücksichtigung von *Opium für Ovid*', in *Yoko Tawada. Poetik der Transformation: Beiträge zum Gesamtwerk*, ed. by Christine Ivanović (Tübingen: Stauffenburg, 2010), pp. 73–100 (p. 74); and Theodore Ziolkowski describes the characters as projections of the author: *Ovid and the Moderns*, p. 216.
19. Ziolkowski, p. 216.
20. van Dijk, p. 74.
21. Ibid.
22. Tawada, *Spielzeug und Sprachmagie*, p. 217. Cited also in van Dijk, p. 74.
23. Tawada, *Spielzeug und Sprachmagie*, pp. 180–81.
24. Gizem Arslan writes about the significance of letters of the alphabet in Tawada's work in 'Metamorphoses of the Letter in Paul Celan, Georges Perec, and Yoko Tawada' (Diss. Cornell University, 2013).
25. Édouard Glissant, *Poetics of Relation*, trans. by Betsy Wing (Ann Arbor: University of Michigan Press, 1997).
26. E.g. Cho-Sobotka; Schmitz-Emans, *Poetiken der Verwandlung*.
27. *Benjamin über Kafka*, p. 30.
28. E.g. Clara Ervedosa, 'Die Verfremdung des Fremden: Kulturelle und ästhetische Alterität bei Yoko Tawada', *Zeitschrift für Germanistik*, 16.3 (2006), 568–80; Sabine Fischer, 'Durch die japanische Brille gesehen: Die fiktive Ethnologie der Yoko Tawada', *Gegenwartsliteratur*, 2 (2003), 59–80; Maria S. Grewe, *Estranging Poetic: On the Poetic of the Foreign in Select Works by Herta Müller and Yoko Tawada* (New York: BiblioBazaar, 2011); Ruth Kersting, *Fremdes Schreiben: Yoko Tawada* (Trier: Wissenschaftlicher Verlag Trier, 2006); Koiran, *Schreiben in fremder Sprache*.
29. Ziolkowski, p. 91. However, Ziolkowski erroneously attributes the quote about not wanting predecessors and successors to 'the unnamed author, who enters her narrative from time to time in the first person' (p. 217). The statement in question is not made by the narrative 'ich' but by the character Coronis, an East European writer living in Germany. In his analysis, Ziolkowski equates the character Coronis and her rejection of 'all attempts to force her into a role either Eastern or Western' (p. 217), with Tawada herself. However, Coronis is not to be equated with Tawada herself, as illustrated by the fact that Coronis is from Eastern Europe, and previously lived under a dictatorship.
30. Christine Ivanović, 'Exophonie und Kulturanalyse: Tawadas Transformationen Benjamins', in *Yoko Tawada. Poetik der Transformation: Beiträge zum Gesamtwerk*, ed. by Christine Ivanović (Tübingen: Stauffenburg, 2010), pp. 171–206. A similar analysis is also made by Susan C. Anderson in 'Surface Translations', p. 54.
31. Schmitz-Emans, *Poetiken der Verwandlung*, p. 181.
32. E.g. Cho-Sobotka, p. 174; Sieglinde Geisel, 'Kopfkissenbuch der Verwandlung: Die Anverwandlung literarischer Motive und Wahrnehmungsweisen von Ovid und Sei Shonagon in Yoko Tawadas Opium für Ovid', *Text + Kritik*, 191/192 (2011), 47–53 (p. 47); Schmitz-Emans, *Poetiken der Verwandlung*, p. 180.
33. Several people have made this point, for example, Susan Anderson cites Albrecht, Breger, Fischer, Kersting, Kraenzle, Mejcher-Neef, Wägenbauer, Weigel and Yıldız as people who have demonstrated ways in which Tawada's work criticizes dualistic and Eurocentric thinking about cultural difference. See also: Brett de Bary, 'Deixis, Dislocation, and Suspense in Translation: Tawada Yōko's The Bath', in *The Politics of Culture: Around the Work of Naoki Sakai*, ed. by Richard F. Calichman and John Namjun Kim (Oxford and New York: Routledge, 2010), pp. 40–51 (pp. 40–42).
34. Published in Yoko Tawada, *Talisman* (Tübingen: Konkursbuchverlag, 1996).
35. Yoko Tawada, *Tokeru machi sukeru michi* (Tokyo: Nihon Keizai Shinbun Shuppansha, 2007), p. 131. Cited in Tomiko Kuribayashi, 'Nomadic Narratives: Yoko Tawada's Japanese-German Fiction', in *Traversing Transnationalism: The Horizons of Literary and Cultural Studies*, ed. by Pier Paolo Frassinelli, Ronit Frenkel, and David Watson (Amsterdam: Rodopi, 2011), pp. 137–54 (p. 152).
36. The connection between *Opium für Ovid* and Shōnagon's *Pillow Book* is discussed in Geisel, 'Kopfkissenbuch der Verwandlung'.
37. *The Pillow Book of Sei Shōnagon*, ed. and trans. by Ivan I. Morris (New York and Chichester: Columbia University Press, 1991), pp. 9–10.
38. Published in Slaymaker, pp. 13–20 (p. 14).

39. Ibid.
40. Dieter Hasselblatt, *Zauber und Logik: Eine Kafka Studie* (Cologne: Verlag Wissenschaft und Politik, 1964), p. 61.
41. Joy Hendry, *Wrapping Culture: Politeness, Presentation, and Power in Japan and Other Societies* (Oxford and New York: Oxford University Press, 1999).
42. Gabriele Brandstetter, 'Gesichter und Texturen: Zu einer Physiognomik der Falte — Rainer Maria Rilke, Aby Warburg, Yoko Tawada', in *Schrift und Bild und Körper*, ed. by Ulrike Landfester (Bielefeld: Aisthesis, 2002), pp. 87–121 (p. 115).
43. Ibid., p. 149.
44. Ibid., p. 114.
45. Yumiko Washinosu, '*Sumidagawa no shiwaotoko* oder Text der Trans-Formation', in *Yoko Tawada. Poetik der Transformation: Beiträge zum Gesamtwerk*, ed. by Christine Ivanović (Tübingen: Stauffenburg, 2010), pp. 101–12 (p. 109).
46. Roland Barthes, *Empire of Signs*, trans. by Richard Howard (New York: Hill and Wang, 1983), p. 78. Cho-Sobotka cites this line in a German translation, in which the word 'Falte' is used (p. 219).
47. Walter Benjamin, 'Die Aufgabe des Übersetzers' (1921), in *Gesammelte Schriften*, IV.1: *Kleine Prose, Baudelaire-Übertragungen*, ed. by Rolf Tiedemann and Hermann Schweppenhäuser (Frankfurt a.M.: Suhrkamp, 1991), pp. 9–21 (p. 15).
48. Brandstetter, p. 116.
49. Gilles Deleuze, *The Fold: Leibniz and the Baroque* (Minneapolis: University of Minnesota Press, 1993), p. 3. *The Fold* was first published in French in 1988, in English translation in 1993, in Japanese translation in 1998, and in German translation in 2000. It is not clear whether Tawada had read the book at the time of writing *Opium für Ovid*, but it is possible.
50. Ibid., p. 3.
51. Ibid., p. 9.
52. Ibid.
53. Ibid., p. 98.
54. Simon O'Sullivan, 'Fold', in *The Deleuze Dictionary: Revised Edition*, ed. by Adrian Parr (Edinburgh: Edinburgh University Press, 2010), pp. 107–08.
55. Hansjörg Bay, 'A und O. Kafka — Tawada', in *Yoko Tawada. Poetik der Transformation: Beiträge zum Gesamtwerk*, ed. by Christine Ivanović (Tübingen: Stauffenburg, 2010), pp. 149–70 (pp. 160–64).
56. Leslie Adelson, 'Rusty Rails and Parallel Tracks: *Trans-Latio* in Yoko Tawada's *Das nackte Auge* (2004)', in *Un/Translatables*, ed. by Catriona MacLeod and Bethany Wiggin (Evanston, IL: Northwestern University Press, forthcoming, 2016).
57. Roland Barthes, *Writing Degree Zero and Elements of Semiology*, trans. by Annette Lavers and Colin Smith (Beacon Press: Boston, 1967), pp. 76–77.
58. Tawada, *Ein Gast* (Tübingen: Konkursbuchverlag, 1993), p. 58.
59. Yoko Tawada, *Überseezungen* (Tübingen: Konkursbuchverlag, 2002), p. 29.
60. An overview is provided by Claudia Breger, Irmela Krüger-Fürhoff, and Tanja Nusser, eds, *Engineering Life: Narrationen vom Menschen in Biomedizin, Kultur und Literatur* (Berlin: Kulturverlag Kadmos, 2008).
61. Botho Strauß, *Die Nacht mit Alice als Julia ums Haus schlich* (Munich: C. Hanser, 2003), p. 107.
62. Sara Ahmed, *The Cultural Politics of Emotion* (New York: Routledge, 2004).
63. Karl Marx, 'Zur Kritik der Hegel'schen Rechts-Philosophie: Einleitung', in *Deutsch-französische Jahrbücher*, ed. by Arnold Ruge and Karl Marx (Paris: Bureau der Jahrbücher, 1844), pp. 71–85 (p. 72).
64. V. I. Lenin, *Revolution, Democracy, Socialism: Selected Writings*, ed. by Paul Le Blanc (London: Pluto Press, 2008), p. 193.
65. Patricia T. Clough, 'The Affective Turn: Political Economy, Biomedia and Bodies', *Theory, Culture and Society*, 25.1 (2008), 1–22 (p. 1).
66. Fredric Jameson, *Postmodernism, Or, The Cultural Logic of Late Capitalism* (Durham, NC: Duke University Press, 1991), p. 10.
67. Ibid., p. 15.

68. Ibid., p. 16.
69. Rei Terada, *Feeling in Theory: Emotion after the 'Death of the Subject'* (Cambridge, MA and London: Harvard University Press, 2001), p. 158.
70. Yoko Tawada, 'Missing Heels', in *The Bridegroom Was a Dog*, trans. by Margaret Mitsutani (Tokyo, New York, and London: Kodansha International, 1998).
71. Hiltrud Arens, 'Das kurze Leuchten unter dem Tor oder auf dem Weg zur geträumten Sprache: Poetological Reflections in Works by Yoko Tawada', in *Yōko Tawada: Voices from Everywhere*, ed. by Doug Slaymaker (Lanham: Lexington Books, 2007), pp. 59–76 (p. 71).
72. Elisabeth Grosz, *Volatile Bodies: Towards a Corporeal Feminism* (Bloomington: Indiana University Press, 1994), p. 3.
73. Sharalyn Orbaugh, 'The Body in Contemporary Japanese Women's Fiction', *The Woman's Hand: Gender and Theory in Japanese Women's Writing*, ed. by Paul Schalow and Janet Walker (Stanford University Press, 1996), pp. 119–64 (p. 125).
74. Klaus-Peter Köpping, '"Bauch haben": Die Inszenierung von Gemeinschaftsgefühl in Japan', in *Emotionalität: Zur Geschichte der Gefühle*, ed. by Claudia Benthien, Anne Fleig, and Ingrid Kasten (Cologne: Böhlau, 2000), pp. 213–37 (p. 229).
75. Ibid., p. 229.
76. Ibid., p. 233.
77. Ibid., p. 218.
78. Ibid., p. 234.
79. Interview with Linda Koiran, cited in Koiran, *Schreiben in fremder Sprache*, p. 380.
80. John Namjun Kim, 'Ethnic Irony: The Poetic Parabasis of the Promiscuous Personal Pronoun in Yoko Tawada's "Eine leere Flasche" (A Vacuous Flask)', *The German Quarterly*, 83.3 (2010), 333–52 (p. 340).
81. Yoko Tawada, 'Metamorphose des Heidenrösleins — Ein Versuch über Goethe', in *Sprachpolizei und Spielpolyglotte* (Tübingen: Konkursbuchverlag, 2007), pp. 48–55 (esp. 54–55). Tawada's essay is discussed in Aeka Ishihara, 'Warum kann der Knabe die Rose nicht in der Natur belassen? Tawada und Goethes *Heidenröslein*', in *Yoko Tawada. Poetik der Transformation: Beiträge zum Gesamtwerk*, ed. by Christine Ivanović (Tübingen: Stauffenburg, 2010), pp. 113–24; and in Christina Szentivanyi, '"Tawada Yoko does not exist"/"Dichter sind Alchimisten" — Transformatives Fließen in Texten Yoko Tawadas', ibid., pp. 441–48.
82. Goethe wrote a botanical account of metamorphosis, 'Versuch die Metamorphose der Pflanzen zu erklären', in 1790, and the poem 'Metamorphose der Pflanzen' in 1798. However Tawada's characterization of Goethe's poem as striving towards a final, perfect identity is not supported by Goethe scholarship. On Goethe's model of subjectivity see esp. Stefan Keppler, *Grenzen des Ich: Die Verfassung des Subjekts in Goethes Romanen und Erzählungen* (Berlin: Walter de Gruyter, 2006).
83. Hans Eichhorn draws attention to the opening sentence in his 'Die unerträgliche Leichtigkeit der Poesie: Marginalien zu Yoko Tawadas *Opium für Ovid*', *Text + Kritik*, 191/192 (2011), 43–46.

ENDINGS AND BEGINNINGS: TOWARDS A CONCLUSION

❖

Metamorphosis is not about finality but about change. Tales of metamorphosis do not dwell upon the ending of one bodily form, but look towards new modes of existence. Even when metamorphosis leads to death, as it does for Gregor Samsa, we look towards change, and to the new life that is beginning for Grete. The pictures of a silk worm's metamorphic life-cycle that accompany the chapters of this book can be considered a reminder of the ongoing process of change. Accordingly, the chapters should not be seen as disparate entities, but as interlinked through their engagement with and transformation of shared issues. In such a book it is only appropriate that the conclusion does not aim to assert definitive truths about the role of metamorphosis in literature, but instead to reflect upon the confluences and shifts in writers' engagement with transforming identities, bodies, and affects.

Metamorphosis has been understood as a process of radical and rapid bodily change, most frequently referred to as a 'Verwandlung'. Whereas Ovid's 'Metamorphosen' are rooted in classical metaphysics, as examples of the world's continual flux, in the secular tales of 'Verwandlung' that I have explored, metamorphosis is not part of an attempt to explain nature, but is an engagement with the inexplicable. In many cases, there is no discernible reason for the metamorphosis, but only a 'hole in the text', as Tawada put it when describing Kafka's *Die Verwandlung*. In an age in which God is dead, as Nietzsche claimed, metamorphoses no longer reflect divine justice, but are instead instances of strangeness in the irrational fabric of the world.

Fantastic literature is a key genre for modern metamorphosis texts. Unlike myth or fairy tale, the fantastic mixes familiar, everyday reality with experiences that do not fit with one's view of reality. Reader and protagonist characteristically hesitate as to whether the extraordinary events are real or illusory.[1] The strong affects of shock, horror, or confusion belong to the confrontation with the loss of everyday certainties. Fantastic literature has roots in the Romantic movement. However, whereas Hoffmann's characters hesitate over the reality of the metamorphoses, in later texts, such as Kafka's *Die Verwandlung*, hesitation is often missing. For Gregor, the metamorphosis is categorically not a dream. However, the reader may still experience uncertainty over the status of the metamorphosis, meaning that we may still read Kafka's texts as fantastic, albeit as a new form of fantastic literature.[2] Kafka's work may even be seen as a precursor to surreal texts, in which bizarre and absurd metamorphoses are experienced by the protagonist as unremarkable, as is often the case in Tawada's work. Unlike Tawada's *Opium für Ovid*, however, Erpenbeck's *Geschichte vom alten Kind*, written around the same time, presents the metamorphosis as radically unnatural. The different affects of the texts — the surprise and humour of Tawada's text, versus the uncanny enigma of Erpenbeck's — may be linked to the different positioning of metamorphosis.

The ambiguity over the reality of the metamorphosis, apparent in Hoffmann's and Kafka's texts, may be linked to the texts' focalization through individual perception, reflecting the ambiguous status of objective, external reality in post-Kantian thought. While Hoffmann blurs the distinction between actual and imagined metamorphosis, Kafka's more radical focalization through Gregor's perspective reflects the view in empirical psychology of this period that reality is always mediated through consciousness. The reality of the metamorphosis is thus dependent only on whether Gregor and his family experience it as such. For both Hoffmann and Kafka, an interest in the ways in which we mediate and perceive the world, and indeed transform reality, is part of their profound interest in metamorphosis more broadly, both as subject matter and as literary practice.

Metamorphosis offers an alternative perspective through which to view the world, but not always an escape from real-life concerns. Even in Hoffmann's *Der goldene Topf*, where metamorphosis reveals the existence of the utopian realm of Atlantis, the narrator continues to face mundane hardship, although he has learnt the art of imaginative transformation. For Gregor Samsa, on the other hand, the escapist possibilities that had seemed to open up through metamorphosis do not lead to freedom. Although metamorphosis is about change, it is not necessarily a call for change. Sometimes, the horror of metamorphosis is a way of articulating resistance towards change. The texts' differing use of metamorphosis reflects wider attitudes towards the transformation of identities and bodies, as well as changing understandings of what it is to be human, of the role of literature and the expression of affect.

Transforming Identities

Metamorphosis raises the longstanding philosophical problem of personal identity — how we can remain the same person despite spatio-temporal change. For Aristotle, the problem could be dealt with by distinguishing between 'essential' changes, such as death, and 'accidental' changes, such as greying hair. The straightforward idea that a person can remain the same despite certain 'accidental' changes allowed Ovid to claim that the spirit persists intact throughout the characters' metamorphic changes. However, by the time we reach the Romantic period, the concept of a persisting, immaterial spirit can no longer be asserted as a certainty. In attempting to account for personal identity using, for example, Locke's concept of a person as a single, unified consciousness, the potential for breaks in consciousness — and for losing one's personal identity — becomes apparent. In sleeping, dreaming, drunken, or irrational states, the possibility of radically altered personhood arises.

In all the literary texts I examined, metamorphosis happens in states of loosened consciousness. In contrast to classical literature, there is often no reason or purpose for the metamorphosis, but rather, metamorphosis is used to explore the fragility of personal identity. In Hoffmann's 'Der goldne Topf', Anselmus's awareness of the metamorphic realm begins when daydreaming under the elder tree. When the door knocker transforms into the face of an evil woman, Anselmus has just been drinking a strong liqueur. In Kafka's *Die Verwandlung*, Gregor transforms during uneasy dreams, and in Kafka's 'Bericht für eine Akademie', the ape Rotpeter starts to speak after drinking schnapps. In Kaschnitz's story, the metamorphosis takes place in the dream-like landscape of childhood memory, while in Erpenbeck's novella the transformation happens while the girl is in a sleepy state in a hospital bed. The title of Tawada's book, *Opium für Ovid: Ein Kopfkissenbuch von 22 Frauen*, makes reference both to sleeping, and to a mind-altering drug, both of which are central to the processes of metamorphosis around which the book revolves.

Not only does metamorphosis highlight the ways in which personal identity may be broken, but it also engages with conflicts between different forms of social identity. For Hoffmann, metamorphosis articulates a conflict that is central within his work: the conflict between artistic fulfilment and social acceptability. Metamorphosis, like art itself, can allow access to a higher or deeper self, and can intimate depths of feeling that are only affected superficially in philistine society. Hoffmann's metamorphoses do not only involve accessing the wonders of a poetic realm, however. They may also reveal the danger of emotional experience that is unaligned with reality, or they may simply satirize the gulf between the true artist and bourgeois affectedness.

A conflict between superficial, bourgeois identity and inner, affective experience is also explored through Gregor's metamorphosis in *Die Verwandlung*. However, although the metamorphosis does intimate new forms of affective and aesthetic experience, it is most importantly a means of confronting repressed corporeality. Similarly, in chapter 3, the confrontation with unwelcome corporeality is central. In the texts by Erpenbeck and Kaschnitz, the child's fat, abject body suggested the presence of repressed aspects of the psyche. Metamorphosis was a way of forcibly bringing to light an identity that had previously remained hidden.

The texts from Hoffmann to Erpenbeck suggest a dualistic split between a person's social or familial identity with its associated duties and expectations, and a deeper self with a hidden affective force. Yet in Yoko Tawada's work, the many metamorphoses do not reveal a deeper self, but instead engage with multiple ways in which identities can be challenged and transformed. Rather than opposing essence and appearance, identity in Tawada's work might be described, following the terminology of Deleuze, as a 'swarm of appearances'. Yet even in the earlier texts, while metamorphosis may engage with the conflict between essence and superficial identity, it also undermines such distinctions by suggesting fluidity between the different forms of identity, and often powerlessness as certain identities and modes of being are forced onto the protagonists. All the metamorphosis texts raise the suggestion that we are not fully in control of our identities, but rather, we are continually subject to the identity ascriptions of others, and we are continually changed through unexpected circumstances that are not of our making.

A sense of changing identity can, in particular, result from social transition and geographical boundary crossing. Like other authors for whom metamorphosis is central, such as Ovid or Nabokov, all of the authors I explored have had close personal experience with geographical, cultural or social displacement. Hoffmann's frequent relocations due to personal and political upheaval, and Kafka's insecurities surrounding social mobility, contribute to both authors' preoccupation with changing identities and with metamorphosis. In chapter 3, both authors' interest in ways of dealing with unwanted past identities and the prospect of radical change are partly shaped by their experience of political upheaval and extreme social change. For Yoko Tawada, the experience of crossing between places and languages opens up an interest in boundary-crossing, destabilized identities, and metamorphosis. An account of metamorphosis in literature is at the same time an account of identities transforming as individuals cross geographical, cultural, and social boundaries, and are jolted out of their familiar existence.

An affinity between metamorphosis and the experience of changing social environments has been noted before, for example by Marina Warner, who examines the possibility of metamorphosis arising in 'cross-cultural zones'.[3] However, Willem de Blécourt criticizes Warner's claim as an 'unsubstantiated observation' that suffers from a 'denial of indigenous notions'.[4] It is important not to ignore 'indigenous notions' of metamorphosis, but Warner's claim need not exclude writers' engagement with existing traditions of metamorphosis. Writers' engagement with existing traditions may be motivated, however, by personal interest in changing identities under conditions of social, cultural, and geographical movement. Certainly broad claims about the affinity between metamorphosis and cultural crossing are difficult to support, but, like Warner, I have found strong reasons to consider social and cultural transition an important factor for writers' engagement with changing identities and bodies. When exiled poet Nelly Sachs claimed that 'An Stelle von Heimat | Halte ich die Verwandlungen der Welt' [Instead of home | I hold the transformations of the world], she was referring to the replacement of a secure sense of homeland with the poetic practice of transformation and an interest in the motif of metamorphosis.[5] Indeed, the radical political changes affecting German society over the past two centuries can be regarded as particularly fertile ground for metamorphosis.

Changing identities can be a cause for anxiety and horror, as in *Die Verwandlung*, or it can promise freedom from the restrictions of fixed identity. Opposition towards essentialist models of identity — identity as fixed, stable essence — has increased in recent decades with critical work that takes issue with notions such as 'women's experience' as a homogeneous category.[6] Instead, diversity and changeability come to assume a prominent role: for example, critical theorists Gilles Deleuze and Felix Guattari's concepts of 'nomadology' and 'becoming' have inspired critical work such as Rosa Braidotti's *Nomadic Subjects* (1994) and *Metamorphoses* (2002), built around an affirmation of fluid identities. However, there are also problems with purely affirmatory accounts of flux and metamorphosis, in that it becomes easy to lose sight of the ways in which identification matters in our lives. That is, identities matter as a way of structuring attachments that can be enriching as well as restrictive, and that continue to shape social life.[7] Literary tales of metamorphosis address both sides of the debate: they may affirm fluid, nomadic, identity-less existence, or claim a value in identity, belonging, and in the discovery of the affects that seem to emanate from a deeper self.

Transforming Humans

In the texts I explored, human to animal metamorphosis tends to be a physical transformation, yet when an animal becomes a human, as in Hoffmann's and Kafka's ape tales, it is primarily mental capacities and linguistic abilities that are transformed. The difference reveals a longstanding association between animality and corporeality, and between humanity and the mind. Becoming animal, when explored in depth in tales such as *Die Verwandlung*, can mean a re-evaluation of bodily sensations, but the mind is not completely refigured. In Kafka's text, becoming animal allows for an exploration of attributes that have been excluded from human social life, such as sexual and appetitive urges. As in Kafka's text, human–animal metamorphosis generally reveals little about the nature of the animal mind, but much about how it feels for a human to be trapped within an animal body. Conversely, narratives of animals becoming human are less concerned with corporeal change, and more with what it means to acquire human abilities. In both Hoffmann's and Kafka's ape tales, human abilities are not necessarily superior, and are often accompanied by negative affects.

The view that becoming animal is a degrading prospect, as Hegel claimed, is based on an assumption of human superiority. Yet becoming animal is not always, or not purely, degrading — instead it can open up forgotten modes of corporeal being, as in Kafka's *Die Verwandlung*.[8] Moreover, both Hoffmann and Kafka challenge human superiority through their ape tales, in which the apes copy ('ape') vulgar behaviour, thus revealing their 'progress' to human existence to be a hollow achievement. Most importantly, becoming human or relinquishing humanity means gaining or losing voice. Losing verbal language can be a frightening, degrading prospect, as it is for Gregor Samsa, but it can also pose a positive alternative, by opening up an unrealized capacity for non-linguistic, affective communication.

The idea of affects inhabiting the pre-linguistic has a long tradition in the West: Herder, for example, claims that language originates in emotional expression (*Abhandlung über den Ursprung der Sprache*, 1772). Indeed, the advent of language often marks the origin of the human, with speaking, human rationality being seen as a progression from unspeaking, animal emotionality. 'Regression' to a non-linguistic state can also be seen as offering an alternative to the ills of civilization, as a return to what Rousseau called the 'state of nature'. Since metamorphosis may explore that which has been lost in civilized, linguistic society, it can offer a 'critique of language', as Irving Massey claims.[9] However, since Massey focuses on the loss of language, he is led to conclude that metamorphosis is a 'morbid subject'.[10] In contrast, I have considered what is gained after losing human language, namely, a non-verbal language of emotion.

Bodily and Temporal Transformations

Metamorphosis poses a challenge to the longstanding tradition of privileging of the human mind over the animal body. For Plato, to know something purely means ignoring all bodily concerns, and viewing objects with the mind alone (*Phaedo*, p. 12). It is not difficult to see why Plato also upheld the idea of metempsychosis after death, which makes bodies irrelevant to the endurance of the spirit. Yet representations of metamorphosis force us to return to the body as a central concern. When Gregor Samsa continues to worry about his job after having found himself radically transformed, Kafka makes comically apparent just how profoundly Gregor ignores his body. It is only through the metamorphosis that Gregor starts attending to his corporeal existence and to the bodily urges that had long been suppressed. Metamorphosis acts as a reminder of bodily existence in a world that has almost forgotten bodily needs.

Chapters 3 and 4 placed emphasis on women's bodily experience and on cultural stereotypes about female bodies. Two aspects of bodily identity were of particular importance: gender and age. Gender plays a role in many metamorphosis texts, not only those that are directly about gender transformation. In chapter 3, the metamorphoses are mapped onto the transition from girlhood to womanhood, and at the same time are depicted as a form of acquiring female identity. The unusual emphasis on the neutral gender of the girl prior to the metamorphosis also draws on the idea of the pre-metamorphic state as a gender-less pupa-like existence, which can also be found, for example, in Nabokov's or Tawada's work.[11] Theorists Deleuze and Guattari consider the transition from girl to woman a particularly important site of metamorphosis, and regard the little girl, as Elizabeth Grosz put it, as a privileged site of 'a culture's most intensified disinvestments and recastings of the body'.[12] For them, the idea of becoming woman is the most symbolically resonant form of 'becoming', a central concept in their work. However, the texts I explored in chapter 3 challenge a purely affirmatory account of becoming woman, by suggesting the continued investment in childhood identity, and the difficulty of breaking from an unwanted past.

Chapter 3 also examined metamorphosis as sudden transformation of age: although maturation and ageing are everyday human experiences of bodily change, tales of metamorphosis rapidly speed up or reverse this process. Because bodily change comes into sharper focus at particular points in a life-cycle, such as at puberty, these transitional periods often become the sites of metamorphosis. Metamorphosis can also be mapped on to moments of coming into or out of being: metamorphoses are often conceptualized as moments of death or rebirth. By linking metamorphosis to extreme moments of life-transition, such texts engage with affectively saturated processes of corporeal change.

By changing the pace of bodily change to something unusually rapid, metamorphosis can appear to subvert ordinary temporality, often challenging notions of development or progress. Instead, metamorphosis acts as a moment of crisis. In Kaschnitz's and Erpenbeck's stories, the abrupt contrast between the child's body and adult identity marks a gulf between past and present. After metamorphosis, access to the past may be blocked, or alternatively, metamorphosis may function as a reversal and recollection of a past that had been forgotten or repressed. Metamorphosis may also undercut the continuity between present and future, as a foreclosing of an expected future path, or a regression to a past state. Regressive metamorphosis not only includes transformation into a child, but transformation into an animal, understood as a regression to an earlier evolutionary state. Kafka's *Die Verwandlung*, for example, has been read both as a regression to 'lower' animal existence and as an escape to a state of infant dependency. However, although such regression may seem to offer an escape, it can also mean having to confront undesirable or repressed aspects of the self.

When metamorphosis is about individual moments of crisis it is often narrated in the form of the short story or novella. As a single, striking event, metamorphosis may act as the focal point of a short narrative, either as striking premise, whose consequences are then explored, or as turning point and anagnorisis towards the end of the narrative. Such narratives may be seen as experiments in engaging with a single outlandish idea, as in chapters 2 and 3. However, when the metamorphoses are multiple, and part of an engagement with multiple identities and continual change, as in chapter 4 and partly in chapter 1, then metamorphoses may be part of a longer, interlocking narrative.

In the texts I explored, metamorphosis sometimes happens at the start of the story (*Die Verwandlung*), and sometimes at the end (those of Kaschnitz and Erpenbeck). Friedmann Harzer claims that metamorphosis tends to come at the end when the metamorphosis is a psychological one, and therefore leaves no room for further narration.[13] However, most metamorphoses are psychological as well as corporeal, in the sense that they alter a person's experiences and identity. In the stories by Kaschnitz and Erpenbeck, the final metamorphosis does involve psychological change, but it is not simply the profound psychological change that brings the narrative to a conclusion. In both cases, the metamorphosis involves the revelation of a hidden identity, which, once revealed, resolves the narrative tension that has been built up throughout. In Kaschnitz's story, the revealing of a past identity gives the narrative a sense of circularity, whereas in Erpenbeck's the revelation of the girl's identity is accompanied by her claim to have completely forgotten the past, meaning that the narrative can go nowhere and must end.

While the texts I have explored involve individuals undergoing radical change, the texts' exploration of personal crisis can often be related to wider processes of social and political change. Under conditions of radical social and political upheaval, it is not only identities that may be called into question, but concepts of temporality, particularly the idea of progress from past to present. Social upheaval, like metamorphosis, undermines the continuity between past and present and raises the prospect of a future that is radically different.

Literary Transformations

Metamorphosis is often used to explore literary processes, since both involve inhabiting alternative existences. Indeed, bodily transformations are often paralleled with the imaginative or literary capacity to transform the way in which we perceive the world. For example, 'Der goldne Topf' is about Anselmus's need to develop a poetic sensitivity in order to become aware of metamorphosis and to enter another, wonderful realm. By copying manuscripts for Lindhorst, Anselmus learns to recognize the alternative, animal forms of those around him, and discovers the wonders of a 'Leben in der Poesie' [life in poetry]. The many metamorphoses in Hoffmann's texts are testament to the value Hoffmann places on imagination. In Hoffmann's work, metamorphosis can also be an animistic process of transforming something through bringing it to life. In 'Der goldne Topf', Anselmus's initiation into the imaginative realm involves an experience of nature coming alive. In Kafka's *Die Verwandlung*, the interior focus on the consequences of a single transformation mirrors Kafka's writing practice, which involves intense engagement with another being's perspective and affects.

The motif of caterpillar–butterfly metamorphosis can also act as a metaphor for writing. The life-cycle of the silk-moth allows for particularly apt comparison: like the silk worm, the writer spins threads to form a narrative, which ends as a complete, self-enclosed cocoon. Within the space of the cocoon, metamorphosis occurs: both the writer's enacting of metamorphosis through the writing process, but also the affective transformation of the reader upon reading the text. When writing is considered as a form of metamorphosis, the process of change is foremost: writing is not creation *ex nihilo*, but a process of re-shaping the material of everyday life, stories and literary texts, or linguistic expressions.

Not only do the texts often offer parallels between metamorphosis and literary writing, but they often make explicit the literary nature of the metamorphosis: that is, the way in which the scenario of metamorphosis arises through an imaginative act. In several of the texts I explored, language acts as inspiration for the metamorphosis: the expression 'nachäffen' [to ape] is central in Hoffmann's and Kafka's stories of ape–human metamorphosis, in which an ape becomes human through 'aping' human behaviour. In *Die Verwandlung*, the metaphorical use of 'Ungeziefer' as an insult is transformed into the imaginative scenario of actually being an 'Ungeziefer'. Being an 'Ungeziefer' is not so much about being a specific animal as about being abject. Through metaphor, metonymy, or linguistic ambiguity, creative possibilities arise that form a source for many metamorphosis stories. Such language play works best when it surprises through unexpected connections. Likewise, part of the surprise and satisfaction of metamorphosis tales is the unexpected transformation of affectively laden language into radical corporeal experience.

Affective Transformations

Affects transform bodies, and for this reason, metamorphosis stories are often also about affective transformation. In 'Der goldne Topf', Anselmus must learn to engage a different set of affects — the feelings of wonder and transcendence — in place of the mundane aggravations that hold him back from awareness of metamorphosis. In Hoffmann's work, the imaginative bodily metamorphoses within the stories often arise through the characters' affective transformation.

The kinds of affects that arise in metamorphosis texts provide insight into particular understandings of metamorphosis, identity, and change. First of all, metamorphosis surprises. For Descartes, wonder is the first of all the passions, for it is what we experience when we are surprised and moved, and which may then led to other passions.[14] The experience of wonder is a defining feature of tales of metamorphosis, which revolve around the shock of radical change. Such moments of shock pull us from impassionate disregard into the affective engagement upon which our values, concerns, and identities are formed.

After wonder, metamorphosis evokes a range of emotions. In particular, the confronting of different bodily existence prompts existential emotions: emotions based on acute awareness of one's position within an environment. Whereas in Ovid's *Metamorphoses* emotions such as jealousy, love, or rage lead to the transformations, in the modern texts I have explored, there may be no obvious reason for the transformation. Yet the possibility of metamorphosis is itself the generator of intense fears and desires surrounding an individual's identity. At least since Romanticism, the focalization through an individual's perspective has shifted attention from metamorphosis as plot device, to metamorphosis as a way of engaging with an individual's affective confrontation with changing body and identity.

The possibility of metamorphosis can evince horror and anxiety, but also positive responses, such as desire or longing. The intense awareness of the self during moments of personal change also allows for feelings of shame or guilt, since these feelings inhabit the gap between an actual and an ideal identity. Disgust and abjection are also key, since they involve pushing away an unwanted other that seems to have the potential for intruding into or contaminating the self. Abjection, in particular, is often regarded as being involved in the formation of the self. In chapter 3, the positioning of the two child figures as abject was part of a rejection of an unwanted past identity.

Metamorphosis also tends to evoke affects that are not always easy to place. The change and uncertainty that is part of metamorphosis brings with it mixed emotions. As Nabokov put it, metamorphosis does not involve 'the crude anguish of physical death but the incomparable pangs of the mysterious mental manoeuvre needed to pass from one state of being to another'.[15] Fluctuating affects often accompany unsettled identities and are a core aspect of literary engagement with metamorphosis. However, affects can be displayed very differently in different sociohistorical contexts. Tracing some of the shifts in the affective style of literary texts can also provide insight into changing configurations of self and identity. Metamorphosis texts, in particular, allow for close attention to configurations of identity and to different responses to the prospect of changing bodies and identities.

Cycles of Change

In modern German literature, metamorphosis articulates desires and fears over the possibility of identities becoming unstable. Hoffmann's Romantic texts might be seen as part of the start of this new engagement with metamorphosis, revealing desires for self-realization, but also fears over the loss of autonomy. The modern self with its depths of individual thought and intense feeling makes possible the metamorphoses within Hoffmann's texts. It is affects, understood as sublime and transgressive forces, that allow the individual to confront their inner depths or outer limits. Metamorphosis can thus be both self-realization made possible by poetic sensibility, but also a loss of autonomy through uncontrolled affect. The model of emotions as both intimating access to a 'higher' or 'deeper' self, but also as external forces threatening the self has been particularly influential. I argued that this model of emotion emerges alongside a configuration of modern identity as unstable and open to metamorphosis, once the external casing is shuffled off to reveal new, inner depths.

In Kafka's work, metamorphosis can also be a way of exploring unstable identity and the gulf between a real inner self and a social exterior. However, the individual crisis of metamorphosis is not articulated through the overt affects of Romantic literature, but rather, affects move below the surface to the forgotten realms that have been excluded from social life, the realms of the animal. Overt affective display is no longer a sign of the true individual, but of affectedness and social disreputability. By becoming animal, Kafka's figures access socially unsanctioned aspects of corporeal and affective existence. As a regression to an earlier stage of individual and evolutionary development, prior to the advent of language, such metamorphosis also engages with anxieties over the impossibility of communication. Chapter 2 thus represents the animal stage of this book, in which the literary imagination of being animal allows exploration of difficult aspects of human existence.

Chapter 3 foregrounds corporeality by examining texts that revolve around child figures that are invested with great affective charge. However, affects are neither overtly expressed as in Hoffmann, nor pushed under the surface as in Kafka, but follow a pattern of repression and release. The figures are positioned as abject, but the negative affects appear disproportionate and difficult to understand because of the repression of their original object. This affective pattern creates a tension which mirrors the narrative structure involving metamorphosis as a final revelation of identity. In these texts, affects are liable to erupt suddenly from an otherwise emotionally detached narrative. I argued that these moments of affectivity provide insight into the characters' pasts, which otherwise remain inaccessible. This chapter represents the pupal stage of my book, in which an abject animal-like body has spun itself into a protective cocoon, cutting itself off from the past, and hiding its true form. In this state, bodies and affects have to be reconfigured, pointing towards a radically different future, which remains enigmatic.

In Tawada's work metamorphosis still has the capacity to evoke fears and desires, but the possibility of an unstable subject and of identities becoming fragmented or multiple is no longer threatening. This means that the intense affectivity of metamorphosis is loosened, and emphasis shifts to a reflective engagement with the ways in which identities and bodies alter and transform under different social, cultural, and political conditions. Tawada's texts allow for an affirmation of unfixed identities, and with it comes an affirmation of metamorphosis. Although the 'ver' of 'Verwandlung' can have the sense of going awry, this does not mean that metamorphosis must be a horrific prospect and a morbid subject. As Tawada shows, metamorphosis can surprise and delight, with narratives that are playful and open to the new and unexpected. This model of metamorphosis emerges alongside a model of the subject that embraces the release from a stable, singular, unified identity. Chapter 4 examined how Tawada's work engages with and transforms older metamorphosis texts, thereby enacting metamorphosis as a literary process. In this sense, the chapter represents the metamorphic stage of the book as a whole, in which that which has gone before is reconfigured and emerges as something unexpected and different. At this stage, the subject no longer appears to have a stable basis but flies away as something as ephemeral and fleeting as a butterfly.

With this, we look into the unknown. But not towards an end, but towards new beginnings, new transformations, new ways of imagining moving identities. Even when we consider metamorphosis as part of an unending cycle of change, it still surprises, it still seems strange and unlikely, and it is this that gives the texts their power to affect and to transform. While the texts I have explored do this in different ways within different socio-cultural contexts, I have not regarded them as fixed products of historical moments, but I have, rather, emphasized their active potential. Stories of metamorphosis transform and are transformed as they come into contact with the readers who engage and reflect through a metamorphic imagination.

Notes to the Conclusion

1. Tzvetan Todorov, *The Fantastic: A Structural Approach to a Literary Genre*, trans. by Richard Howard (Ithaca: Cornell Paperbacks, 1975), p. 26.
2. Peter Cersowsky, *Phantastische Literatur im ersten Viertel des 20. Jahrhunderts: Untersuchungen zum Strukturwandel des Genres, seinen geistesgeschichtlichen Voraussetzungen und zur Tradition der 'schwarzen Romantik' insbesondere bei Gustav Mayrink, Alfred Kubin und Franz Kafka* (Munich: Fink, 1983), pp. 159–63.
3. Marina Warner, *Fantastic Metamorphoses, Other Worlds: Ways of Telling the Self* (Oxford and New York: Oxford University Press, 2002), p. 17.
4. Willem de Blécourt, 'Animal Shapeshifting. Between Literature and Everyday Life. An Introduction', in *Tierverwandlungen: Codierungen und Diskurse*, ed. by Willem de Blécourt (Tübingen: Francke, 2011), pp. 7–12 (p. 10).
5. Nelly Sachs, 'Banquet Speech' [1966], in *Nobel Lectures, Literature 1901–1967*, ed. by Horst Frenz (Amsterdam: Elsevier Publishing Company, 1969), pp. 619–20 (p. 620).
6. Paula Moya, 'Introduction', in *Realist Theory and the Predicament of Postmodernism*, ed. by Paula Moya and Michael R. Hames-Garciá (Berkeley: University of California Press, 2000), pp. 1–28 (pp. 2–6).
7. E.g. ibid., pp. 8–9. Moya argues for 'reclaiming identity', not through returning to an essentialist model of identity which is complicit with positivist assumptions, but through a postpositivist realist approach. See also Satya Mohanty, 'The Epistemic Status of Cultural Identity: On Beloved and the Postcolonial Condition', in *Realist Theory and the Predicament of Postmodernism* ed. by Paula Moya and Michael R. Hames-Garciá (Berkeley: University of California Press, 2000), pp. 29–66.
8. See Introduction.
9. Irving Massey, *The Gaping Pig: Literature and Metamorphosis* (Berkeley, Los Angeles, and London: University of California Press, 1976), p. 1.
10. Ibid.
11. Nabokov says that 'the caterpillar is a *he*, the pupa an *it*, and the butterfly a *she*' ('Nabokov's Butterflies, On Transformation', p. 54). Similarly, Tawada, in *Opium für Ovid*, explores the idea of transformation happening in sleep, a time in which everyone is androgynous (p. 71).

12. Elisabeth Grosz, *Volatile Bodies: Towards a Corporeal Feminism* (Bloomington: Indiana University Press, 1994), p. 175.
13. Friedmann Harzer, *Erzählte Verwandlung: Eine Poetik epischer Metamorphosen (Ovid, Kafka, Ransmayr)* (Tübingen: Niemeyer, 2000), pp. 38–39.
14. René Descartes, *The Passions of the Soul* [1649], trans. by Stephen Voss (Indianapolis: Hackett Publishing Company, 1989), book II, article 76.
15. Vladimir Nabokov, *Transparent Things* (London: Penguin, 2011), p. 100.

BIBLIOGRAPHY

Main Primary Texts

ERPENBECK, JENNY, *Geschichte vom alten Kind*, Text und Commentar, Buchners Schulbibliothek der Moderne (Bamberg: Buchners, 2008)
HOFFMANN, E. T. A., *Sämtliche Werke*, 6 vols, ed. by Wulf Segebrecht and others (Frankfurt a.M.: Deutscher Klassiker, 1985–2004)
KAFKA, FRANZ, *Gesammelte Werke*, Kritische Ausgabe, 12 vols, ed. by Hans-Gerd Koch (Frankfurt a.M: Fischer, 1994)
KASCHNITZ, MARIE LUISE, *Das dicke Kind und andere Erzählungen*, Text und Commentar, ed. by Asta-Maria Bachmann and Uwe Schweikert (Frankfurt a.M: Suhrkamp Basis-Bibliothek, 2002)
TAWADA, YOKO, *Opium für Ovid: Ein Kopfkissenbuch von 22 Frauen* (Tübingen: Konkursbuchverlag, 2000)
—— *Verwandlungen. Tübinger Poetik Vorlesungen* (Tübingen: Konkursbuchverlag, 1998)

Other Primary Literature

ADORNO, THEODOR W., 'Aufzeichnungen zu Kafka', in *Gesammelte Schriften*, ed. by Rolf Tiedemann, X.1: *Prisms* (Frankfurt am Main: Suhrkamp, 1997), pp. 254–87
ADORNO, THEODOR and MAX HORKHEIMER, *Dialektik der Aufklärung* (Frankfurt a.M.: Fischer, 1986)
APULEIUS, *The Golden Ass* (Or: *The Metamorphoses*), trans. by Sarah Ruden (New Haven: Yale, 2011)
BENJAMIN, WALTER, 'Die Aufgabe des Übersetzers', in *Gesammelte Schriften*, ed. by Rolf Tiedemann and Hermann Schweppenhäuser, IV.1: *Kleine Prose, Baudelaire-Übertragungen* (Frankfurt a.M.: Suhrkamp, 1991), pp. 9–21
—— *Benjamin über Kafka: Texte, Briefzeugnisse, Aufzeichnunen*, ed. by Hermann Schweppenhäuser (Frankfurt a.M.: Suhrkamp, 1981)
—— 'Über den Begriff der Geschichte', in *Gesammelte Schriften*, ed. by Rolf Tiedemann and Hermann Schweppenhäuser, I.2: *Abhandlungen 2* (Frankfurt a.M.; Suhrkamp, 1980), pp. 691–700
—— 'Über das Mimetische Vermögen', in *Gesammelte Schriften*, ed. by Rolf Tiedemann and Hermann Schweppenhäuser, VII.2: *Nachträge* (Frankfurt a.M.: Suhrkamp, 1989), pp. 791–92
DARRIEUSSECQ, MARIE, *Truismes* (Paris: P.O.L., 1997)
DARWIN, CHARLES, *The Expression of Emotions in Man and Animals* (Chicago: University of Chicago Press, 1969)
—— *On the Origin of Species* (Cambridge MA: Harvard University Press, 1975)
DESCARTES, RENÉ, *The Passions of the Soul* [1649], trans. by Stephen Voss (Indianapolis: Hackett Publishing Company, 1989)
EICHENDORFF, JOSEPH VON, *Sämtliche Gedichte und Versen*, ed. by Hartwig Schultz (Frankfurt a.M.: Deutscher Klassiker, 2006)

ERPENBECK, JENNY, *Dinge, die verschwinden* (Berlin: Galiani, 2009)

—— 'Erinnerung ist nur ein Blick zurück', *derStandard.at*, interview with Adalbert Reif, 6 Nov. 2009 (Printed edition 8–11–2009) <http://derstandard.at/1256744249081/Album-Interview-Erinnerung-ist-nur-ein-Blick-zurueck> [accessed 7 May 2015]

—— *Heimsuchung* (Frankfurt a.M.: Eichborn, 2008)

—— 'Man kann sich sein Verhältnis zur Vergangenheit nicht aussuchen', *Planet Interview*, interview with Maren Schuster and Martin Paul, 1 September 2008 <http://www.planet-interview.de/interviews/jenny-erpenbeck/34662/> [accessed 7 May 2015]

—— *The Old Child and The Book of Words*, trans. by Susan Bernofsky (London: Portabello, 2008)

FREUD, SIGMUND, *Gesammelte Werke*, ed. by Anna Freud, 18 vols (Frankfurt a.M. Fischer, 1948–99)

GOETHE, JOHANN WOLFGANG VON, *Sämtliche Werke, Briefe, Tagebücher und Gespräche*, 40 vols (Frankfurt a.M.: Dt. Klassiker, 1993–2011)

—— *The Sorrows of Young Werther*, trans. by Michael Hulse (London: Penguin, 1989)

GRIMM, JAKOB and WILHELM GRIMM, *Kinder und Hausmärchen: Ausgabe letzter Hand*, ed. by Heinz Rölleke (Stuttgart: Reclam, 2009)

GRIMMELSHAUSEN, HANS JAKOB CHRISTOFFEL VON, *Der abenteuerliche Simplicissimus Teutsch* (Stuttgart: Reclam, 1986)

HAECKEL, ERNST, *Die Welträtsel* [1899] (Norderstedt: Books on Demand, 2008)

HEBBEL, FRIEDRICH, 'Tagebuch 9. Januar 1842', *Werke*, IV, ed. by Gerhard Fricke, Werner Keller, and Karl Pörnbacher (Munich: Hanser. 1966), p. 458

HEGEL, GEORG WILHELM FRIEDRICH, *Phänomenologie des Geistes*, in *Werke*, III, ed. by Eva Moldenhauer and Karl Markus Michel (Frankfurt a.M.: Suhrkamp, 1986)

—— *Vorlesungen über die Ästhetik II*, in *Werke*, XIV, ed. by Eva Moldenhauer and Karl Markus Michel (Frankfurt a.M.: Suhrkamp, 1999)

—— *Werke*, 20 vols, ed. by Eva Moldenhauer and Karl Markus Michel (Frankfurt a.M.: Suhrkamp, 1986–2001)

HEINE, HEINRICH, *Sämtliche Schriften*, ed. by Klaus Briegleb, 6 vols (Munich: Deutscher Taschenbuchverlag, 1968–76)

HERDER, JOHANN GOTTFRIED, *Abhandlung über den Ursprung der Sprache* (Berlin: Christian Friedrich Voss, 1772)

—— 'Zum Sinn des Gefühls', in *Schriften zu Philosophie, Literatur und Kunst im Altertum*, ed. by Jürgen Brummack and Martin Bollacher, IV (Frankfurt a. M.: Deutscher Klassiker, 1994), pp. 233–42

HOFFMANN, E. T. A., *The Golden Pot and Other Tales*, trans. by Ritchie Robertson (Oxford: Oxford University Press, 2008)

HOFMANNSTHAL, HUGO VON, *Erfundene Gespräche und Briefe*, ed. by Ellen Ritter, XXXI: *Sämtliche Werke. Kritische Ausgabe*, 40 vols, ed. by Rudolf Hirsch and Heinz Otto Burger (Frankfurt a.M.: Fischer, 1991)

KAFKA, FRANZ, *Aphorisms* (New York: Schocken, 2015)

—— *Briefe*, 3 vols, ed. by Hans-Gerd Koch (Frankfurt a.M.: Fischer, 1999–2005)

—— *Briefe an Felice und andere Korrespondenz aus der Verlobungszeit*, ed. by Erich Heller and Jürgen Born (Frankfurt a.M.: Fischer, 1976, repr. 2003)

—— *Briefe an Milena*, ed. by Jürgen Born and Michael Müller (Frankfurt a.M.: Fischer, 1983)

—— *The Diaries of Franz Kafka, 1910–1913*, trans. by Joseph Kresh (New York: Schocken, 1948)

—— *The Diaries of Franz Kafka, 1914–1923*, trans. by Martin Greenberg (with the assistance of Hannah Arendt) (New York: Schocken, 1949)

—— *Tagebücher*, ed. by Hans-Gerd Koch, Michael Müller, and Malcolm Pasley (Frankfurt a.M.: Fischer, 1990)

—— *Tagebücher in der Fassung der Handschrift*, ed. by Michael Müller (Frankfurt a.M.: Fischer, 1983)
—— *The Metamorphosis and Other Stories*, trans. by Joyce Crick (Oxford: Oxford University Press, 2009)
—— *A Hunger Artist and Other Stories*, trans. by Joyce Crick (Oxford: Oxford University Press, 2012)
KANT, IMMANUEL, *Kritik der Urteilskraft* [1790] (Hamburg: tredition, 2011)
LENIN, V. I., *Revolution, Democracy, Socialism: Selected Writings*, ed.by Paul Le Blanc (London: Pluto Press, 2008)
LOCKE, JOHN, *An Essay Concerning Human Understanding* [1690] (Penguin: London, 1997)
MARX, KARL, 'Zur Kritik der Hegel'schen Rechts-Philosophie: Einleitung', in *Deutsch-französische Jahrbücher*, ed. by Arnold Ruge and Karl Marx (Paris: Bureau der Jahrbücher, 1844), pp. 71–85
MERIAN, MARIA SIBYLLA, *Metamorphosis Insectorum Surinamensium* (Selbstverlag: Amsterdam, 1705)
NABOKOV, VLADIMIR, *Lectures on Literature*, ed. by Fredson Bowers (San Diego, New York, and London: Harcourt, 1982)
—— 'Metamorphosen', in *Masken, Metamorphosen*, Literaturmagazin, 45, ed. by Delf Schmidt (Reinbek bei Hamburg: Rowohlt, 2000), pp. 45–46
—— 'Nabokov's Butterflies, On Transformation', *The Atlantic Monthly*, 285.4 (2000), 54
—— *Transparent Things* (London: Penguin, 2011)
NIETZSCHE, FRIEDRICH, *Sämtliche Werke*, Kritische Studienausgabe, ed. by Giorgio Colli and Mazzino Montinari, 15 vols (Munich: Dt. Taschenbuch, 1999)
OVID, *Metamorphoses*, Oxford Classical Texts (Oxford: Oxford University Press 2004)
—— *Metamorphoses*, trans. by A. D. Melville (Oxford: Oxford University Press, 1987)
PLATO, *Phaedo*, trans. by David Gallop (Oxford: Oxford University Press, 2009)
RILKE, RAINER MARIA, *Werke: Kommentierte Ausgabe in vier Bänden*, ed. by Manfred Engel, Ulrich Fülleborn, Horst Nalewski, and August Stahl (Leipzig: Insel Verlag, 1996)
SACHS, NELLY, 'Banquet Speech' [1966], in *Nobel Lectures, Literature 1901–1967*, ed. by Horst Frenz (Amsterdam: Elsevier Publishing Company, 1969)
SCHELLING, FRIEDRICH WILHELM JOSEPH VON, 'Ideen zu einer Philosophie der Natur', in *Schellings Werke: Nach der Original in neuer Anordnung*, ed. by Manfred Schröter, 12 vols (Munich: Beck, 1965), I, 77–350
—— *Von der Weltseele* (Hamburg: Perthes, 1798)
SEBALD, W. G., *Luftkrieg und Literatur: Mit einem Essay zu Alfred Andersch* (Munich: Hanser, 1999)
—— *Die Ringe des Saturn: Eine englische Wallfahrt* (Frankfurt a.M.: Eichborn, 2001)
SHŌNAGON, SEI, *The Pillow Book of Sei Shōnagon*, ed. and trans. Ivan I. Morris (New York and Chichester: Columbia University Press, 1991)
STEINTHAL, HEYMANN, *Abriss der Sprachwissenschaft*, Part 1: *Die Sprache im Allgemeinen*, 1: *Einleitung in die Psychologie und Sprachwissenschaft* (Berlin: Olms, 1881)
STRAUSS, BOTHO, *Die Nacht mit Alice als Julia ums Haus schlich* (Munich: C. Hanser, 2003)
TAWADA, YOKO, *Ein Gast* (Tübingen: Konkursbuchverlag, 1993)
—— *Henshin no tame no Opiumu* (Tokyo: Kodansha, 2001)
—— 'Missing heels', *The Bridegroom Was a Dog*, trans. by Margaret Mitsutani (Tokyo/ New York/ London: Kodansha International, 1998)
—— *Das Nackte Auge* (Tübingen: Konkursbuchverlag, 2004)
—— *Spielzeug und Sprachmagie in der europäischen Literatur: eine ethnologische Poetologie* (Tübingen: Konkursbuchverlag, 2000)
—— *Sprachpolizei und Spielpolyglotte* (Tübingen: Konkursbuchverlag, 2007)
—— *Talisman* (Tübingen: Konkursbuchverlag, 1996)

—— *Tokeru machi sukeru michi* (Tokyo: Nihon Keizai Shinbun Shuppansha, 2007)
—— *Überseezungen* (Tübingen: Konkursbuchverlag, 2002)
TROJANOW, ILIJA, *Der Weltensammler* (Munich: Hanser, 2006)
TIECK, LUDWIG, *Der blonde Eckbert/Der Runenberg* (Stuttgart: Reclam, 1984)
UEXKÜLL, JAKOB VON, *Streifzüge durch die Umwelten von Tiere und Menschen: Ein Bilderbuch unsichtbarer Welten* (Frankfurt a.M.: S. Fischer, 1970)
—— *Umwelt und Innenwelt der Tiere* (Berlin: Springer, 1909)
WELLS, H. G., *The Island of Doctor Moreau* (Toronto: Broadview, 2009)

Secondary Literature

ABEL, ELIZABETH, 'Revisionary Revelations: Women and Self-Worth in Two West-German Short Stories', in *The German Mosaic: Cultural and Linguistic Diversity in Society*, ed. by Carol Aisha Blackshire-Belay (Westport: Greenwood, 1994), pp. 63–71
ABRAHAM, ULF, *Franz Kafka: Die Verwandlung* (Frankfurt a.M.: Moritz Diesterweg, 1993)
ABU-LUGHOD, LILA, and CATHERINE LUTZ, eds, *Language and the Politics of Emotion* (Cambridge: Cambridge University Press), 1990)
ADELSON, LESLIE A., 'The Future of Futurity: Alexander Kluge and Yoko Tawada', *The Germanic Review*, 86.3 (2011), 153–84
—— 'Rusty Rails and Parallel Tracks: Trans-Latio in Yoko Tawada's *Das nackte Auge* (2004)', in *Un/Translatables*, ed. by Catriona MacLeod and Bethany Wiggin (Evanston, IL: Northwestern University Press, forthcoming, 2016)
AGAMBEN, GIORGIO, *The Open: Man and Animal* (Stanford: Stanford University Press, 2004)
AHMED, SARA, *The Cultural Politics of Emotion* (New York: Routledge, 2004)
ALCOFF, LINDA MARTÍN, 'Introduction: Identities: Modern and Postmodern', in *Identities: Race, Class, Gender and Nationality*, ed. by Linda Martín Alcoff and Eduardo Mendieta (Malden, MA: Blackwell, 2003), pp. 1–8
ALT, PETER-ANDRÉ, *Begriffsbilder: Studien zur literarischen Allegorie zwischen Opitz und Schiller* (Tübingen: Niemeyer, 1995)
—— *Franz Kafka. Der ewige Sohn. Eine Biographie* (Munich: Beck, 2005)
—— *Kafka und der Film: Über kinematographisches Erzählen* (Munich: Beck, 2009)
ALTIERI, CHARLES, *The Particulars of Rapture: An Aesthetics of the Affects* (Ithaca: Cornell University Press, 2003)
ANDERS, GÜNTHER, *Kafka — Pro und Contra* (Munich: Beck, 1951)
ANDERSON, MARK, *Kafka's Clothes: Ornament and Aestheticism in the Habsburg Fin de Siècle* (Oxford: Clarendon, 1992)
ANDERSON, SUSAN C., 'Surface Translations: Meaning and Difference in Yoko Tawada's German Prose', *Seminar: A Journal of Germanic Studies*, 46.1 (2010), 50–70
ARENS, HILTRUD, 'Das kurze Leuchten unter dem Tor oder auf dem Weg zur geträumten Sprache: Poetological Reflections in Works by Yoko Tawada', in *Yōko Tawada: Voices from Everywhere*, ed. by Doug Slaymaker (Lanham and Plymouth: Lexington Books, 2007), pp. 59–76
ARMSTRONG, PHILIP, *What Animals Mean in the Fiction of Modernity* (London: Routledge, 2008)
ARSLAN, GIZEM, 'Metamorphoses of the Letter in Paul Celan, Georges Perec, and Yoko Tawada' (Diss. Cornell University, 2013)
ASKER, D. B. D., *Aspects of Metamorphosis: Fictional Representations of the Becoming Human* (Amsterdam: Rodopi, 2001)
BAKHTIN, M. M., 'Forms of Time and of the Chronotope in the Novel: Notes towards a Historical Poetics', in *The Dialogic Imagination: Four Essays*, trans. by Caryl Emerson and Michael Holquist (Austin: University of Texas Press, 2004), pp. 84–258

BARTHES, ROLAND, *Empire of Signs*, trans. by Richard Howard (New York: Hill and Wang, 1983)
—— *Writing Degree Zero and Elements of Semiology*, trans. by Annette Lavers and Colin Smith (Boston: Beacon Press, 1967)
BARY, BRETT DE, 'Deixis, Dislocation, and Suspense in Translation: Tawada Yōko's *The Bath*', in *The Politics of Culture: Around the Work of Naoki Sakai*, ed. by Richard F. Calichman and John Namjun Kim (Oxford and New York: Routledge, 2010), pp. 40–51
BAY, HANSJÖRG, 'A und O. Kafka — Tawada', in *Yoko Tawada. Poetik der Transformation: Beiträge zum Gesamtwerk*, ed. by Christine Ivanović (Tübingen: Stauffenburg, 2010), pp. 149–70
BERENBAUM, MAY, 'Fatal Attraction', in *Insect Lives*, ed. by Hoyt and Schultz (New York, John Wiley & Sons, 1999), pp. 219–22
BERGER, FRANZ SEVERIN and CHRISTIANE HOLLER, *Trümmerfrauen: Alltag zwischen Hamstern und Hoffen* (Vienna: Ueberreuter, 1994)
BLACKMAN, LISA, *Immaterial Bodies: Affect, Embodiment, Mediation* (London: Sage, 2012)
BLÉCOURT, WILLEM DE, 'Animal Shapeshifting. Between Literature and Everyday Life. An Introduction', in *Tierverwandlungen: Codierungen und Diskurse*, ed. by Willem de Blécourt (Tübingen: Francke, 2011), pp. 7–12
BOA, ELIZABETH, 'Günter Grass and the German Gremlin', *German Life and Letters*, 23.2 (1970), 144–51
—— *Kafka: Gender, Class and Race in the Letters and Fictions* (Oxford: Clarendon Press, 1996)
BORN, JÜRGEN, *Kafkas Bibliothek: Ein beschreibendes Verzeichnis* (Frankfurt a.M.: Fischer, 1990)
BOWIE, ANDREW, 'Friedrich Wilhelm Joseph von Schelling', *Stanford Encyclopedia of Philosophy* (Winter 2010 Edition), ed. by Edward N. Zalta, <http://plato.stanford.edu/archives/win2010/entries/schelling/> [accessed 2 Apr. 2013].
BRAIDOTTI, ROSA, *Metamorphoses: Towards a Materialist Theory of Becoming* (Cambridge: Polity Press, 2002)
—— *Nomadic Subjects: Embodiment and Sexual Difference in Contemporary Feminist Theory* (New York: Columbia University Press, 1994)
BRANDT, BETTINA, 'The Unknown Character: Traces of the Surreal in Yoko Tawada's Writings', in *Yōko Tawada: Voices from Everywhere*, ed. by Doug Slaymaker (Lanham and Plymouth: Lexington Books, 2007), pp. 111–24
BRANDSTETTER, GABRIELE, 'Gesichter und Texturen: Zu einer Physiognomik der Falte — Rainer Maria Rilke, Aby Warburg, Yoko Tawada', in *Schrift und Bild und Körper* ed. by Ulrike Landfester (Bielefeld: Aisthesis, 2002)
BREGER, CLAUDIA, IRMELA KRÜGER-FÜRHOFF, and TANJA NUSSER, eds, *Engineering Life: Narrationen vom Menschen in Biomedizin, Kultur und Literatur* (Berlin: Kulturverlag Kadmos, 2008)
BREGER, CLAUDIA, 'Mimikry als Grenzverwirrung: Parodistische Posen bei Yoko Tawada', in *Über Grenzen: Limitation und Transgression in Literatur und Ästhetik*, ed. by Claudia Benthien and Irmela Krüger-Fürhoff (Stuttgart: Metzler, 1999), pp. 176–206
BRIDGWATER, PATRICK, *Kafka, Gothic and Fairytale* (Amsterdam and New York: Rodopi, 2003)
BRISON, SUSAN, *Aftermath: Violence and the Remaking of a Self* (Princeton: Princeton University Press, 2002)
BRITTNACHER, HANS RICHARD, *Ästhetik des Horrors: Gespenster, Vampire, Monster, Teufel und künstliche Menschen in der phantastischen Literatur* (Frankfurt a.M.: Suhrkamp, 1994)
BROD, MAX, *Über Franz Kafka* (Frankfurt a.M.: Fischer, 1966)
BROWN, H. M., *E. T. A. Hoffmann and the Serapiontic Principle: Critique and Creativity* (Rochester, NY: Camden House, 2006)
BRUCH, HILDE, *Eating Disorders: Obesity, Anorexia Nervosa and the Person Within* (London: Routledge and Kegan Paul, 1973)

BRUNNER-UNGRICHT, GABRIELA, *Die Mensch–Tier Verwandlung: eine Motivgeschichte unter besonderer Berücksichtigung des deutschen Märchens in der ersten Hälfte des 19. Jahrhunderts* (Bern: Land, 1998)

BYNUM, CAROLINE WALKER, *Metamorphosis and Identity* (New York and Cambridge, MA: Zone/MIT Press, 2001)

CANETTI, ELIAS, *Das Gewissen der Worte: Essays* (Munich: Hanser, 1983)

CERSOWSKY, PETER, *Phantastische Literatur im ersten Viertel des 20. Jahrhunderts: Untersuchungen zum Strukturwandel des Genres, seinen geistesgeschichtlichen Voraussetzungen und zur Tradition der 'schwarzen Romantik' insbesondere bei Gustav Mayrink, Alfred Kubin und Franz Kafka* (Munich: Fink, 1983)

CHO-SOBOTKA, MYUNG-HWA, *Auf der Suche nach dem weiblichen Subjekt: Studien zu Ingeborg Bachmanns 'Malina', Elfriede Jelineks 'Die Klavierspielerin' und Yoko Tawadas 'Opium für Ovid'* (Heidelberg: Universitätsverlag Winter, 2007)

CLARKE, BRUCE, *Allegories of Writing: The Subject of Metamorphosis* (Albany: State University of New York Press, 1995)

—— *Posthuman Metamorphosis: Narrative and Systems* (New York: Fordham, 2008)

CLOUGH, PATRICIA T., 'The Affective Turn: Political Economy, Biomedia and Bodies', *Theory, Culture and Society*, 25.1 (2008), 1–22.

CLOTTES, JEAN, *Chauvet Cave: The Art of Earliest Times*, trans. by Paul G. Bahn (Salt Lake City: University of Utah Press, 2003)

CORNGOLD, STANLEY, *Complex Pleasure: Forms of Feeling in German Literature* (Stanford: Stanford University Press, 1998)

—— *Franz Kafka: The Necessity of Form* (Ithaca/ London: Cornell University Press, 1988)

—— 'The Metamorphosis: Metamorphosis of the Metaphor', in *Franz Kafka: The Necessity of Form* (Ithaca, NY: Cornell University Press, 1988), pp. 47–89

—— and BENNO WAGNER, *Franz Kafka: The Ghosts in the Machine* (Evanston: Northwestern University Press, 2011)

COSGROVE, MARY and ANNE FUCHS, 'Introduction', in *Memory Contests: The Quest for Identity in Literature, Film and Discourse since 1990*, ed. by Anne Fuchs (Rochester, NY: Camden House, 2007), pp. 1–24

CSENGEI, ILDIKO, *Sympathy, Sensibility and the Literature of Feeling in the Eighteenth Century* (Basingstoke: Palgrave Macmillan, 2012)

DELEUZE, GILLES, *The Fold: Leibniz and the Baroque* (Minneapolis: University of Minnesota Press, 1993)

DELEUZE, GILLES and PIERRE FÉLIX GUATTARI, *Kafka: Towards a Minor Literature* (Minneapolis: University of Minnesota Press, 1986)

DENNEHY, TOBIAS, 'Weise Einfältigkeit vom unteren Ende der Hierarchieleiter: Jenny Erpenbecks nüchterne und anstrengende "Geschichte vom alten Kind"', *Literaturkritik*, 2 (2000), <http://www.literaturkritik.de/public/rezension.php?rez_id=835> [accessed 4 December 2015]

DENTE, CARLA, and others, eds, *Proteus: The Language of Metamorphosis* (Aldershot: Ashgate, 2005)

DETERDING, KLAUS, *E. T. A. Hoffmanns Leben und Werke* (Würzburg: Königshausen & Neumann, 2010)

DIJK, KARI VAN, '"Starting out with fragments": Zur androgynen Poetologie Yoko Tawadas unter besonderer Berücksichtigung von *Opium für Ovid*', in *Yoko Tawada. Poetik der Transformation: Beiträge zum Gesamtwerk*, ed. by Christine Ivanović (Tübingen: Stauffenburg, 2010), pp. 73–100

DODERER, KLAUS, *Die Kurzgeschichte in Deutschland: Ihre Form und ihre Entwicklung* (Darmstadt: Wissenschaftliche Buchgesellschaft, 1977)

DOUGLAS, MARY, *Purity and Danger: An Analysis of Concepts of Pollution and Taboo* [1966] (Abingdon: Routledge Classics, 2007)

EICHHORN, HANS, 'Die unerträgliche Leichtigkeit der Poesie: Marginalien zu Yoko Tawadas *Opium für Ovid*', *Text + Kritik*, 191/192 (2011), 43–46

EITLER, PASCAL, 'Der "Ursprung" der Gefühle — reizbare Menschen und reizbare Tiere', in *Gefühlswissen: eine lexicalische Spurensuche in der Moderne*, ed. by Ute Frevert and others (Frankfurt a.M.: Campus, 2011), pp. 93–120

ERVEDOSA, CLARA, 'Die Verfremdung des Fremden: Kulturelle und ästhetische Alterität bei Yoko Tawada', *Zeitschrift für Germanistik*, 16.3 (2006), 568–80

FISCHER, SABINE, 'Durch die japanische Brille gesehen: Die fiktive Ethnologie der Yoko Tawada', *Gegenwartsliteratur*, 2 (2003), 59–80

FLATLEY, JONATHAN, *Affective Mapping: Melancholia and the Politics of Modernism* (Cambridge, MA: Harvard University Press, 2008)

FOUCAULT, MICHEL, *Madness and Civilisation: A History of Insanity in the Age of Reason* (London: Tavistock, 1967)

FREVERT, UTE and OTHERS, *Gefühlswissen: eine lexicalische Spurensuche in der Moderne* (Frankfurt a.M.: Campus, 2011)

GALLAGHER, DAVID, *Metamorphosis: Transformations of the Body and the Influence of Ovid's Metamorphoses on Germanic Literature of the Nineteenth and Twentieth Centuries* (Amsterdam and New York: Rodopi, 2009)

GEISEL, SIEGLINDE, 'Kopfkissenbuch der Verwandlung: Die Anverwandlung literarischer Motive und Wahrnehmungsweisen von Ovid und Sei Shonagon in Yoko Tawadas *Opium für Ovid*', *Text + Kritik*, 191/192 (2011), pp. 47–53

GERHARDT, KRISTINA, 'The Ethics of Animals in Adorno and Kafka', *New German Critique*, 97, 33.1 (2006), 159–79

GILMAN, SANDER, *Franz Kafka* (London: Reaktion, 2005)

—— *Obesity: The Biography* (Oxford: Oxford University Press, 2010)

GLISSANT, EDOUARD, *Poetics of Relation*, trans. by Betsy Wing (Ann Arbor: University of Michigan Press, 1997)

GREGG, MELISSA and GREGORY J. SEIGWORTH, 'Introduction', in *The Affect Theory Reader*, ed. by Melissa Gregg, Gregory J. Seigworth, and Sara Ahmed (Durham, NC: Duke University Press, 2010), pp. 1–28

GREWE, MARIA S., *Estranging Poetic: On the Poetic of the Foreign in Select Works by Herta Müller and Yoko Tawada* (New York: BiblioBazaar, 2011)

GROSZ, ELISABETH, *Volatile Bodies: Towards a Corporeal Feminism* (Bloomington: Indiana University Press, 1994)

GÖTTSCHE, DIRK, ed., *'Für eine aufmerksamere und nachdenklichere Welt': Beiträge zu Marie Luise Kaschnitz* (Stuttgart and Weimar: Metzler, 2001)

HARZER, FRIEDMANN, *Erzählte Verwandlung: Eine Poetik epischer Metamorphosen (Ovid, Kafka, Ransmayr)* (Tübingen: Niemeyer, 2000)

HASSELBLATT, DIETER, *Zauber und Logik: Eine Kafka-Studie* (Cologne: Verlag Wissenschaft und Politik, 1964)

HENDRY, JOY, *Wrapping Culture: Politeness, Presentation, and Power in Japan and Other Societies* (Oxford and New York: Oxford University Press, 1999)

HERZOG, WERNER, dir., *Cave of Forgotten Dreams* (IFC Films/Sundance Selects, 2010. Film)

HILSCHER, EBERHARD, 'Hoffmanns poetische Puppenspiele und Menschenmaschinen', *Text + Kritik*, 3.2 (1992), 20–31

HÖFLE, PETER, 'Einleitung', in *Einfach Kafka* (Frankfurt a.M.: Suhrkamp, 2008), pp. 7–16

HOYT, ERICH and TED SCHULZ, eds, *Insect Lives: Stories of Mystery and Romance from a Hidden World* (New York: John Wiley & Sons, 1999)

HUYSSEN, ANDREAS, *After the Great Divide: Modernism, Mass Culture, Postmodernism* (Bloomington, IN: Indiana University Press, 1986)

ISHIHARA, AEKA, 'Warum kann der Knabe die Rose nicht in der Natur belassen? Tawada und Goethes *Heidenröslein*', in *Yoko Tawada. Poetik der Transformation: Beiträge zum Gesamtwerk*, ed. by Christine Ivanović (Tübingen: Stauffenburg, 2010), pp. 113–24

IVANOVIĆ, CHRISTINE, ed., *Yoko Tawada. Poetik der Transformation: Beiträge zum Gesamtwerk* (Tübingen: Stauffenburg, 2010)

—— 'Exophonie und Kulturanalyse: Tawadas Transformationen Benjamins' *Yoko Tawada. Poetik der Transformation: Beiträge zum Gesamtwerk*, ed. by Christine Ivanović, (Tübingen: Stauffenburg, 2010) pp. 171–206

JACKSON, ROSEMARY, *Fantasy: The Literature of Subversion* (London and New York: Routledge, 1981)

JAMES, SUSAN, *Passion and Action: The Emotions in Seventeenth-Century Philosophy* (Oxford: Oxford University Press, 1997)

JAMESON, FREDRIC, *Postmodernism, Or, The Cultural Logic of Late Capitalism* (Durham NC: Duke University Press, 1991)

JONES, KATIE, 'Ganz gewöhnlicher Ekel? Disgust and Body Motifs in Jenny Erpenbeck's *Geschichte vom alten Kind*', in *Pushing at Boundaries: Approaches to Contemporary German Women Writers from Karen Duve to Jenny Erpenbeck*, ed. by by Heike Bartel and Elizabeth Boa, German Monitor, 64 (Amsterdam and New York: Rodopi, 2006)

KEPPLER, STEFAN, *Grenzen des Ich: Die Verfassung des Subjekts in Goethes Romanen und Erzählungen* (Berlin: Walter de Gruyter, 2006)

KERSTING, RUTH, *Fremdes Schreiben: Yoko Tawada* (Trier: Wiss. Verlag Trier, 2006)

KIM, JOHN NAMJUN, 'Ethnic Irony: The Poetic Parabasis of the Promiscuous Personal Pronoun in Yoko Tawada's "Eine leere Flasche" (A Vacuous Flask)', *The German Quarterly*, 83.3 (2010), 333–52

KOIRAN, LINDA, *Schreiben in fremde Sprache: Yoko Tawada und Galsan Tschinag* (Munich: Iudicium, 2009)

KOPPENFELS, MARTIN VON, *Immune Erzähler: Flaubert und die Affektpoetik des modernen Romans* (Munich: Wilhelm Fink Verlag, 2007)

KÖPPING, KLAUS-PETER, '"Bauch haben": Die Inszenierung von Gemeinschaftsgefühl in Japan', in *Emotionalität: Zur Geschichte der Gefühle*, ed. by Claudia Benthien, Anne Fleig, and Ingrid Kasten Cologne: Böhlau, 2000), pp. 213–37

KRAENZLE, CHRISTINE, 'The Limits of Travel: Yoko Tawada's Fictional Travelogues', *German Life and Letters*, 61.2 (2008), 244–60

—— 'Mobility, Space and Subjectivity: Yoko Tawada and German-Language Transnational Literature' (Diss. University of Toronto, 2004)

—— 'Travelling without Moving: Physical and Linguistic Mobility, Translation, and Identity in Yoko Tawada's *Überseezungen*', *Transit*, 2.1 (2006), 1–15

KREMER, DETLEF, *Romantische Metamorphosen: E. T. A. Hoffmanns Erzählungen* (Stuttgart: Metzler, 1993)

—— *E. T. A. Hoffmann: Erzählungen und Romane* (Berlin: Schmidt, 1999)

KRISTEVA, JULIA, *Powers of Horror: An Essay on Abjection*, trans. by Leon S. Roudiez (New York: Columbia University Press, 1982)

KURIBAYASHI, TOMOKO, 'Nomadic Narratives: Yoko Tawada's Japanese-German fiction', in *Traversing Transnationalism: The Horizons of Literary and Cultural Studies*, ed. by by Pier Paolo Frassinelli, Ronit Frenkel, and David Watson (Amsterdam: Rodopi, 2011) pp. 137–54

LACAN, JACQUES, 'Some Reflections on the Ego,', *International Journal of Psychoanalysis*, 34 (1951), 11–17

LAUER, GERHARD, 'Spiegelneuronen: Über den Grund des Wohlgefallens an der Nachahmung'. *Rücken der Kulturen*, ed. by by Karl Eibl, Katja Mellmann, and Rüdiger Zymner (Paderborn: Mentis, 2007), pp. 137–63

LOEB, ERNST, 'Bedeutungswandel der Metamorphose bei Franz Kafka und E. T. A. Hoffmann: Ein Vergleich', *The German Quarterly*, 35.1 (1962), 47–59

LUCHT, MARC, and DONNA YARI, eds, *Kafka's Creatures: Animals, Hybrids and other Fantastic Beings*, (Lanham: Lexington, 2010)
MARX, LEONIE, *Die deutsche Kurzgeschichte* (Stuttgart: J. B. Metzler, 2005)
MASSEY, IRVING, *The Gaping Pig: Literature and Metamorphosis*, (Berkeley, Los Angeles, and London: University of California Press, 1976)
MEJCHER-NEEF, ANNEMARIE, 'Yoko Tawada: *Talisman*', *Frauen in der Literaturwissenschaft: Rundbrief*, 49 (1996), 68–69
MENNINGHAUS, WINFRIED, *Ekel: Theorie und Geschichte einer starken Empfindung* (Frankfurt a.M.: Suhrkamp, 1999)
MAYER, PETRA, 'Hoffmanns poetischer Bullenbeißer — eine Ausgeburt des Grotesken. Nachricht von den neuesten Schicksalen des Hundes Berganza', *E. T. A. Hoffmann-Jahrbuch* ed. by Hartmut Steinecke and others, vol. 15 (2007) pp. 7–24.
MEYER-SICKENDIEK, BURKHARD, *Affektpoetik: Eine Kulturgeschichte literarischer Emotionen* (Würzburg: Königshausen und Neumann, 2005)
MILLER, WILLIAM IAN, *The Anatomy of Disgust* (Cambridge, MA: Harvard University Press, 1997)
MINDEN, MICHAEL, 'Kafka's *Josefine, die Sängerin oder Das Volk der Mäuse*', *German Life and Letters*, 62.3 (2009), 297–310
MOHANTY, SATYA, 'The Epistemic Status of Cultural Identity: On Beloved and the Postcolonial Condition', in *Realist Theory and the Predicament of Postmodernism*, ed. by Paula Moya and Michael R. Hames-Garciá (Berkeley: University of California Press, 2000), pp. 29–66
MOYA, PAULA, 'Introduction', in *Realist Theory and the Predicament of Postmodernism*, ed. by Paula Moya and Michael R. Hames-Garciá (Berkeley: University of California Press, 2000), pp. 1–28
MOYA, PAULA and MICHAEL R. HAMES-GARCIÁ, eds, *Realist Theory and the Predicament of Postmodernism* (Berkeley: University of California Press, 2000)
MURNANE, BARRY, 'Ungeheuere Arbeiter: Moderne Monstrosität am Beispiel von Gregor Samsa', in *Monster: zur ästhetischen Verfassung eines Grenzbewohners*, ed. by Roland Borgards, Christiane Holm, and Günter Oesterle (Würzburg: Königshausen & Neumann, 2009), pp. 289–308
NAGEL, THOMAS, 'What is it like to be a bat?', *The Philosophical Review*, 84.4 (1974), 435–50
NEUMANN, GERHARD, 'Romantische Aufklärung: Zu E. T. A. Hoffmanns Wissenschaftspoetik', in *Aufklärung als Form: Beiträge zu einem historischen und aktuellen Problem*, ed. by Helmut Schmiedt and Helmut J. Schneider (Würzburg: Königshaus– & Neumann, 1997)
NICKLAS, PASCAL, *Die Beständigkeit des Wandels: Metamorphosen in Literatur und Wissenschaft* (Hildesheim: Olms, 2002)
NOBILE, NANCY, '"So morgen wie heut": Time and Context in Jenny Erpenbeck's *Geschichte vom alten Kind*', in *Gegenwartsliteratur*, II, ed. by Paul Michael Lützeler and Stephan K. Schneider (Tübingen: Stauffenburg, 2003), pp. 283–84
NUSSBAUM, MARTHA, *Upheavals of Thought: The Intelligence of Emotions* (Cambridge: Cambridge University Press, 2003)
ORBAUGH, SHARALYN, 'The Body in Contemporary Japanese Women's Fiction', in *The Woman's Hand: Gender and Theory in Japanese Women's Writing*, ed. by Paul Schalow and Janet Walker (Stanford University Press, 1996), pp. 119–64
O'SULLIVAN, SIMON, 'Fold', in *The Deleuze Dictionary: Revised Edition*, ed. by Adrian Parr (Edinburgh: Edinburgh University Press, 2010), pp. 107–08
PARKINSON, ANNA, 'Aptitudes of Feeling: Ekphrasis as Prosthetic Witnessing in Anne Duden's *Judas Sheep*', *New German Critique*, 112.38 (2011), 39–63
PARKES, STUART and JOHN J. WHITE, eds, *German Monitor: Gruppe 47 Fifty Years On* (Amsterdam: Rodopi, 1999)

PERLOFF, MARJORIE, 'Foreword', in *Yōko Tawada: Voices from Everywhere*, ed. by Doug Slaymaker (Lanham: Lexington Books, 2007), pp. vii–ix

PINFOLD, DEBBIE, *The Child's View of the Third Reich in German Literature: The Eye among the Blind* (Oxford: Oxford University Press, 2001)

PULVER, ELSBETH, *Marie Luise Kaschnitz* (Munich: C. H. Beck, 1984)

REBER, URSULA, *Formenverschleifung: zu einer Theorie der Metamorphose* (Paderborn: Fink, 2009)

RICHARDS, ANNA, 'Suffering, Silence and the Female Voice in German Fiction around 1800', *Women in German Yearbook*, 18 (2002), 89–100

ROBERTSON, RITCHIE, *Kafka: Judaism, Politics, and Literature* (Oxford: Clarendon, 1985)

ROSSBACH, NIKOLA, '"Gepeinigt von Phantasie": Autobiographische Kindheitsentwürfe bei Marie Luise Kaschnitz', in *'Für eine aufmerksamere und nachdenklichere Welt': Beiträge zu Marie Luise Kaschnitz*, ed. by Dirk Göttsche (Stuttgart and Weimar: Metzler, 2001), pp. 49–64

RYAN, JUDITH, *The Vanishing Subject: Early Psychology and Literary Modernism* (Chicago: Chicago University Press, 1991)

SAID, EDWARD, *Orientalism* [1978] (New York: Vintage, 1994)

SALISBURY, JOYCE E., *The Beast Within: Animals in the Middle Ages* (New York: Routledge, 1994)

SANDNER, DAVID, *Fantastic Literature: A Critical Reader* (Westport: Praeger, 2004)

SCHEER, MONIQUE, 'Topographien des Gefühls', in Ute Frevert and others, *Gefühlswissen: Eine lexikalische Spurensuche in der Moderne* (Frankfurt a.M.: Campus, 2011), pp. 41–64

SCHERER, K. R., 'Appraisal Theories', in *Handbook of Cognition and Emotion*, ed. by T. Dalgleish and M. Power (Chichester: Wiley, 1999), pp. 637–63

SCHMITZ-EMANS, MONIKA, *Franz Kafka. Epoche — Werk — Wirkung* (Munich: C. H. Beck, 2010)

—— 'Metamorphose und Metempsychose: Zwei konkurrierende Modelle von Verwandlungen im Spiegel der Gegenwartsliteratur', *Arcadia*, 40 (2005), 390–413

—— *Poetiken der Verwandlung* (Innsbruck: Studienverlag, 2008)

SCHWAB, GABRIELE, 'Words and Moods: The Transference of Literary Knowledge', SubStance, Vol.26 No.3, No. 84, 1997, pp. 107–27.

SKULSKY, HAROLD, *Metamorphosis. The Mind in Exile* (Cambridge, MA and London: Harvard University Press, 1981)

SLAYMAKER, DOUG, ed., *Yōko Tawada: Voices from Everywhere* (Lanham: Lexington Books, 2007)

SOKEL, WALTER H., *The Myth of Power and the Self: Essays on Franz Kafka* (Detroit: Wayne State University Press, 2002)

—— 'Nietzsche and Kafka: The Dionysian Connection', in *Kafka for the Twenty-First Century*, ed. by Stanley Corngold and Ruth V. Gross (Rochester, NY: Camden House, 2011), pp. 64–74

—— 'Towards the Myth [Festrede]', *Journal of the Kafka Society of America*. June/Dec. 1998, pp. 7–15

—— *The Writer in Extremis: Expressionism in Twentieth-Century Literature* (Stanford: Stanford University Press, 1959)

SPILKA, MARK, 'Kafka's Sources for *The Metamorphosis*', *Comparative Literature*, 11 (1959), 289–307

SUVIN, DARKO and CARLA DENTE, 'Some Thoughts on Metamorphosis: An Interview with Darko Suvin', in *Proteus: The Language of Metamorphosis* ed. by Carla Dente and others (Aldershot: Ashgate, 2005), pp. 13–22

SZENTIVANYI, CHRISTINA, '"Tawada Yoko Does Not Exist"/"Dichter sind Alchimisten" — Transformatives Fließen in Texten Yoko Tawadas', in *Yoko Tawada. Poetik der Transformation: Beiträge zum Gesamtwerk*. ed. by Christine Ivanović (Tübingen: Stauffenburg, 2010), pp. 441–48

TACHIBANA, REIKO, *Narrative as Counter-Memory* (New York: State University of New York Press, 1998)
TATAR, MARIA M., *The Hard Facts of the Grimms' Fairy Tales* (Princeton: Princeton University Press, 2003)
—— 'E. T. A. Hoffmann's "Der Sandmann": Reflection and Romantic Irony,' *Modern Language Notes*, 95 (1980), 585–608
—— 'Mesmerism, Madness and Death in Hoffmann's "Der goldne Topf"', *Studies in Romanticism*, 14.4 (1975), 365–89
TAYLOR, CHARLES, *Sources of the Self: The Making of Modern Identity* (Cambridge, MA: Harvard University Press, 1989)
TERADA, REI, *Feeling in Theory: Emotion after the 'Death of the Subject'* (Cambridge. MA and London: Harvard University Press, 2001)
TODOROV, TZVETAN, *The Fantastic: A Structural Approach to a Literary Genre*, trans. by Richard Howard (Ithaca: Cornell Paperbacks, 1975)
TYLER, LISA, 'Revisionary Revelations: Women and Self-Worth in Two West-German Short Stories', *The German Mosaic: Cultural and Linguistic Diversity in Society* ed. by Carol Aisha Blackshire-Belay (Westport: Greenwood, 1994), pp. 63–71
WARNER, MARINA, *Fantastic Metamorphoses, Other Worlds: Ways of Telling the Self* (Oxford and New York: Oxford University Press, 2002)
WASHINOSU, YUMIKO, 'Sumidagawa no shiwaotoko oder Text der Trans-Formation' *Yoko Tawada. Poetik der Transformation: Beiträge zum Gesamtwerk*, ed. by Christine Ivanović (Tübingen: Stauffenburg, 2010), pp. 101–12
WATKINS, HOLLY, *Metaphors of Depth in German Musical Thought: From E. T. A. Hoffmann to Arnold Schoenberg* (Cambridge: Cambridge University Press, 2011)
WEBBER, ANDREW, *The Doppelgänger: Double Visions in German Literature* (Oxford: Clarendon, 1996)
WEIGEL, SIGRID, 'Shylocks Wiederkehr: Die Verwandlung von Schuld in Schulden', in *Fünfzig Jahre danach: Zur Nachgeschichte des Nationalsozialismus*, ed. by Sigrid Weigel and Birgit R. Erdle (Zürich: VDF, 1996), pp. 165–92
WETHERELL, MARGARET, *Affect and Emotion: A New Social Science Understanding* (London: Sage, 2012)
—— ed., *Identity in the 21st Century: New Trends in Changing Times* (Basingstoke: Palgrave Macmillan, 2011)
WIRTZ, ISABEL, 'Jenny Erpenbeck: Geschichte vom alten Kind', *Bayrischer Rundfunk Online*, 28 December 2000
WÖLLNER, GÜNTER, *E. T. A. Hoffmann und Franz Kafka: Von der 'fortgeführten Metapher' zum 'sinnlichen Paradox'* (Berne: Haupt, 1971)
YILDIZ, YASEMIN, *Beyond the Mother Tongue: The Postmonolingual Condition* (New York: Fordham University Press, 2012)
ZILCOSKY, JOHN, '"Samsa war Reisender": Trains, Trauma, and the Unreadable Body', in *Kafka for the Twenty-First Century* ed. by by Stanley Corngold and Ruth V. Gross (Rochester, NY: Camden House, 2011), pp. 179–97
ZIMMERMANN, GISBERT, 'Maikäfer in Deutschland: geliebt und gehasst. Ein Beitrag zur Kulturgeschichte und Geschichte der Bekämpfung', *Journal für Kulturpflanzen*, 62.5 (2010), 157–72
ZIOLKOWSKI, THEODORE, *Ovid and the Moderns* (Ithaca, NY: Cornell University Press, 2005)
ZUPANČIČ, ALENKA, *The Shortest Shadow: Nietzsche's Philosophy of the Two* (Cambridge, MA: MIT Press, 2003)

INDEX

❖

abjection 88, 90–91, 167
Abraham, Ulf 72
Abu-Lughod, Lila and Catherine Lutz 9, 146
Adelson, Leslie 121, 122, 143
Adorno, Theodor 65
  and Max Horkheimer 5, 68
affect 9–11, 21, 159, 160, 166–69 (*see also* emotions)
  cultural theories of 9, 146
    intense 40, 113, 159
  lack of 93, 112, 143, 148
    Romantic 24, 27
  transformation of 22–25, 31
  as transformative 11, 144–49
  use of term 10
Ahmed, Sara 146
Akinari, Ueda 137
Altieri, Charles 10
anagnorisis 1, 98, 117, 165
Anders, Günther 60
Anderson, Susan 122, 149
animal transformations
  ape 8, 41–42, 69–71, 163, 166
  butterfly/ moth 88, 96, 111–12
  dog 43–45, 65, 77, 79
  fish 137
  pig 8
animal studies 65
animism 19, 25, 34, 130
Apuleius, *The Golden Ass* 7, 14, 41
Arabian Nights 1
Arens, Hiltrud 150
Aristotle 5, 9, 160
Asker, D. B. D. 12
Aue, Hartmann von, *Gregorius* 67
Authorship 125, 135–37, 141

Bachmann-Medick, Doris 121
Bakhtin, Mikhail 7
Baldanders 8
Barthes, Roland 137
  Le degré zéro de l'écriture 143
  L'Empire des Signes 139–40
Bay, Hansjörg 141
Beer-Hofmann, Richard 13
Benjamin, Walter
  'Die Aufgabe des Übersetzers' 126, 132, 140
  'Über den Begriff der Geschichte' 115
  on Kafka 81, 131

mimetic capacity 63
  discussed by Tawada 150
Bildungsroman 7, 19, 111, 153
Blécourt, Willem de 162
bodily experience 6–7, 14, 65–68, 110–12, 164–65
Braidotti, Rosa 162
Brandstetter, Gabrielle 139–40
Brentano, Clemens 13
Broch, Hermann 13
Brod, Max 71
Brown, Hilda 32
Bruch, Hilde 106
Brunner-Ungricht, Gabriela 26
butterfly motif 88, 96, 111–12
Bynum, Caroline Walker 12

Callot, Jacques 22, 40
Calvino, Italo 13
Camus, Albert, *L'Étranger* 143
Canetti, Elias 7
caterpillar motif 91–92, 111
Cho-Sobotka, Myung-Hwa 127, 134, 136–37, 139
Cervantes, Miguel de 42
Cixous, Hélène 6
Clarke, Bruce 13, 31
Clough, Patricia 11, 147
cocoon motif 96, 111–12, 136–37
Conrad, Joseph 13
Corngold, Stanley 56, 60, 62, 78
  and Benno Wagner 61
corporeality *see* bodily experience
Cosgrove, Mary 114
creation *ex nihilo* 8, 136, 166

Dante, Alighieri 5
Daphne 129–30
Darrieussecq, Marie, *Truismes* 8
Darwin, Charles 12, 13, 69
  The Expression of the Emotions in Man and Animals 81
  On the Origin of Species 81
Deleuze, Gilles 97, 128, 161
  and Félix Guattari 73, 162, 164
  The Fold: Leibniz and the Baroque 140–41
Descartes, René 5, 167
Dickens, Charles, *The Pickwick Papers* 92
Dijk, Kari van 126–27, 144
disgust 65–68, 70, 71, 91, 101, 167
Doderer, Klaus 88

Doppelgänger 20

Eichendorff, Joseph Freiherr von 25
emotions 9–10, 167 (*see also* affect)
   and animality 80
   appraisal theory 11
      as external forces 4, 39, 145, 168
Enlightenment 3–4, 5, 19, 35, 48
Erpenbeck, Jenny 87–88
   Dinge, die verschwinden 87
      Geschichte vom alten Kind 7, 87–88, **98–110**, 110–17, 160, 161, 164
   Heimsuchung 88
Erpenbeck, John 107
escapism 30
evolution 12, 68–71, 81
expressionism 60

fairy-tales, *see Märchen*
fantastic literature 20, 29, 30, 58, 123, 159–60
Flatley, Jonathan 10
folds 137–41
Foucault, Michel 35
Freud, Sigmund 55, 93
   'Das Unheimliche' 34, 36, 37–38, 57, 89
   on trauma 105, 113
      Die Traumdeutung 13
Fuchs, Anne and Mary Cosgrove 114

Gallagher, David 12
GDR 99, 101, 103, 108–09, 116
'Gemüt' 48–50
Gilman, Sander 92, 106
Glissant, Édouard, *Poetics of Relation* 128
globalization 120–22
Goethe, Johann Wolfgang
   'Die Braut von Korinth' 36
   'Heidenröslein' 153
   on Hoffmann 21
   Die Leiden des jungen Werthers 63, 77–78
   'Metamorphose der Pflanzen' 13, 153
   on the novella 68, 99
   Wilhelm Meisters Lehrjahre 92
golem 127
Gotthelf, Jeremias, *Die schwarze Spinne* 12
Göttsche, Dirk 96–97
Grass, Günter, *Die Blechtrommel* 116
Gregg, Melissa and Gregory J. Seigworth, 11
Grimm, Jakob and Wilhelm
   'Das junggeglühte Männlein' 103
      Kinder- und Hausmärchen 19
Grimmelshausen, *Simplicissimus* 8
Grosz, Elisabeth 150, 164
Guattari, Félix 162, 164

Haeckel, Ernst 71
   Die Welträtsel 76

Haraway, Donna 124
Harzer, Friedmann 13, 165
Hasselblatt, Dieter 58
Hebbel, Friedrich 50
Hegel, Georg Wilhelm Friedrich 5, 97, 163
Heine, Heinrich 21
Hendry, Joy 138
Herbst, Alban Nikolai 13
Herder, Johann Gottfried 21
   'Ursprung der Sprache' 42, 163
Hesse, Hermann 12
Hodrová, Daniela, *Città Dolente* 126, 142
Hoffmann, E.T.A. 4, 8, 14, 15, 20, 55
   'Nachricht von den neuesten Schicksalen des Hundes Berganza' 21, 40, **42–45**, 49, 77
   'Don Juan' 24
   Fantasiestücke in Callots Manier 20, 21, 22, 29, 33
   'Das fremde Kind' 130
   'Der goldne Topf' 21, **22–33**, 34, 160, 161, 166
   Die Lebens-Ansichten des Katers Murr 49, 131
   Meister Floh 34
   'Nachricht von einem gebildeten jungen Mann' [Milo] 21, 40, **41–43**, 48, 49, 69
   Nachtstücke 33, 34
   'Rat Krespel' 24
   'Der Sandmann' 21, **33–40**, 46–47
   Die Serapionsbrüder 36–37
   Undine 20
   Klein Zaches, genannt Zinnober 47–48
Hofmannsthal, Hugo von 64
Hölderlin, Friedrich 142
Homer 13, 79
humanity 5–6, 163

identity:
   gender 6, 34, 93, 100, 112, 152, 164
   modern 4, 14, 21, 54, 168
   personal 3–4, 6, 11, 12–13, 14, 18, 19, 160
   social 4
intertextuality 8, 13, 14, 15, 121, 128–35, 139
Io 74, 76
Ivanović, Christine 132

Jackson, Rosemary 33
Jameson, Frederic 148–49
Jones, Katie 101
Joyce, James 13

Kafka, Franz 13, 14, 15, 47, 55–56, 129
   and E.T.A. Hoffmann 41, 43, 47, 55
   works:
      Der Bau 64, 73
      'Ein Bericht für eine Akademie' 5, 56, 69–73, 76, 131, 144, 161
      'Blumfeld, ein ältere Junggeselle' 126, 130–31
      'Brief an den Vater' 76
      'Elf Söhne' 127

'Forschungen eines Hundes' 65, 77, 79, 131
'Hochzeitsvorbereitungen auf dem Lande' 63
'Ein Hungerkünstler' 66, 81
In der Strafkolonie 58
'Josefine, die Sängerin' 63, 77, 79
'Unglücklichsein' 59–60, 89
Das Urteil 58, 63, 64
'Das Schweigen der Sirenen' 79
'Die Sorges des Hausvaters' 63
Der Verschollene 56
Die Verwandlung 6, 12, 47, **56–82**, 108, 114, 125, 131, 137, 142, 144, 160, 161, 163, 165, 166
'Vor dem Gesetz' 73
Kant, Immanuel 24, 28, 160
Kaschnitz, Marie Luise, 'Das dicke Kind' 6, **87–98**, 110–17, 164
 'Lupinen' 97, 161
Keats, John 13
Kim, John Namjun 152
Klee, Paul, *Angelus Novus* 115
Koppenfels, Martin von, *Immune Erzähler* 93
Köpping, Klaus-Peter 151
Kremer, Detlef 31, 32–33, 38, 47
Kristeva, Julia 88, 91

Lacan, Jacques 97
La Mettrie, *L'Homme Machine* 46
language crisis 64, 76
language, losing *see* voicelessness
language play 8–9, 12, 41, 43, 62, 121, 166
Leda 129
Lenin, V.I. 146
Locke, John 4, 160
Loeb, Ernst 47

machine-like existence 5, 37, 45–46, 55, 68
madness 35–36
Mann, Thomas 12
Märchen 19, 20, 22, 29, 57–58, 102
Marx, Karl 129, 146
Marx, Leonie 111
Massey, Irving 12, 33, 163
memory contests 114
Menninghaus, Winfried 59
Merian, Maria Sibylla 15
'Metamorphose' 2
Metamorphosis
 alchemical 31, 38
 animal, *see* animal transformations
 animistic 34
 as allegory of writing 31, 136, 165–66
 as 'Ausweg' 72–73
 as bodily process 6, 164
 cabbalistic 31, 38
 cybernetic (*see also* machine-like existence) 13, 55
 degrading 5, 6, 44, 75, 78, 80, 163
 through hormones 124, 145

as literary process 7–9, 135–37, 165–66
perceptual 25–29
protean 20
as regression 7, 68, 82, 163, 165
metaphor 8, 9, 32–33, 41, 60–62, 78, 129, 136, 150, 166
metempsychosis 6, 164
metonymy 9, 33, 130–31, 166
mimesis 7, 63
Minden, Michael 79
modernism 54–55
monstrosity 60, 68, 108
Murnane, Barry 78
music 20, 24, 25, 31, 41, 45, 46, 48, 77–80, 82, 127
muteness, *see* voicelessness

Nabokov, Vladimir 62, 112, 125, 162, 164, 167
Nagel, Thomas 12
Narcissus 95
Naturphilosophie 29, 35
Nicklas, Pascal 13
Nietzsche, Friedrich 78, 142
 Zur Genealogie der Moral 41, 42, 66
 Also sprach Zarathustra 38
Nobile, Nancy 99, 102, 107, 108
novella 68, 99, 111, 165
Nussbaum, Martha 82

obesity 92, 106
Opium Wars 124, 133
Orbaugh, Sharalyn 150
Ovid, *Metamorphoses* 3, 12, 13, 14, 41, 74, 76, 128–35, 167

Parkinson, Anna 10
Plato 5, 9, 13, 164
postcolonialism 124, 135
posthumanism 13
postmodern literature 13, 122, 135, 148–49
Pulver, Elsbeth 88, 96, 98

de Quincey, Thomas 47

Ransmayr, Christoph 13
Rausch 133–36, 141–42, 145, 148, 152
Reber, Ursula 13
rhizomatic relationships 128
Richards, Anna 112
Rilke, Rainer Maria:
 Die Aufzeichnungen des Malte Laurids Brigge 55
 Duineser Elegien 72
Robertson, Ritchie 64, 68
Romanticism 4, 14, 19–21, 80
Romantic irony 30, 39
Roßbach, Nikola 92–93
Rousseau, Jean-Jacques 163
Ryan, Judith 54–55

Sachs, Hans 8

Sachs, Nelly 12, 96, 111, 162
Sacher-Masoch, Leopold von 67
Schelling, Friedrich Wilhelm Joseph 28
    Von der Weltseele 29
Schmitz-Emans, Monika 12, 55, 133
Schubert, Gotthilf Heinrich von 24
'Schuld' 65, 104, 106
Schwab, Gabriele 80
Sebald, W. G.:
    Luftkrieg und Literatur 103
    Die Ringe des Saturn 8
Serapiontic principle 37
silk/silkworms 138
Shakespeare 13
shame, *see* 'Schuld'
Shikibu, Murasaki, *The Tale of Genji* 134–35
Shōnagon, Sei, *The Pillow Book* 134–35
short story 88, 99, 111, 165
Skulsky, Harold 11
Sokel, Walter 60, 64, 73, 78
Stefan, Verena, *Häutungen* 6
Steinthal, Helmut 76
Strauß, Botho, *Die Nacht mit Alice* 145
Stunde Null 98
subjectivity 8, 10, 11, 21, 29, 54, 64, 82, 140–41, 143, 149, 153
    lack of/ crisis in 105, 107, 110, 112, 115, 117
sublime 24

Tachibana, Reiko 114
Tatar, Maria 24
Tawada, Yoko 8, 15, 120–21
    on Hoffmann 130
    comparison with Kafka 141
    on Kafka 58, 130–31, 136, 141–42
    works:
        Das Bad 150–51
        'Eigentlich darf man es niemandem sagen, aber Europa gibt es nicht' 134
        'Der Faltenmann von Sumida Fluss' 139
        'Eine leere Flasche' 152
        Ein Gast 143
        'Missing Heels' 149
        Das Nackte Auge 143, 149
        Opium für Ovid 122–54, 160, 161
        Spielzeug und Sprachmagie 121, 130–31, 142
        Sprachpolizei und Spielpolyglotte 153
        Talisman 151
        'Tawada Yoko does not exist' 135
        Überseezungen 144, 147, 149
        Verwandlungen 122, 125, 136, 144, 149–50, 152–53
Taylor, Charles 4, 14, 50, 54
Temporality 7, 13, 68–71, 110, 115, 164–65
Terada, Rei, *Feeling in Theory* 148–49
Tieck, Ludwig, 'Der blonde Eckbert' 102, 131
Todorov, Tzvetan 29, 58
translation 8, 122, 132, 140, 143, 149
trauma 105, 113–14
Trojanow, Ilija, *Der Weltensammler* 120
Tyler, Lisa 95, 97

Ueda Akinari 137
Uexküll, Jakob von 65, 69
uncanny, *see* Freud, 'Das Unheimliche'
'Ungeziefer' 8, 60–61, 166

'Verwandlung' 2, 159, 168
voicelessness 6, 74–77, 112, 163

Warner, Marina 5, 13, 98, 162
wartime experience 96, 103, 106
Washinosu, Yumiko 139–40
Webber, Andrew 31
Weigel, Sigrid 104, 121
Wells, H. G. 13
    The Island of Doctor Moreau 80
Wende 108
Wöllner, Günter 46
Woolf, Virginia, *Orlando* 12
wounds 70, 136

Yildiz, Yasemin 124

zero point 142–43
Zilcosky, John 75
Zinner, Hedda 98
Ziolkowsky, Theodore 126, 127, 132
Zupančič, Alenka 38

www.ingramcontent.com/pod-product-compliance
Lightning Source LLC
LaVergne TN
LVHW061251060426
835507LV00017B/2023